GUIDING THE FAMILY
Practical Counseling
Techniques

Bernice Bronia Grunwald, M.Ed.

Instructor, Alfred Adler Institute
Chicago, Illinois

Best wishes!
Hal McAbee

Harold V. McAbee, Ed.D.

Professor, Counseling Psychology
Director, The Adler-Dreikurs Institute of Human Relations
Bowie State College
Bowie, Maryland

ACCELERATED DEVELOPMENT INC.
Publisher

Muncie,   Indiana

p. 225
p 281
? ques.

GUIDING THE FAMILY
Practical Counseling Techniques

Library of Congress Catalogue Card Number: 84-70098

International Standard Book Number: 0-915202-43-3

© Copyright 1985 by Accelerated Development Inc.

Cover Design: Barbara Valakos

Technical Assistants: Michelle Crowe
                      Tanya Dalton
                      Judy McWilliams
                      Sheila Sheward

Order additional copies from

Accelerated Development Inc.
Publishers   Tel (317) 284-7511
3400 Kilgore Avenue, Muncie, Indiana 47304

DEDICATION

We gratefully dedicate this book to our respective spouses

Joseph Achim Grunwald
and
Norma Lou McAbee

PREFACE

Many therapists and counselors constantly are trying to help parents with problems relating to their children. After using several different texts in order to assemble basic materials for courses in Family Counseling, it became obvious to the authors a basic text in the field based on principles of Adlerian Psychology did not exist. That is the major reason that this book was written.

The purpose of this book is to provide a model of counseling skills that will enable counselors, teachers, social workers, and others, who are working with parents and children, to help them live with each other in harmony and enjoyment. In this book the authors discuss in detail techniques which, if properly applied, will bring about positive changes in family relationships which at present are often based on open warfare. Suggested are actions that counselors should take in specific situations and recommendations the counselor may propose to parents and to children.

Many parents feel defeated, guilty, angry, and terribly worried. These feelings are increased by the present tendency to blame parents and to hold them responsible for their childen at home and in school. Because of this, psychological guidance for parents is urgent in today's society.

A counselor's first concern is to help parents realize that mistakes they may have made were due to lack of knowledge and not to lack of responsibility or love for their children. Parents need help understanding their own misleading concepts of their roles as parents. Parents must and can be helped to understand that, in spite of their best intentions, they often contribute to, if not create, the friction and alienation that exists between them and their children. Parents need to be helped to learn how to be democratic without becoming permissive and without allowing their children to put them into their service and to tyranize them. This book attempts to teach counselors how to help families to establish relationships based on democratic principles which must be applied to all the members in the family regardless of age.

The emphasis in this book is mostly on "how to do it." Content is organized in a step-by-step procedure, guiding the beginning counselor in understanding of the client and how to elicit acceptable agreements among family members. The focus is on the counselor's role as a moderator and a friend who shows respect and empathy for problems that the client brings and, at the same time, retains professional authority and skills.

While each chapter contains specific applications to particular problems of family dissension, the focus of the book remains on the total philosophy of relationships. In each chapter the application of specific, basic principles are stressed. However, each chapter has a focus on different aspects of the counseling procedure with guidelines and recommendations.

Case studies are presented to illustrate how the counselor will proceed, step-by-step, in helping families with their problems. Most of our interpretations and suggestions have been illustrated with examples which the authors fathered through years of their work with families. These examples were either taken from notes or transcribed from tapes. All names have been changed.

In conclusion, a textbook cannot possibly contain discussions applicable to all problems that may arise in a family, but it can provide the counselor with knowledge and skills, techniques, and approaches, that can lead to insights in family relationships and how the counselor can help families solve their problems.

The authors are aware that many Adlerians counsel both in private settings and publicly in front of groups of students, lay persons, and professionals. Basic principles and techniques throughout this volume apply in either type of setting.

November, 1984

Bernice Bronia Grunwald

Bernice Bronia Grunwald, M.Ed.

Harold V. McAbee

Harold V. McAbee, Ed.D.

ACKNOWLEDGMENTS

We are appreciative of the indispensable role played by colleagues in the writing of the book. We were thrilled by the reaction of the readers, seasoned professors, as well as students, who wrote or told us their reaction to the book and their suggestions for improvements. A number of colleagues read and commented on whole sections of the manuscript and we owe them a special debt and gratitude—Dr. Raymond Corsini of Hawaii and Dr. Richard Kopp of the California School of Professional Psychology. Dr. Corsini has represented an ideal to us in writing and in personal integrity. We are greatly honored by his foreword to this edition. Special thanks to Betty Haeussler, faithful and painstaking secretary, without whose help the manuscript would never have been completed.

In addition, we would like to express our appreciation to the multitude of families who provided us with the experiences and much material for this book.

Bernice Bronia Grunwald, M.Ed.

Harold V. McAbee, Ed.D.

FOREWORD

Throughout the many years of my college and university education and then after that through my many years of experience as a clinical psychologist, over and over again, I heard comments from fellow students, from professors, and from clinicians to the effect: "Parenting should be taught; being a parent is one of the most difficult tasks, and someone should make certain that parents know what to do." "How can we get parents to learn how to rear children?"—and comments of that sort.

To meet these needs, many books have been printed, organizations have been started, and all kinds of attempts have been made to educate parents—and others who are involved in rearing children. The net effect of all these efforts are unknown, but hopefully they will help to make people better parents, to have happier homes, and children who are healthier and more useful to the community.

Love is absolutely not enough. Love can stifle, envelop, and even damage a child. How many crimes have we family counselors seen committed in the name of love! It is respect, and love which is called for to make parenting happy and successful. Not that love need be a negative influence, but it just isn't enough. We need love and respect, and I am convinced of the two that respect is the more important.

In Bronia Grunwald's and Harold McAbee's *Guiding the Family* we find a book which fits into the oldest tradition of family counseling, a complex of concepts that originally came from Dr. Alfred Adler, a Vienese psychiatrist, who started the first family counseling centers in the early 1920s. Since then, there have been thousands of Adlerian family counseling centers throughout the world and hundreds of articles and dozens of books based on these ideas. Adlerian family counseling ideas were brought to America in the 1930s by a remarkable man, teacher to both Mrs. Grunwald and Dr. McAbee, Dr. Rudolf Dreikurs.

These two students of Adlerian ideas have had the benefit of continued exposure to the ideas of a great many of their colleagues, and also the benefit of working with thousands of families in need, and in *Guiding the Family* they have been able in a convincing manner to summarize their experiences and knowledge for the benefit of both parents and counselors. While the book is directed primarily to a professional audience, and should become *the* textbook for family counselors, it can have a direct personal benefit to parents and others who are tangentially involved in the field of family counseling—physicians, lawyers, ministers, teachers, nurses, and others who work with parents with problems.

A number of important points about this book:

1. It is very simply and clearly written.

2. It is theoretically and philosophically sound. In reading it I was not able to find, despite my most critical attention, a single statement with which I could find disagreement.

3. It is eminently practical. Practically every page has something valuable and unusual.

Guiding the Family should become a classic in this field and could well become the single most important text in the field of family counseling. I recommend it without any reservation.

Raymond J. Corsini, Ph.D.
Senior Counselor
Family Education Centers of Hawaii

GUIDING THE FAMILY:
PRACTICAL COUNSELING TECHNIQUES

CONTENTS

IV PSYCHOLOGICAL PREMISES 43

V DIAGNOSTIC TECHNIQUES—
GATHERING SIGNIFICANT DATA 67

FIGURES

GUIDING
THE
FAMILY

HISTORICAL OVERVIEW

Because this book advocates methods used by Adler's and Dreikurs' approach to counseling families, the authors consider it fitting to provide the reader a short overview of Alfred Adler and his basic philosophy to human relationships.

Alfred Adler was a psychiatrist who lived and worked in Vienna, Austria, during the first quarter of this century. He died in Scotland in 1937.

He was a social psychiatrist, more concerned in preventive education than in curing sick people. Adler's interest was in re-educating individuals and in this way influencing society and its values. He was mainly concerned with helping people to live together as equals with concern for each other's welfare. Adler considered most people as discouraged rather than sick, and therefore, placed great emphasis on encouraging individuals, on restoring faith in their potentials and abilities to cope with and overcome most of life's problems.

Adler recognized that most problems that parents and children were having were a direct outgrowth of their poor relationships. He also realized that the disintegration of the family which became apparent at the beginning of the 20th century was generally the result of a changing society, one which was moving from a traditional, autocratic posture to a democratic basis with equal rights for all people. He felt that this greatly affected the relationship that parents had with their children. He realized that the traditional methods of rearing children became outdated and ineffective as society became more democratic.

In his practice as a psychiatrist, Adler came to realize that many problems which he encountered in adults were a result of improper training during their childhood. He found that this concept was especially true in adults who were pampered and overprotected when they were children. These individuals were usually poorly prepared to cooperate with others and face life realistically.

After World War I, Adler also became aware that teachers were having more problems with students than before. While studying these problems, he realized more and more that problems parents had with their children at home and those that teachers had with their students in the classroom were interwoven and interrelated. He recognized as an impossible task to help so many parents and teachers who needed guidance and assistance on an individual one-to-one basis. Thus Adler's idea for an open child guidance center was born where he could reach many parents, teachers, and would-be parents. Because these basic problems in many families were so similar, and because they were the result of a lack of education of adults in the understanding of children and how they unwittingly contributed to those problems, Adler felt that counseling in public would educate many people during the time that he could educate just one family or teacher.

In 1922 Adler had organized his first child guidance center within the community. It met with such enthusiasm and such success that the movement grew to over 30 such centers, mostly located in public schools and conducted by psychologists whom he had trained. These centers became very popular and were observed by parents, teachers, school principals, social workers, and all other people who were interested in childhood education. Parents and teachers who struggled with problem children united in their difficulties. While members of the audience identified with families being counseled, they realized their own inadequate methods for resolving problems which were similar to parents who were being counseled. Adler invited the audience to participate and to share their own experiences, successes, or failures in their methods for resolving problems and to help encourage the family. This took away any stigma or shame that parents on stage might have felt. They did not feel alone and the interest of the people in the audience was encouraging to them.

People who have not experienced open child guidance centers are often prejudiced and actually horrified at the idea of discussing one's problems in the open before others. Only those who have attended such counseling sessions become aware of its effectiveness. All participants learn the principles of relationships based on equality and mutual respect, on better communication, and of loving children without "smothering" them and crippling them in their personality development.

These centers were closed in 1934 when the Facists came to power in Austria.

Adler had always hoped that some day these kinds of centers would be established in the United States. His hopes came true when one of his ardent followers, Dr. Rudolph Dreikurs, came to Chicago in 1937. He soon established his first Child Guidance Center at the Abraham Lincoln School. Soon other centers opened. Dreikurs trained many counselors from many parts of the world in the methods of Adlerian family counseling, and today one finds hundreds of Adlerian-Dreikursian family counseling centers all over the United States, Canada, Israel, Greece, and in many other countries of Europe. Dreikurs' contributions, chronicled much more completely elsewhere, included the systemization and expansion of many of Adler's basic tenets. Although Dreikurs believed that most of his basic ideas were Adlerian in origin, Dreikurs felt that systematic organization and techniques of application were necessary in order to teach others how to use effectively Adler's ideas in counseling and therapy. Codification of the four goals of misbehavior and the technique of effectively revealing these to a misbehaving child were among the most useful of Dreikurs' many contributions. The application of Dreikur's approach will be discussed extensively in this book. Dreikurs systematized an interview schedule for gathering pertinent information needed in lifestyle (personality) assessment. He contributed the "hidden reason" and "two points on a line" techniques as means to aid the counselor to quickly show the client that he/she is understood. Dreikurs ably demonstrated and taught these concepts and other confrontation techniques that have proven to be so effective.

Dreikurs believed firmly with Adler that encouragement was essential to improvement of behavior and human relationships. He clarified this concept and wrote two books on the topic. Dreikurs may have been the first to use the group approach in therapy, beginning with a group of alcoholics in 1925. He also stimulated many practitioners to use multiple therapy and this practice is common today. The development of the system of Natural and Logical Consequences and application of these techniques may be Dreikurs' finest contributions. This approach contains the principles of discipline congruent with the democratic society.

Finally, Dreikurs left a great legacy of literature and many well trained followers in the field who carry the Adlerian-Dreikursian movement forward.

CHAPTER I

ADLERIAN THEORY AND FAMILY COUNSELING

RATIONALE

Professional personnel working in the field of human behavior need to be well versed in theory. A number of reasons exist as to why this is necessary. Although the study of theory is in ill repute in some schools that prepare counselors and other professionals in the field of human relationships, it is inconceivable that counselors and other similar professional persons can be effective without utilizing a set of psychological principles that explain the dynamics of human behavior.

One aim of this book is to furnish this needed understanding. As theory is discussed, the practical application of this theory is explained. The authors firmly hold that several *a priori* reasons exist for counselors understanding a firm theoretical basis for their practice.

Without a basic construct from which to make assumptions, one cannot understand nor assist those who come for help. Counseling often is ineffective because counselors do not understand their client's behavior psychologically and, therefore, cannot help clients understand themselves and what motivates them to behave as they do. Counselors, who lack this training, are in no position to align their goals with clients and work together effectively.

Having a firm belief in a particular model of human behavior will lend consistency to the counselor's efforts because it will provide direction to take in setting short-and long-term goals with the client. This psychological orientation will give definition and structure to the information needed to assist the client. The theoretical knowledge helps the counselor in structuring the counseling session and formulating techniques that elicit appropriate or useful information which are needed to assist the client. Then theoretical bases will enable the counselor to assist the disruptive client families to understand how they are functioning and how to apply effective corrective measures. If the corrective action is inappropriate or incongruent with the theoretical base, it will not be effective. For example, many counselors, who are not trained in Adlerian principles, believe that human behavior is basically instinctive in nature and that one of the instincts is anger typified by aggression. They suggest that a corrective treatment would be to provide opportunities for the angry child to express anger. This approach will not be effective because the client can generate an untold amount of anger if it suits the purpose. This corrective approach is completely contrary to Adlerian theory which holds that all behavior is purposive or goal oriented.

Being well versed in theory enables the family counselor to apply a basic tenet to many specific situations and thereby raise the level of competency. It elevates the level of activity from technical to professional. Having a strong commitment to a theoretical base will assist the family counselor in remaining consistent when faced with new or unique situations in ongoing counseling. It furnishes the basis for congruent treatment and thereby provides the counselor with support and courage for following convictions in difficult cases.

Counselors frequently encounter situations that are completely unique to their experiences. Holding to a consistent theoretical base in counseling will help the counselor keep biases from intruding inappropriately on otherwise common sense, logical judgments that may be inconsistent with the theoretical base.

To those who say, "It sounds fine in theory, but it won't work in practice," these authors comment, "that if the theory is sound, and properly applied, the results probably will be effective." This statement is offered with the conviction of over fifty years of combined counseling experience by these authors.

BASIC PRINCIPLES OF
INDIVIDUAL/ADLERIAN PSYCHOLOGY
APPLIED TO FAMILY COUNSELING

Adlerian or Individual Psychology rests on the basic philosophy of a democratic culture. Basic tenets include ideas that all people are equal, that mutual respect should exist among all living persons, and that every individual has the freedom of personal choice as long as it does not harm others. The thoughtful reader will note the extension of these ideas in principles and application throughout this volume.

Principles of Adlerian Psychology have been codified to twelve basic tenets by Heinz Ansbacher and Rowena Ansbacher (1956). These twelve tenets, though simple, have a profound affect on the approach of any counselor who uses them. While power rests in their simplicity, which is deceptive, great skill is required to apply them effectively. The value and usefulness of these principles will become more apparent as the reader progresses through this volume.

The following statements of Adlerian principles have been paraphrased from Ansbacher codifications. These statements have been selected as being most cogent for application to family counseling situations.

1. All human activity is designed to help the individual overcome basic feelings of inferiority and attain feelings of superiority or perfection.

Explanation. Adler (Ansbacher & Ansbacher, 1956) held that all individuals have inferiority feelings beginning in childhood. These are attributed to the obvious biological dependence for survival. A second major reason for inferiority feelings is the realization that one is relatively insignificant when compared to the world at large and the universe. A third major reason is a product of the modern world—the complex social, business, and industrial world. The complexity and specialization of the world in these modern times subjects almost everyone to a high level of dependency in order to insure existence. Most individuals respond to the challenge by belonging to many social and economic organizations in attempts to prove and insure their worth and overcome their sense of inferiority and insecurity. Adler (Ansbacher & Ansbacher, 1956) pointed out that as long as individuals strove to overcome life's problems, inferiority feelings were probably advantageous. Only when the individual has lost the courage to overcome problems, do such feelings interfere with effective functioning. The striving for superiority to overcome life's problems is the basic Adlerian explanation for motivation. It is the Adlerian way of explaining compensation and overcompensation, i.e., overcoming inferior feelings by means of achievement.

2. The human striving to overcome feelings of inferiority is directed toward the individual's ideal. This ideal sets the ultimate goal or self-ideal for the individual toward which to strive; it represents perfection. The ideal is a fiction in the philosophical sense in that it exists only in the imagination as may be contrasted with a concrete real.

Explanation. This principle accounts for later analysis that Adlerian Psychology is a theological, goal-oriented theory of human behavior. This principle is that every individual uses mental and emotional faculties to analyze his/her environment, draw conclusions, and establish goals for attainment. This concept is the basic principle that holds that an individual's behavior is not explained, or controlled by heredity or environment. It infers also the premise that the individual chooses (creates) what will be done in order to attain established goals. More important, however, it provides the theory of human behavior that explains why every individual is unique and different. It is the only acceptable explanation of vast panorama of individual differences found in people in the view of these authors. Every individual creates an ideal self and methods for striving toward it and every individual creates one that is unique.

The counselor has the task to discover each client's goals and striving techniques for reaching them; how these goals influence the client's behavior and how these ideals and behaviors influence others, i.e., family, workmates, community, and so forth.

The concept that the self-ideal is fictional explains the eternal striving of the perfectionist who can never seem to quite reach a satisfactory level of achievement. If the goal is reached, a higher goal is set. Parents and teachers are known for raising levels of expectations when children attain one level. "My parents are never satisfied," is a comment often heard from children. This is basically discouraging to them. The counselor needs to be alert to new demands by the parent as the identified client moves from one level of achievement to another. This principle also explains the dissatisfaction of the highly ambitious individual's self-inflicted standards or goals. They never quite attain their ultimate goal, i.e., a satisfactory level of achievement, because it is fictional. They, then, become discouraged. Unfortunately, such individuals seldom realize that some of their goals are fictional and unattainable. This situation keeps many in a continuous state of dissatisfaction with themselves and with others. The family counselor has the responsibility to educate, to help parents and children understand the dynamics of such eternal unsatisfactory striving, and to help them to accept themselves as they are and give up their striving for the ideal (fictional) self.

3. Psychological goals of the individual usually are unknown to self. This was Adler's idea of the unconscious mind.

Explanation. The counselor should reveal the purposes of the client's behavior and feelings. The purpose is frequently a fictitious concept of what one must be in order to feel successful, i.e., "I must be first or I don't count." The counselor also must help clients choose positive, alternative ways to pursue their goals when they are on a mistaken path. For example, one who seeks exorbitant power might be led to attain the goal by becoming a leader that helps rather than dominates. The mistaken pursuit or pursuit of mistaken goals results in making difficulty for the client. The counselor reveals the unconscious goals to clients largely through various confrontation techniques (see Chapter IV). The effectiveness of corrective measures for misbehaving individuals will be dependent on the accuracy of goal assessment of the client's misbehavior by the counselor.

4. Various aspects of the individual such as the conscious, unconscious, physical, mental, and emotional, are all part of a unified system moving toward the same psychological goal. This was Adler's view of the holistic nature of man.

Explanation. This principle indicates Adler's view that the individual is a unified whole and strives toward the goal(s), whether or not understood, with every aspect of his/her being. This is the holistic view of persons originated by Smuts and developed by Adler and others. It suggests also that the individual cannot be understood except as a united whole. The implication is for the counselor to consider all aspects of the client's view of life and self in relation to goals. To attempt to work with an individual's emotional, sexual, or intellectual needs in isolation is useless. The real question is how the client uses each of these attributes in moving toward one and the same goal—the ideal self. This theory gave birth to Adler's name for his school of thought—Individual Psychology, i.e., every person is indivisible and cannot be divided into different entities for the purpose of understanding the person's behavior.

5. Every individual subjectively perceives and interprets all phenomena through own unique screen which Adler called the apperceptive schema.

Explanation. This Adlerian principle firmly establishes Individual Psychology as a subjective psychology. Inclusion of the apperceptive schema idea in the structure of the Adlerian system, precludes by definition, the idea of so-called objective thinking. Adlerians recognize that some individuals make fewer or more mistakes than others, but that, as Ansbacher and Ansbacher (1956) stated, "Nobody knows the ultimate correct (exact) view of the world."

The counselor must first learn attitudes of the individual and view of self and the world in order to understand various strivings (activities) of the individual. The counselor then has the possibility of re-educating the individual concerning mistaken concepts and ways of behaving.

6. An understanding of the individual can be derived only from his/her relationships to others. The ability of the individual to function effectively in society depends on the development of the quality known as social interest. Social interest is not an inborn trait, but must be developed through education of the individual.

Explanation. Adler was adamant in insisting that a meaningful understanding of an individual's functioning could only be derived by examining the person in the social context. A person's functioning in life can be understood only in relationships to other human beings. Such relationships are essential for survival of the individual and the species. The individual's meaning and purpose result from interpretations of interaction with others. The individual then can select various activities and movements that may enable the person to survive. The counselor's job becomes one of educating individuals to understand and change from mistaken ways of interacting to positive and effective ways of interacting with others in order to develop social interest. The development of social interest in the client is a major task for the counselor. Most families that the counselor will encounter contain one or more members who lack the courage or techniques of functioning positively within the family or other groups. Thus, helping the individual and family members to understand the folly of mistaken behaviors, not in the social interest, becomes a primary task. An especially important counselor function is to teach the value of and techniques of acting in the social interest to members of the family. Family members must come to understand the value of making contributions to the group. All of these factors play a major factor in the individual's overcoming the sense of inferiority and development of sound mental health.

7. An adjunct of the foregoing theory is that all life problems of an individual become problems of the general social group. As individuals develop values and value systems, these become values for the social group.

Explanation. From their interaction, people form values and standards. These, in turn, become expectations for individuals to achieve and, in turn, influence goal setting for themselves and others. A simple example is the development of value of education. Early in the history of mankind, individuals with inquisitive minds discerned that the creation and accumulation of some knowledge were of value. These concepts further developed into the idea that education of the masses was good for the social group and compulsory education eventually resulted. Individuals acting out against this commonly accepted social value become problems for themselves and the larger group. Such acting out is further illustrated by the problems created when the child mistakenly rebels against achievement in school.

GOALS OF DISTURBING BEHAVIOR

Dreikurs (1957) made many major contributions to Adlerian therapy and counseling. Many of these included systemization of Adler's basic concepts which have been most useful in teaching the application of these ideas. Perhaps the most useful to family counselors was his typology of goals of disturbing behavior seen commonly in children (Dreikurs, 1957). Dreikurs' original scheme has been augmented by additions by Dreikurs, Grunwald, and Pepper (1971) which have broadened the application of the Dreikurs' four goals of children's misbehavior in various ways. Bullard's (NASAP, 1973) work also focused on the four goals in positive as well as negative interpretations.

Dreikurs, consistent with the goal oriented behavior theory in Individual Psychology, pointed out that every action of the child has a purpose. The child's purpose is to make a place for self in the group. Both Adler and Dreikurs believed that finding a place and an acceptance in the group were primary to all behavior; it insured survival. Dreikurs further pointed out that the well-adjusted child achieved that place by making contributions to and meeting requirements of the group. However, should the child be denied or fail to perceive opportunities to meet group standards for acceptance, he/she would avail self of one of several goals of disturbing behavior in order to achieve the purpose.

Dreikurs (1957) originally titled the four goals as the "four goals of disturbing behavior," apparently because such behavior on the part of the children usually disturbed parents or teachers. These also have been variously termed as goals of misbehavior, the maladjusted goals, mistaken goals, and children's goals of behavior. These are four in number: *Attention Getting, Power, Revenge,* and *Assumed Disability.* Dreikurs further specified that these are immediate in nature and apply to current behavior interactions between the child and another person—most often a parent or teacher.

Children turn to achieving goals of disturbing or mistaken behavior as alternative ways of seeking acceptance or finding a place in the group when positive means have not been successful for them. Small children most often resort to a large variety of attention getting devices in order to be noticed or accepted. If these devices seem to be successful and if the child feels accepted, he/she will continue to behave at this level. However, should the various attention getting activities fail to satisfy the child, and if there should be a lack of opportunity to contribute to the welfare of the group as a means of being accepted, the child may turn to achieving power as a means to belong. The child may very well begin to think, "If no one really pays any attention to me, I will become the boss and then I'll be noticed. After all, Mom and Dad and my teacher have their way and it seems to give them an important place." Should the striving for power and control work, power-seeking children may incorporate this goal into their lifestyle and more or less operate this way in most situations for the remainder of their lives. (Sweeney, 1981)

Should various attempts at gaining power fail, the child may decide that few people, if any, will do as he/she wants or expects, that no one cares about him/her. The child generally feels hurt by this rejection and frustration of attempts to gain the goal of power and will seek retaliation or revenge. Revenge may take mild or strong forms. This is the goal level at which very discouraged children and youth become vicious, delinquent, and often turn to vandalism, stealing, and other destructive or useless activities.

If the misbehaving child or youth finds a satisfactory place with these destructive activities, possibly he/she will lead an extremely unhappy life or may become an habitual criminal, alcoholic, or drug addict at the worst. Should none of the first three goals furnish the child the needed sense of belonging, the child may give up the struggle and feign a disability. This assumed disability of the normal child usually results in giving up on the struggle to find a place in the group and often results in the adult world giving up on the child.

Dreikurs (1957) further pointed out in explaining the four goals that the child could pursue these in both constructive (positive) ways and destructive (negative) ways. Dreikurs (1957) also stated that the child could obtain the goal in a variety of ways and that the goal might very well change in different situations. The best clues as to the intent (goal) of the child are the reaction (what the adult did in the situation) and affect (emotional response) on the part of others.

Dreikurs' concept and detailed formulation of these four goals are the most helpful techniques available for the Adlerian trained family counselor. Explicit detail for practical application of these four-goals concept will be found in Chapter IV.

PAMPERED CHILDREN

This section contains some major reasons why so many children adopt useless, even destructive behaviors and strive for the mistaken goals of disturbing behavior. Pampering and spoiling may be the most serious impediment to the child's normal development. Many adults who cannot cope with life's problems have been pampered and spoiled when they were children. People often refer to children as being pampered or spoiled without being aware of what these expressions actually imply. These classifications of children are commonly used because they are similar in nature and often overlap. But, upon closer examination, we find that different categories of pampering and spoiling exist and that each has a distinct affect on the child's personality development. In our present society many children are pampered and spoiled. In a sense, this has become accepted as a "normal" way of rearing children.

We are often asked: "What is better for the child's personality development, to grow up in a pampered way in a permissive home atmosphere or in a strict, authoritarian environment?" When people put this question to the late Rudolf Dreikurs, he would reply, "You may as well ask me what is better—to be hung or shot?" Neither motivates a change of values, behavior, self-worth, nor the fictitious goal the child has set for self in order to find a place and be recognized and accepted.

Why parents pamper children. Let us first examine why parents pamper and spoil their children. The following basic reasons are synthesized. Parents pamper to shield the child from unpleasant experiences, believing that this prevents the child from developing fears, feelings of inadequacy, or being unloved. This is especially true in parents who are strongly attached to their children and who feel that giving the child much love is the key to the child's happiness. Some parents know that what they do may be pleasant for the child at the moment but do not realize that it may do the child harm in the long run. Parents' tolerance for frustration is low; they suffer when the child is deprived of receiving what is wished and, hence, the parents give in to the child. In the final analysis, these parents pamper themselves in the process of pampering and spoiling the child. How often do counselors hear a parent say, "I know that I should not have done this, but I just couldn't help myself. It hurt me so much to see my child cry."

Then, we have parents who want to be regarded as the "best" parent a child can have; to be loved by the child and to be completely dependent on the parent. When parents give in to the child that cries, the reason is not so much that difficulty comes from parents seeing the child in tears, but parents being threatened that the child may consider them bad and withdraw affection. This dependency on the child's love by the parent is often exploited by the child. A child may literally blackmail parents who refuse to give in by saying "I hate you. You are a bad mother/father." Some children even may go so far as to accuse the parent with, "I am sure that you are not my parent; you probably adopted me or you wouldn't be so mean." This is often more than the parent can endure and, therefore, allows the child to have what is wanted. The tragedy does not lie so much in what the child says or does as in the parents' falling for this trick because of their tremendous need to be loved under all circumstances.

Many parents spoil their children because they do not want to deprive them of the things that they themselves were deprived of when they were children. This is especially true in regard to material things. Some parents overemphasize the status that goes with material possessions. They feel inferior when they believe that their child possesses less than the child of the neighbor. It becomes extremely important to such parents to show the community in which they live that they are as well off as the best or the most wealthy.

A ten-year old boy, aware that his parents competed with the others in the community, told his parents that most of the children in his class wore special brand gym shoes and that he felt ashamed to wear his plain, old gym shoes. The next day, the mother took her son to the store where he could choose the shoes that he claimed the other students wore. Later the mother learned that her son had lied to her. The counselor discussed this with the boy.

Counselor: *What is this business about the gym shoes that upset your mother?*

Boy: *Well, I told her that I was ashamed to wear the ones I had.*

Counselor: *Is that the reason why she is upset?*

Boy: *Not exactly. I did not tell her the whole truth.*

Counselor: *Care to talk about it?*

Boy: *Well, I lied to her.*

Counselor: *You must have had a reason.*

Boy: *Well, yes. I liked these new gym shoes and I knew that she wouldn't buy them for me if I told her that I wanted new ones. So I lied.*

Counselor: *What would have happened if you had told the truth; that you did not like the ones you have?*

Boy: *Oh, she would never have bought them. She would have told me that's too bad and that would have been it.*

We see from this example that children recognize their parents' feelings and values. This boy knew how important it was for his mother to show the others in the community that they were on equal grounds materially.

To cite another example:

Fourteen year old Isaak suddenly stopped inviting his friends to his house. The parents thought that he had had a falling out with his friends and asked him about it. He told them that he was ashamed to invite his friends to his crummy house with the old furniture. This upset the parents and they promptly bought new furniture. It was not the boy's values, but his feelings of being socially inferior because his home was not as nice as his friends' that upset them.

These two examples are not isolated situations but the kind that happen frequently in some communities. Perceived values of neighbors, shame, and feelings of inferiority parents experience when they can't keep up economically with others drives them to compete. This distorts the child's values in general and may instill inferiority feelings. It encourages the child to view self as always being entitled to be on the receiving end while disregarding how this may affect others.

Pampered children have a very poor tolerance for frustration. They must have what they want immediately or they either throw tantrums or punish parents by turning to drugs, sexual abuse, or not learning in school. These children rarely stay at a task for very long. They are not used to exerting themselves to accomplish anything. Thus, pampered children often are found to be underachievers in school. These children grow up in a hot-house atmosphere in which the natural order that exists in "regular" homes does not exist for them. Their lack of self-reliance often causes them to break down under any demand for the discharge of responsibilities, especially if this is under hardship.

Types of Pampering

Overindulgence. The children to whom everything is given belong to this category. If parents deny these children's wishes, they throw temper tantrums and manipulate parents to give in through provocative behaviors (breaking things, threatening to run away). These children often measure their self-worth by the number of things they are getting. They associate getting with being loved and important. Because these children were reared to "get," they may feel threatened in the relationship when parents deny something. These are the "gimmee" children, the ones who greet everyone with, "What did you bring me?" An example.

> *Five year old Randy had a temper tantrum because visitors did not bring him a present. He asked them to leave the house and not come back unless they brought him a gift. The parents felt embarrassed but also somewhat sorry for the child. They promised to buy the toy he had wished for the next day if he behaved now.*

Children may become tyrants if permitted to dictate to their parents in such a manner. If denied, they may produce symptoms of extreme anger, disorderliness, unwillingness to go to school, and even enuresis.

Overpermissiveness. A distinction exists between the child that is reared in an indulgent way and the one that is reared in an overpermissive manner. The latter does not always get the material things wanted, but is allowed to do as he/she pleases with complete disregard as to how those actions affect others. This is often the result of the psychology that advocates the importance of letting the child "express" self and not to be exposed to frustration. Such children often put everyone in the household into their services. They leave their things all over the house; they scribble on walls or on furniture; they come and go as they please, disregarding the time when mother serves meals, and so forth.

A mother came for counseling because of her older daughter, Hanna, who did poorly in school. About her younger daughter, Tanya, she said that she was a very imaginative child who could occupy herself for hours. Then, she told the counselor how ingenious Tanya was by giving the following example:

> *Tanya was trying to sew a wedding gown for her doll. She could not find any lacy material for the dress, so she had the bright*

idea of cutting off a piece of the lace curtains in her room and made the doll dress. Mother thought that this showed great imagination. When asked about the curtain and the disregard for common property, this mother replied: "You can always buy a new curtain, but you can never undo the harm when you frustrate the child. The curtain does not matter."

We have counseled parents whose children are allowed to paint on the walls of any room, who are not stopped from hammering nails into furniture, and others who ate an entire cake, leaving nothing for other members of the family. Nothing was said in order not to frustrate the child. Often these children learn how to get out of unpleasant situations and to protect themselves by setting up excuses in advance.

"Teacher doesn't like me, that's why I have poor grades," or "I couldn't do the assignment. I was not in class when the teacher explained this lesson."

"I couldn't hear what mother wanted because she was too far away."

"I couldn't straighten up the room because mother announced it was time to get ready for dinner, so I left everything."

What happens to these children is never the fault of what they do but always of what somebody else does. Such children find their places in life through such excuses and have a very difficult time in learning responsibility.

Overdomineering. Overdomineering parents do not give the child an opportunity to learn from mistakes because the parents make all the decisions. This child cannot take a step without the parent's directions such as the following:

"First do your homework and get it out of the way, then you can go out and play. Don't play with Susan, she is not your kind. I'd rather you'd make friends with Mary. Don't read the comic strip, you don't learn anything from it. I would prefer you would read the history book and be prepared for tomorrow."

Such parents tell the child how to handle their allowance, how to spend it, and how much to save and for what. Such children grow up without confidence in their own judgment. They always need someone to tell them what to do and how to do it. This lack of confidence in their ability to make intelligent decisions prevents them from achievement based on decision making. Often they know the answer, yet leave the question unanswered out of fear of making a mistake. There are many children who score low on achievement tests because of this fear. Yet, teachers often do not realize that the scores on such tests are misleading.

Children who grow up in overdomineering homes also may become rebels when they get older. They may rebel openly or covertly against the domineering parents. An example.

> *Twelve-year old Ronnie was the son of a policeman. His father made all the decisions for him. He decided what books Ronnie should read, how much time he should spend reading and when the boy had finished the book, the father quizzed him to make sure that his son had really read it. As Ron put it when the counselor spoke to him, "My father gave me the third degree like I was a criminal who is trying to withhold information." When Ronnie entered junior high school he began to rebel. He refused to go to his room and when he went, refused to read. His school work suffered. The father punished him with house arrest and often with the strap, but no amount of punishment diminished his rebellion. When we talked to Ronnie, he said: "My father is stubborn and so am I. If he can keep up harassing me, I can keep up with my resistance. He can't bully me." Here we encounter open rebellion. But not all youngsters have Ronnie's courage and determination. They rebel covertly through not listening, not working in school, defying all authority. Some escape into drugs, or alcohol, and others may even become serious delinquents and get involved with the police. Defying authority of adults gives these children a feeling of superiority.*

In the case of Ronnie, the counselor had to concentrate on changing the relationship between the father and the son. The father was advised not to get involved with homework or with chores. The counselor suggested that the father find time to do pleasant things with his son, discuss with him his own work as a policeman, and perhaps even ask Ron's advice in some matters. The emphasis was on talking and listening to each other. The father was helped to discuss his own feelings of inadequacy; his fear of the opinion of the community to whom he was supposed to present a model citizen; how threatened he was about what the community will think of him, rather than of his son, if the latter behaved in an antisocial manner. Ron and his father began to really talk. The boy felt that for the first time he was treated like an equal and developed compassion for his father. It was not easy for this father to make such drastic changes in his relationship with the son. At first, he felt that this meant for him to relinquish his authority as a father, but he gradually began to realize that it was difficult for him to give up his "power" held as a representative of the law. As Ron began to respond somewhat to his father, and as the father began to feel less threatened, the counselor was in a position to work out some of the problems the parents had with Ron in regard to the acceptance of responsibilities. The father completely stopped choosing books for Ronnie and quizzing him about them. Ronnie agreed to help with household chores, but only during the weekend. The parents agreed. When the counselor met with the family two weeks later, the mother reported that her son was doing more than he had originally agreed. He occasionally helped with the chores during the week. The parents expressed appreciation without making Ronnie feel guilty for not helping more during the week. Ron was much happier. He reported that his father now counsels families by helping them with problems they have which were similar to those he had with his father. This delighted the boy. The father also rather enjoyed his new role.

Overprotection as pampering. Overprotection and overdomination are somewhat related, but on a closer examination we can observe quite different patterns of pampering and a distinct difference in how this affects the child. Overdomineering parents instill in the child a fear of using judgment because they teach the child that parents know what is best and will decide. Overprotective parents overestimate possible dangers and constantly point them out to the child.

> *"Do not run or you may fall; do not venture far away from home because you may get lost; don't go on the class field trip because the bus may have an accident; don't go near a dog or cat because it may bite or scratch you. Chew your food or you may choke when you swallow it; don't go out when it rains or you will catch cold."*

Some parents succeed in getting their children excused from physical education, especially daughters, because exercises are too strenuous. Because of this overprotection, many children do not have normal social contact with other children in school or neighborhood. They do not participate in activities that many others do. This may add to their loneliness and dependency on the parents. Such children often live in constant fear and develop lack of faith in their own capabilities.

Children function better if they are brought up in an atmosphere of mutual respect and consideration and have the opportunity to develop self-reliance and independence. Children need leadership, but the kind of leadership which guides and influences them to enjoy independence and cooperation. When we counsel parents, emphasis is placed on a democratic relationship, one which encourages participation and responsibility. The counselor should help parents realize that pampering and spoiling do not prepare children to meet the demands of life.

Many people love to spoil children, shower them with affection, and overprotect them. Parents usually do not stop to consider the long-range consequences that pampering and spoiling have on the child. Parents who enjoy pampering their children have sympathy, but they must become aware of the high price paid for such mistakes and how much more difficult it will be to correct these mistakes.

Often, pampering and spoiling the child are far less the result of consideration for the child, as the parents claim, but of giving in to the parents' own needs to be such good and loving parents. For example:

> Nine-year old Ralph would not go to bed unless his parents also retired. They let him decide when everyone should go to bed. At one point in the evening he would say, "Time to go bed." Everyone would then go to his respective bedroom. The parents came for family counseling not because of this practice, but because of Ralph's problems in school where he would do no work and often go home without permission. Ralph would suddenly appear at home saying that he had enough of school that day and had decided to come home. When the counselor investigated the relationship between the boy and his parents, it was discovered how he generally dictated to the parents including the time to go to bed. The parents, especially the father, could see no wrong in this. He said that it took Ralph only a few minutes to fall asleep and, "What's wrong in showing your child how much you love him and how willing you are to do things that would give him pleasure?" The parents could see no correlation between Ralph's behavior in school and his rearing at home. The counselor and the parents had to work for a long time before the parents were willing to let the boy suffer consequences of his misbehavior. It hurt them to do so; this was a greater problem than the harm they did to their child. The counselor had to help the parents work through their own feel-

ings and low frustration tolerance before they were ready to let go of the dependency of Ralph's dependency on them.

The counselor cannot usually expect parents, like the ones described previously, to change completely even if they now understand that they prevent the child from normal development. An abrupt change may be threatening to both parent and child. Changes should begin slowly. In this case, the parents told Ralph that it was time for him to go to bed disregarding their own bedtime. They gave Ralph several choices as to the time he should go to his room. Later, choices were added as to when he would do his homework and watch television. Gradually, other responsibilities were added. Ralph did not take changes without putting up a fight. The parents were prepared for this rebellion and encouraged by the counselor to remain firm and consistent. The counselor also confronted Ralph, disclosing his goal in keeping his parents busy with him and remaining boss of the family. Ralph was told of the recommendations that were given to the parents and invited to suggest when he would like to begin accepting responsibilities and become independent. At first, Ralph did not believe the counselor. He said that his parents would never listen to such advice and that the counselor had no right to get mixed into what was not the counselor's business. But, as weeks passed Ralph began to show changes in some areas. The parents felt encouraged which, in turn, also encouraged them to continue coming to counseling sessions.

Parents often overprotect their children out of a fear that children will not be able to cope with situations if left to their own devices, or that children will feel unloved if the parents don't give in to the children's wishes. The parents mean well, but what they do not realize is that giving unnecessary service to a child, who can well do things for self, is indirectly conveying that the child is incapable, helpless, and inferior. Giving in to the child out of fear that the child will feel unloved, reinforces the child's skill in manipulation of parents.

Finally, the overprotective parent often unknowingly teaches the child not to assume responsibilities for self and to depend on others. An example:

Toni was the youngest of three brothers. He was eight when his family came for counseling. They complained that Toni refuses to get dressed by himself; that he insists the mother should tie his shoes, and that he is a learning and behavior problem in school. Mother was a little concerned about his behavior at home, but she was worried about his problems in school. Father felt that mother was making a sissy out of the boy, but he himself assumed many responsibilities for the child, like reminding him not to forget to take a pencil to school; to eat his lunch, to listen to the teacher, etc. When it was explained to the parents how their solicitous behavior added to Toni's difficulties in school, and that they would have to stop serving him and insist that he assume responsibilities for himself, Toni became very angry and shouted, "If they love me, they will never listen to you, and if they listen to you, they do not love me, and if they don't love me, I'll run away from home." Mother began to cry, asking Toni how he could possibly think that they don't love him and started a long lecture on how wrong and how unfair he was. Father too was startled and demanded to know if the counselor would suggest that they still go ahead with the recommendations under those circumstances.

One understands how skillfully this boy manipulated his parents and the means he used to keep them under control. The counselor cannot promise that the boy will not run away as he threatened, but the parents have to be helped to understand that they are playing right into the hands of the boy, and that the present problem may never change unless they have the courage to call his bluff or to let him run away and come crawling back. This may mean getting involved with the police, going through a few hours or a day with anxieties, but the final question the parents must ask themselves is, "What sacrifices am I willing to make in order to help my child grow up independently and with a sense of responsibility?"

SUMMARY

Loving and rearing children always calls for emotional sacrifices on the part of the parent. It is not an easy task, but one that parents must go through if they are really concerned with proper training for their child. Counselors can assist parents immeasurably when they help the parents understand why and how children are pampered. The counselor must help parents recognize various pampering techniques such as overindulgence, overpermissiveness, overdomineering, and overprotection. Parents can be motivated to change these approaches when these negative effects of pampering practices are highlighted by the counselor. If the counselor is successful in bringing about changes in the pampering techniques of parents that result in children's negative behaviors, changes in that behavior will follow.

BIBLIOGRAPHY

Ansbacher, H. L., & Ansbacher, R. (Eds.) (1956). *The individual psychology of Alfred Adler.* New York: Basic Books.

Bullard, M. Unpublished paper presented at the 1973 Annual Convention of NSSAP, Toronto, Canada.

Dinkmeyer, D., & McKay, G. (1973). *Raising a responsible child.* New York: Simon & Schuster.

Dreikurs, R., Grunwald, B., & Pepper, F. (1971). *Maintaining sanity in the classroom: Illustrated teaching techniques.* New York: Harper & Row.

Dreikurs, R., Grunwald, B., & Pepper, F. (1982). *Maintaining sanity in the classroom: Illustrated teaching techniques (rev. ed.).* New York: Harper & Row.

Dreikurs, R. (1957). *Psychology in the classroom.* New York: Harper & Row.

Dreikurs, R., & Soltz, V. (1964). *Children: The challenge.* New York: Hawthorn Books.

Ginott, H. (1965). *Between parent and child.* New York: Macmillan.

Sweeney, T. (1981). *Adlerian counseling: Proven concepts and strategies.* Muncie, IN: Accelerated Development.

Walton, F. (1980). *Winning teenagers over.* Columbia, SC: Adlerian Child Care Books.

CHAPTER **II**

THE COUNSELOR

The following premises are to be regarded as a frame of reference within which the counselor will find an individual approach. Although problems of individual families or parent-teacher relationships may be similar, they are never exactly alike. Furthermore, different people will react differently to the counselor's personality, mannerisms, and style. However, some basic considerations are outlined which a counselor should take into account—principles which are safe, contain no risk of offending the client nor diminishing the effectiveness of his/her counseling, and are consistent with Adlerian Psychology.

RESPECT FOR CLIENT

Of utmost importance is the counselor's respect for the client no matter what the age, problem, background, education, religion, color, sex, or particular situation may be. The counselor's own values and ethics must in no way become a hindrance to the counseling procedure.

REMAIN NONJUDGMENTAL

The counselor must at all times remain nonjudgmental. The client must feel that he/she can discuss actions, attitudes, and feelings without fear of being criticized or judged. For example: abortions, giving up a child for adoption, divorce, drinking, smoking, having a criminal record—all of which may conflict with the counselor's own values—must in no way influence the counselor's respect for the client and concern for the latter's problem.

At no time should the counselor tell the client that he/she is not normal, or is sick. People come to the counselor for help and guidance. While no stigma is attached to being an ignorant parent or teacher, a great prejudice is still attached to having a mental illness. However, should the counselor suspect a mental disorder, then the suggestion might be made that the client see someone who has "more experience" with this kind of problem, reassuring the client that Dr. _____will be able to help. This must be done in a matter of fact, nonthreatening manner. The counselor may say:

> *"I would like very much to help you, and I believe that you can be helped. I am just wondering if I am the best person for you. I haven't had much experience with this kind of problem. Would you be willing to see Dr. _____ who is highly experienced with this kind of problem? I believe that you would be very comfortable with him/her."*

If the client agrees, the counselor can ask if it is all right to call Dr. _____immediately and arrange for an appointment.

REFRAIN FROM BLAME SEEKING

The counselor must be careful not to convey the idea that one member of the family is responsible for what may be defined as the problem. Suggestions of who is to blame, which of the children a parent seems to "pick on," or who in the family is more concerned and therefore trying harder to cooperate, opens the way toward provoking or alienating one or more members of the family. Blame seeking serves no positive purpose in counseling. Example:

> Father: *I can't understand how two children can be so different. Helen is always so sweet and she helps without ever complaining. But when you ask Jack to do something, he always grumbles and he complains so much that in the end you regret having asked him. Mostly he doesn't even listen to what it is we ask him to do. He provokes me so that I could strangle him.*

> Counselor: *Yes, from some of the things you told me about Jack, I can see that he is more difficult than Helen, and that his provocations are bound to exasperate you.*

If Jack is present during the session, he is likely to resent the counselor's comments and Jack may now resist all of the counselor's efforts or even deliberately sabotage them. Furthermore, the counselor's remarks are apt to reinforce father's feelings and attitudes toward his son. A more effective reply by the counselor would have been the following:

> Counselor: *May we discuss this problem, Jack? What do you think about what your father just said?*

> OR

> Counselor: *I am sorry to hear that both of you are unhappy. Let's see how we can work out some solutions to this problem. What do you think, Jack?*

The counselor has shown no partiality and, at the same time, has shown confidence in the ability of father and son to resolve their difficulties.

CONFRONT THE CLIENT(S)

Values of confronting the client, i.e., indicating the client's goal in a nonthreatening manner, is an essential step in Adlerian counseling. It also is essential to help the client face the real problem. Being overly cautious and afraid of confronting the client with his/her own part in the problem may stifle the counselor's creativity and spontaneity. Therefore, a real art is essential to combine the spontaneity with careful avoidance of putting the client on the spot or making him/her feel uncomfortable, but still insisting that the client deal with the real issues.

SHOW EMPATHY

The counselor will not help by assuming a patronizing attitude toward the client. Patronizing may imply pity or lack of confidence in the client's ability to deal effectively with the problem, and the client may experience the condescension as insulting. Example of what not to do:

> Mother: *I come home from work so tired, I can hardly stand on my feet. On the way home I usually do some grocery shopping. When I finally come home, I find the house in such a mess; everything is scattered all over the place; the kids are—I don't know where, and my husband comes home and starts giving me arguments for not having dinner ready the moment he enters the house.*

> Counselor: *I am sorry to hear that. Who wouldn't be upset under those circumstances? This is really not fair to you.*

The counselor's response shows "pity" rather than "empathy." This method may discourage the mother even more, and it is bound to reinforce her attitude of "unfairness." The counselor might have said:

> Counselor: *Could it be that you feel responsible that everything gets done properly and on time?*

OR

Counselor: *As I understand it, you would feel better if your children and your husband would give you a hand when you come home tired?*

Such responses move toward understanding of the client's difficulties. The counselor can be sympathetic to the feelings expressed while also helping the client find ways to be more effective with a bad situation.

CONCERNS WITH BEING LIKED

Understandably a counselor wants to be liked by clients. Unfortunately, a counselor's eagerness to be liked (not to be confused with "winning" the client) can cause the counselor to become ineffective by overlooking or not working with the real issue(s).

Over concern with being liked by the client may result in neglect of examination and discussion of the underlying patterns and factors which are responsible for the existing problem. Furthermore, a possibility exists that the client may become overly dependent on the counselor and come to the sessions for reassurance rather than for insight into problems and for learning how to live more effectively with or overcome them.

Counselors are especially prone to make this mistake when they counsel children. In order to be liked by them, counselors often avoid discussing problems which children have with their parents or teachers, avoid confrontation as to the child's goals, and make the counseling session no more than a pleasant visit. An example:

Counselor: *Steve, why did you come to see me?*

Steve: *Because the teacher sent me to you.*

Counselor: *Why?*

Steve: *Because I don't do my work.*

Counselor: *I suppose the work is too hard for you.*

Steve: *Nope.*

Counselor: *It isn't. Don't you like the subject?*

Steve: *No. I hate it.*

Counselor: *Well, if you hate it, I can understand that you don't want to do it. What subject do you like?*

This counselor is more concerned with being liked by the student than helping him/her understand the purpose of his/her behavior. At this point what subject Steve likes is completely irrelevant. Because Steve admitted that the work is not too difficult for him, he may use refusal to work for getting attention or to show his power. The counselor might have stated or posed the following questions. How he proceeds would depend on Steve's response.

Counselor: *You say that you hate the subject, yet you tell me that the work is not too difficult for you. Right? I wonder if you feel that you don't have to do anything that requires work? What do you think?*

OR

Counselor: *Could it be that you do only what you like and that nobody is going to tell you what to do? Why is this so important to you?*

OR

Counselor: *Is it possible that you think that giving in to an adult is a sign of weakness and that you must show how strong you are in your determination?*

OR

Counselor: *What do you suggest that the teacher should do when you don't work?*

OR

Counselor: *Do you think that you and teacher could discuss this problem and come to some agreement? May I suggest this to your teacher?*

The counselor is trying to help Steve realize that he has choices; that it is within his power to change the situation. He/she also is helping Steve to consider the purpose of his behavior and reconsider its importance.

AVOID POWER STRUGGLES

The counselor should avoid getting into a power-struggle with the client. He/she cannot impose his/her own wishes, nor does he/she have the right to insist that the client accept everything the counselor believes, or that the client must do whatever the counselor suggests. Such insistence by the counselor against the will of the client will inevitably result in ineffective counseling. The counselor may appeal, suggest, even plead, but ultimately the decision to use or to reject what is recommended rests with the client.

SHOW DIRECTION AND GOALS

Much of the material in this volume dwells on principles and techniques for application in counseling families. The family counselor should keep a perspective in mind that will serve as a long-range guide throughout the process as he attempts to assist a family in difficulty. The counselor should keep in mind what he/she is trying to achieve with the disrupted family over a series of counseling sessions. Suggested long-range objectives follow.

The counselor must show direction and definite goals if he/she is to gain and maintain the confidence of the family members. The primary goal is to improve relationships in the family.

The counselor's perspective must serve an immediate as well as a long-range goal throughout the counseling process.

An important objective is the promotion of movement and change. While some of the family members may desire change, it does not indicate that all members want it. Children who have been successful through the use of negative behavior are often resistant and do not want any changes, especially changes in their parents. It also may happen that a parent comes for counseling in the hope that the counselor will change "the others" while they themselves do not have to change. The counselor will have to confront them with this possibility and help all family members realize that each must first change himself/herself before any movement or general changes in the family will take place. Each member must think in terms of "what can I do to change the present situation?"

Probably the most important objective is to help the family learn effective problem-solving techniques. In so doing, the family can become an independent, but effectively functioning unit. The Family Council is probably the best approach in teaching family problem-solving techniques. (See Chapter VI.)

CHAPTER **III**

BASIC STEPS IN FAMILY COUNSELING

This book contains many suggestions for the family counselor and the issues discussed are organized under many different and special headings. Material is presented in several basic steps. Dreikurs (1967) outlined four basic elements or goals in therapy and family counseling that he considered essential. These are expanded to seven basic steps in this chapter. Detailed suggestions for the accomplishment of each step or goal are submitted. Counselors will add other techniques as experience is gained in this approach. Each step is specific, indispensable, and each moves logically out of the other. At any moment in the counseling process, any one of the several steps may be more evident than the others, and it may be necessary at any time to move from a logically later step back to a logically prior step in order to continue. In any case, when an effective counseling session is completed, a review of what took place will show that the following Basic Steps were included.

ESTABLISHING RAPPORT

The effective counselor will maintain an open, friendly demeanor, and an obvious interest in the client(s). He/she will show empathy and understanding for the client's situation as he/she moves toward developing mutual confidence and respect. The counselor must be sensitive to possible changes in the relationship during the entire session and take positive steps to restore the client's confidence should it waver.

A positive relationship between counselor and client exists whenever the goals of each are in alignment; when both are on the same side, allies, collaborators in the effort to achieve improvement. Until this position is established, and unless it is maintained throughout the counseling process, it is difficult to work together in order to explore, define, and address problems. This is not to say that much of a fuss and time need be spent on establishing a good relationship. Counselors of different training often spend weeks or months attempting to establish rapport. They often lose the client's confidence in the process. The client becomes further discouraged when weeks have passed with groping in the dark. Adlerian counselors are trained to establish rapport quickly and to help the counselee leave the first session feeling understood and encouraged. The suggestion is that the counselor begin informally and may begin by asking:

> *How do you feel being here?*
> *Is this your first experience talking to a counselor?*
> *I am very glad that you decided to come.*

Would you prefer being called Mr. and Mrs. Brown or would you like it better if we call each other by first name?

If the client prefers to be called by his/her first name, the counselor should give his/her first name. "May I refer to you, Mrs. Brown, as Mom, and to you, Mr. Brown, as Dad?" In ascertaining the client's preference as to how they wish to be addressed, the counselor shows respect and this contributes to building rapport. A simple gesture, a readiness to acknowledge the counselee's choices in the matter of formalitites, or an indication of willingness to proceed on a friendly basis of first names already establishes an atmosphere of equality and the quest for agreement.

To children, "Do you want to shake hands?" The question together with an outstretched hand in greeting communicates respect for the child's choice together with an attitude of friendship. Rarely does a child refuse to shake hands in response, but even then, the way is open to agreement. "O.K., we don't have to."

It is encouraging to have one's difficulties recognized as a *real* difficulty, and to see that one's painful feelings are acknowledged as normal and understandable and that many others have similar difficulties. Parenting is a tough job!

To a parent or child:

This seems to be hard for you to discuss. You seem to have had a bad time and it discouraged you.

OR

You seem to feel very much alone in your predicament. I can understand that this upsets you.

Rapport increases as the client comes more and more to an awareness of the counselor as a collaborator working together to find a more satisfactory way of solving problems. The client does not feel criticized for having difficulties nor is he/she put down for not having the tools to solve them.

GATHERING PERTINENT FACTS

As soon as the foregoing "warm-up" is concluded, the counselor moves directly toward collecting pertinent facts that will assist in understanding the client and problem. It is not necessary to compile a long history of a case in order to understand it. The counselor should focus on the current situation and can do so by directing the parent's attention to answering questions to obtain the following information:

Obtain a general brief description of the problem as the parents see it.

Collect the parent's thumbnail description of each of the children.

Ask the parents to describe a typical day in the life of the family.

Collect detailed information on the family constellation (See Chapter V).

Ask the client on subsequent visits for a review of recommendations made in previous sessions and what happened when these were implemented.

It may not be possible to cover all of the previous elements in one session but, if not, these can be utilized at subsequent sessions. Several of the questions will generally yield sufficient information for the counselor to understand the situation and lend assistance to the family. Chapter V deals more thoroughly with gathering pertinent facts.

PINPOINTING THE ISSUE

While gathering pertinent facts of a case, the counselor will begin immediately to "guess" or make tentative judgments on the goal level of behavior of clients. These tentative judgments will serve as a "working

hypothesis" as the counselor proceeds. He/she may rely on experience with previous cases, interpretation of what has been related, and the family constellation information in order to arrive at some tentative conclusions.

In listening to any account of difficulties, any series of complaints which parents and children present against each other, the counselor must be alert for patterns of feelings or behavior. The "private logic" which accounts for the behavioral patterns of any individual rests on his/her ideas of what is important and what he/she naturally feels inclined to do in a situation (see Chapter IV). Hidden goals must be identified and brought to light. What is meant by the "private logic" and hidden goals is illustrated by the following example.

> Counselor: *Let me see if I understand. You told Helen to clean the table by the time you return from the store. But when you returned and found that she had not done what you told her to do, you got upset and punished her.*
>
> *You also told me that you got very angry when Jimmy ignored your instructions to wear his gloves when he left the house. You then punished him by not allowing him to go out after school.*
>
> *In your opinion, what upset you more, the messy table and the worry about Jimmy's cold hands or the fact that the children did not mind you?*

Pinpointing the real problem will, of course, depend on the parent's response to the question. It is, however, very rare that the parent would be more upset about the messy table or the child's cold hands than about the child's disobedience. This mother may have never before realized the real reason for her anger.

> Counselor: *Could it be that you get upset each time you feel out of control? Are you, perhaps, hurt and angry that the children take your requests so indifferently? Are you worried that this is a reflection on you as a mother? Is this what is really bothering you?*

If the parent agrees, or more likely, agrees that there may be such a possibility, the counselor can "pin-point" the ideas of authority and the notions surrounding it.

Counselor: *Well then, perhaps we could conclude that we are not only talking about Jimmy's gloves or what he does or does not do about them. Perhaps we are talking about your idea of a parent's authority. Possibly that you are afraid that you might lose that authority whenever you can't control his or Helen's behavior, or whenever you can't make the children do what you want them to do?*

In this way, the counselor is encouraging the client to think about things in a new light, helping her to address the real issue of the power struggle with the children, and opening the way toward understanding of how the "need" to be the boss contributes to the conflict. In other words, the counselor helps the client realize that she is playing a part in the problem, and that the problem persists because the mother and the child cooperate in the "fighting."

A standard technique of pin-pointing the issue in Adlerian counseling is that of confrontation of the client. Probably the best known of several techniques of confrontation is the "could it be that...?" question as developed by Dreikurs as an effective means of revealing the mistaken goals to children. Details of applying this and other confrontation techniques are found in Chapter IV.

EXPLORING ALTERNATIVES

The client and the counselor are working together in exploring new possibilities for dealing with the problem effectively. Alternative solutions are always open but often obscured because of the patterns of conflict and discouragement.

Counselor: *Would you be willing to go over the situation again and see if you can picture a more constructive way of dealing with such a problem? What could you do next time?*

The parent and the counselor are now oriented toward imagining behavior which stimulates and elicits cooperation. Any suggestion the parent now makes can be tested by this criterion—does it elicit cooperation? Any proposal which hints of power and coercion can now be called to question as being more likely to lead to resistance, rebellion, and further fighting. Only after the client has been helped to understand self and how he/she functions whenever he/she feels out of control, can the client be motivated to agree to more positive alternatives.

PROMOTING A NEW AGREEMENT, CORRECTIVE MEASURES, AND RECOMMENDATIONS

When the client has come to see his/her part in the troublesome transaction of parent-child conflict, and when it is clear that to continue in the part of the transaction is, in a sense, to "agree" to perpetuating the conflict, the time has come to "change the agreement." Now the counselor is free to help the client to decide upon one or two suggestions for change and to resolve to act on the decision. It will not be of great help to influence the client to change his/her behavior without helping him/her change the basic concept about self and how to judge others who oppose.

The counselor may ask:

Which of the ideas discussed appeal to you? Of all the things we talked about which one strikes you as something you can do right now to improve the situation? Would you be willing to do that plan for a week just as an experiment to see whether or not it will help? Are you willing to apply this principle and to do this one thing the very next time you feel provoked and angry? Have we agreed upon this plan? Will you do it and tell me what happened in the next session?

An agreement to change behavior is already a change in behavior. Blaming the other, feeling bound to act in certain ways because no other choice is apparent, and yielding to pessimism and discouragement are all left behind when one person in the family says, "Yes, I can see one thing which I can do to make the situation better and I will do it."

It is often necessary for the counselor to influence the parent to stop doing some "wrong" things in order to move effectively toward improving relationships in the family. A typical example is to recommend that the parents cease involving themselves in their children's fights. It is most helpful if all members of the family agree on the recommendations and new agreements. However, this is not absolutely necessary if the recommendation is one that one or more members of the family can implement without imposing the decision on others. Again, the example of parents removing themselves from their children's squabbles is a good example.

It is vitally important that clients attempt only as many new agreements that they *know* they can do. Often, only one or two are sufficient. If parents are overloaded with recommendations, they may become confused, fail to follow through and become even more discouraged as a result.

ENCOURAGING THE FAMILY

The counselor should proceed on the basis that every family that comes for counseling needs encouragement. This may begin with the counselor pointing out the strengths that the family can build on. The family will receive some encouragement from the techniques described previously, particularly those recommended for establishing rapport. The counselor, however, would deliberately include encouraging elements. A thorough discussion of encouragement techniques may be found in Chapter VI.

SUMMARY OF SESSION

The counselor should close the session with a brief factual summary which includes the problems as pin-pointed and a review of the recommendations and new agreements to be implemented. The clients should be asked if they feel that they received some help and encouragement and what they might like to focus on at the next session.

After the family has departed, the counselor will find it helpful to make a few brief notes for the agenda for the next interview.

SUMMARY

In summary it should be emphasized that the several basic steps outlined previously may be organized and accomplished in many different configurations and details. However, an analysis of any effective Adlerian counseling session will reveal that these steps have been included. In a series of counseling sessions, one or more of the basic steps will be more evident than others. It is emphasized that the counselor must remain especially sensitive to the establishment and maintenance of rapport through each session. Rapport is primary if the counselor brings about positive changes in the family.

A wide variety of techniques for accomplishing the basic steps are detailed in the chapters following.

REFERENCE

Dreikurs, R. (1967). Goals in therapy, *Psychodynamics, Psychotherapy and Counseling.* Chicago, IL: Alfred Adler Institute.

CHAPTER

PSYCHOLOGICAL PREMISES

CONFRONTATION TECHNIQUES
FOR PSYCHOLOGICAL DISCLOSURE

Use of various confrontation techniques for psychological disclosure is standard procedure of Adlerian trained counselors and therapists. The purpose of confrontation is to reveal the "private logic" of the client. *Private logic may be defined as goals, mistaken ideas, and attitudes toward life, and hidden reasons that people use to justify behavior.* Adler consistently emphasized the difference between private logic and common sense (Dreikurs, 1973). It also is basic Adlerian theory that the individual is not aware of goals as they exist in the unconscious (Ansbacher & Ansbacher, 1964). Dreikurs (1973) also made the point that all private logic comprises the unconscious, thus inferring the necessity to develop techniques for the counselor to assist the client in becoming aware of unconscious, private logic via confrontation. Dreikurs further delineates three psychological processes all of which are part of the private logic. These include: (1) immediate goals of the current situation; i.e., four mistaken goals of misbehavior which also are embedded in the long-range goals; (2) hidden reasons which are justifications for current thought and action; and (3) the long-range goals of the lifestyle as used in psychotherapy (Dreikurs, 1973).

The counselor needs to help the client become aware of the unconscious goals and their influence on behavior. The competent counselor, who reveals the private logic to various members of a family, exercises an effective technique in assisting them to understand each other and how they function. In so doing the counselor can show clients their real intentions or goals, which are hidden reasons and mistaken notions upon which each member operates.

Perhaps even more importantly, the counselor has promoted movement by provoking a response concerning relationships between family members.

The techniques for confrontation for each of the three aspects of private logic are somewhat different. These include short-term disturbing goals of the immediate situation, hidden reason, and long-range goals of the lifestyle. Each provides insight in understanding behavior.

FOUR GOALS OF DISTURBING BEHAVIOR

Disturbing behavior can be classified according to four psychological goals. These are immediate and apply to current interaction. Dreikurs (1957) originally described them as disturbing or maladjusted goals. The four goals appear in other literature as goals of misbehavior, mistaken goals of behavior, and are frequently referred to as Goal 1, Goal 2, Goal 3, and Goal 4. These terms refer to the same conceptual scheme. The Adlerian family counselor will find this technique for classifying children's goals among the most useful of the various methods in helping clients understand the purposes of behavior. Prior to attempted usage, the counselor must first learn every aspect of the four goals of disturbing behavior. The counselor should commit the charts on the following pages to memory so that he/she can quickly classify each specific behavior according to the goal level, that is described in the counseling session.

Children develop various ways to attain their goals when they perceive that they do not have sufficient recognition or find their places in the family through useful contributions. They often divert energies into negative behavior in the mistaken belief that these misbehaviors will result in helping them attain status and acceptance in the group. Children will often strive for mistaken goals even when ample opportunities for positive contributions are available. This attitude is due to lack of courage to try, or a misconception as to their ability to participate positively or a failure to recognize opportunities.

In keeping with the basic theory that all behavior is goal-oriented, Dreikurs (1957) developed an effective plan by which all children's faulty behavior could be classified in these four distinct categories of goals. Dreikurs's schema of four goals of disturbing behavior appears in Figure 4.1.

As Dreikurs (1957) pointed out, all behavior can be categorized as either "useful" or "useless." Whether a behavior is useful or useless depends on whether it makes a contribution to the group by meeting group norms of expectations and requirements. The counselor's first step in use of the schema in interpreting behavior is to ascertain whether the behavior is useless or useful. Secondly, the counselor must determine whether a specific behavior is "active" or "passive" as Dreikurs (1957) also pointed out that all behavior could be classified in these two categories.

Counselors will find that the level of a child's difficulty will operate on a continuum of increased or decreased social interest as shown on the horizontal line at the top of the schema. This may be indicated by vacillation of the child's behavior from useful to useless activities. Such changes in behavior indicate changes in the individual's interest in making contributions to or conforming to group expectations.

Several major clues assist the counselor in pinpointing the goal of misbehavior. Having ascertained the useful or useless and active or

Perfection
+
Adjusted Goal
of Social
Interest   ← (increasing) Continuum of Social Interest (decreasing) →

[handwritten: IDEAL-perfection; felt +; Class]

	Useful Side of Life		Useless Side of Life		Goals of Misbehavior
	Active	Passive	Active	Passive	
	Industrious	Charm, Vain	Tattles	Cries	Attention
	Success	Witty	Show off	Laziness	(Attention
	Over-ambition	Teacher's pet	Nuisance	Clumsy	Getting
	Be first	Sensitive	Bratty	Untidy	Mechanisms)
	Reliable		Minor-	Bashful	
			mischief	Fearful	
			Teases	Dependent	
	Intellectual	Withdrawal	Defiant	Stubborn	Power
	Political		Rebel	Forgets	(Power
	Business		Temper	Dawdles	Struggle)
	Moral		Truant		
	domination		Argues		
			Disobeys		
			Delinquent	Sullen	Revenge
			Vicious	defiance	Getting
			Brutal	Violent	Even
			Steals	passivity	
				Inferiority	Assumed
				complex	Disability
				Hopeless	(Inadequacy)
				Stupid	
				Indolence	

[handwritten annotations: (increasing) ↑ ; Continuum of Courage; cooperate takeover; Ghandi MLK; Poland (Lettwolenda); Martyr; Retaliation; (decreasing) ↓; Final ; felt -]

Felt
Minus
Position

Figure 4.1 Schema of Dreikursian concept of goal centered behavior.

Note. Adapted from *Psychology in the Classroom* by R. Dreikurs. Copyright 1957 by Harper & Row, New York.

passive categories in which a behavior fits, the counselor may then proceed to pinpoint the goal level or levels of a specific behavior. On the schema (Figure 4.1) is indicated various clues to the counselor as dialogue with the parents, the teachers, or the child reveal adult reaction to the behavior. There are four major clues for the counselor to follow in ascertaining the psychological goal of an individual's behavior.

- What the parent or other adult does when the behavior or misbehavior occurs.

- How the parent reacts emotionally.

- The child's response to the series of confrontation questions with the revealing recognition reflex.

- The child's response to corrective measures.

Parents may be readily acquainted with the four goals by becoming familiar with the details found in Figure 4.2.

The counselor must provide instruction in the four goals of misbehavior and how to discern them. In so doing the counselor can teach the parent to avoid the traps set by children. The counselor also needs to reveal to the children that the "games they play" are understood. This revealing is done by confrontation techniques. The child is then helped to find alternate behaviors. The counselor also should convey to the children that he/she will communicate information about the children's "games" to the parents.

The Attention Getting Child. If behaving on the attention getting level on the useful side of life, the child operates on the belief (usually unconscious) that he/she is important *only* if he/she is getting attention. The success-oriented child believes that he/she is accepted or important *only* if he/she is successful. Usually high achievement is lauded by parents and teachers and it tends to prove to a child that "success" will guarantee status. However, the child's social interest and acceptance will be enhanced more if success activities are performed for the contribution made to the group rather than for the attention or power derived from them. Students and counselors often find difficulty in understanding the fine line distinguishing this point, but it is important because often an attention-getting, success-oriented child will cease working if he/she fails to gain adequate recognition.

Goal	Child's Reaction to Reprimand	Corrective Measures from Parent
Attention	Stops disturbing behavior for a while, but then starts all over again May feel satisfied and stop disturbing May realize the absurdity of behavior and give it up	Stop to realize what it is that the child wants from you, and if you sense that he/she wants to keep you busy with him/her, do the opposite from your first reaction. Walk away; tell the child in a friendly way that he/she will have to handle this on his/her own. Watch for moments when the child does not disturb and demand negative attention and then show appreciation. Always give the child positive attention. When the child wants to talk to you, listen and consider what the child is saying. Voice your opinion but do not get into a power struggle.
Power	May resent it and intensify his/her disturbing behavior Is determined to show that he/she is the boss and will do what he/she wants May overtly or covertly demand of the parent "What can you do about it?"	Do not get into a power struggle. Agree with the child that you can't "make" him/her do things, but that you would appreciate him/her helping out in the situation. Watch for opportunities when the child does not fight you and show your appreciation. Find ways to make the child feel important. You may ask the child for advice in an area where you can follow his/her suggestions.

Figure 4.2 Reaction to correction and suggested corrective measures.

Figure 4.2 (continued)

Goal	Child's Reaction to Reprimand	Corrective Measures from Parent
Revenge	Child wants to get even for the hurt he/she experienced from others. May become worse. May tell parent that he/she doesn't like him/her . May threaten to do horrible things. May run out of the room and disappear for a time. May use foul language and become abusive.	Avoid retaliation Help the child realize that he/she tests people to see how much they will take from him/her. Help the child feel needed and wanted. Do not let the child provoke you to a point where you "must get even." Walk away from the situation and cool off. Do not give up on the child.
Assumed Disability (Inadequacy)	There may be no reaction from the child. Child may insist that he/she can't do what the parent requires of him/her. The child may withdraw even more.	Help the child realize that he/she may be mistaken and if an attempt is made, he/she may learn that the task can be accomplished. Give the child easy tasks where the child is bound to succeed. Never say or do anything to reinforce the child's belief that he/she is dumb or incapable. Do not compare the child with other children.

Note. Adopted from *Maintaining Sanity in the Classroom,* Second Edition, by Rudolf Dreikurs, Bernice Grunwald and Floy Pepper. Copyright 1982 by Harper & Row Publishers, New York.

If the child is striving for attention on the useless side of life, he/she may provoke the adult through brattiness, deliberate clumsiness, argumentation, and disobedience (also found in power-seeking children.) Passive children may strive for attention through being lazy, untidy, shy, forgetful, being overly sensitive, or fearful.

The "Power" Acting Child. If attention getting behaviors do not result in the acceptance sought for and a place in the group, the child may become more discouraged. He/she, then, may determine that exercising power will assure a place in the group and status. It is no small wonder that children often desire power. They usually perceive of parents, teachers, other adults, and older siblings as all powerful persons who usually get their own way. Children will pattern behavior after models who are perceived as achieving importance and acceptance. "If I can be the boss and run things like my parents, I'll be important and accepted." Such are the mistaken notions that often spring from an inexperienced child. Efforts to subdue the child in the battle for power will invariably result in the child's victory. As Dreikurs (1957) stated:

> No final "victory" of parents and teachers is possible. In most instances the child will "win out," if only because he/she is not restricted in his/her fighting methods by any sense of responsibility or moral obligation.

Thus, the child won't fight fair and, not having the wide scope of responsibilities that encumber the adult, can spend much more time plotting and executing his/her strategy.

The Revengeful Child. The child who fails in finding a satisfactory place in the group by attention-getting behaviors or power plays, may become convinced that he/she is not liked or accepted and becomes revengeful. This is the sullen, defiant or vicious child who resorts to retaliation to feel that he/she is important. In severely disrupted families, parents often retaliate in return, thereby perpetuating the cycle. Retaliatory or revengeful activities may be verbal or physical, openly brutal or sophisticated. However, the goal is the same—to get even with others.

The Assumed Disability Child. Children who fail to find a place in the group through socially useful contributions, attention getting, power or revengeful activities, will finally give up, become passive, and stop trying. Dreikurs (1957) stated, "He (the child) hides himself behind a display of real or imagined inferiority" (p. 14). If such a child can convince parents or teachers that he/she really cannot perform, demands made on him/her are diminished and much effort and many possibilities of humiliation and failure are reduced. Today's classrooms are full of such children.

RECOGNITION REFLEX

Verification of the accuracy of the counselor's confrontation is the recognition reflex—an involuntary spontaneous reaction by the youngster. This reaction appears in the facial expression as a smile or laughter or other sudden change in expression. Recognition reflex appears when the client becomes consciously aware of his/her true intention or goal. Adolescents and adults are less likely than younger children to react openly with a recognition reflex, but rarely can a telling reflex be avoided. Adolescents and adults who are very discouraged often develop a poker face countenance and are more difficult to "read." Value systems in some subcultures of our society also foster repression of display of emotions thus complicating the work of the counselor. One of the authors had the experience of learning to rely on the dilation of the pupil of the eye as a verification signal in a particular indigenous American population. Experience and development of sensitivity to even minute physical reactions of the client will assist the counselor to overcome such difficulties.

The immediate result of a successful confrontation is an improved rapport and better receptivity on the part of the client as he/she feels understood. The counselor, of course, has a verified base of understanding the goal level of the client and can proceed with appropriate corrective measures.

CONFRONTATION

**Techniques—Four Goals
of Disturbing Behavior**

The purpose of the immediate goal confrontation is to verify the counselor's guess and reveal the client's real goal or intentions for specific behaviors. Such disclosure often is sufficient to influence a change in behavior. However, a change in response by the parents is necessary as well as implementation of a variety of encouragement and other corrective measures.

In eliciting a response from the client as to the accuracy of the counselor's guess, a carefully prescribed procedure is suggested. Experienced counselors may vary the technique, but following the procedure described will bring the best results.

First, the counselor will have collected descriptions of several crisis situations or behaviors during the counseling session. These descriptions must contain very specific information on who did what, what was said, who reacted in what way, and what happened next. The counselor constructs hypotheses or makes guesses as to the client's goal based on this information.

The next important step is to ask the child or other client for permission to reveal or disclose the meaning of the behavior. It is *vital* that the counselor present a friendly, nonaccusatory, almost conspiratorial manner. The counselor can proceed something like this:

> *John, do you have any idea why you behaved like this in these several situations? Usually, John does not know and he is being truthful because his intentions are still at the unaware or unconscious level. The authors also have found that asking if the youngster believes that people have reasons (purposes) for things they do, will usually promote a receptiveness for the whole series of questions involved in the confrontation. This is especially helpful with adolescents. After receiving the usual, "I dunno" reply to the question on why (for what purpose) John acted as he did, the counselor next can say, "I have some ideas about that and want to explain them to you." If there is some hesitancy, the counselor can add, "I may be wrong, but I've known a lot of kids and I would just like to check this out with you," or a similar statement.*

It is important that the counselor receive permission, but it is not absolutely necessary, if the client is to be receptive to the disclosure. On the rare occasion when permission is not forthcoming, the counselor might ask permission to try his/her ideas out on the group if the counseling is in a class on Family Education Center demonstration. The counselor may address himself/herself to the group and ask, "May I tell you why Susan refuses to go to bed when the mother tells her that it is bedtime? Could it be that. . .?'' The counselor then goes through all four goals of disclosure, all the while watching the child's facial expression. If in a private session, the counselor can ask for a minute to jot his/her explanations in notes. Curiosity will almost always stimulate a client to being receptive to hear the counselor's views. If there is a co-counselor in this situation, the two counselors may pause in their dialogue with the client and discuss the meaning of the behavior.

The counselor then proceeds with his/her series of questions and watches for the recognition reflex. It also is essential that the counselor's guesses be put in the form of questions. A note of explanation as to our insistence that the counselor use "Could it be that..." or "I wonder if..." when confronting the child. Such questions are not accusations but indicate that the counselor realizes that he/she may be wrong in the assumption. Youngsters usually respond to such hypothetical questions. We have found that counselors, who confront the child with, "I know why you...you want attention," or "you do this to show that you're the boss," often meet with resentment by the youngster who feels accused and will not respond with a recognition reflex. The most effective approach as recommended by Dreikurs and his students is—"Could it be that..." and complete the question appropriately depending on the mistaken goal in question. More experienced counselors may take shortcuts and only ask one or two questions before an accurate response is shown; however, it is recommended that all four goals be checked in consecutive order as a standard practice. The counselor then poses four, "Could it be...?" questions—one for each of the mistaken goals. It also is helpful to formulate a variety of questions for each goal, but each meaning the same thing. This improves chances of communicating accurately with the client. The counselor might vary the "Could it be...?" introduction with "I wonder if...?" or similar terminology. A variety of confrontation questions are suggested:

Goal One—Attention. *"Could it be that...*
...you want mother to stay busy with you all the time?

...you think that you are not important unless the teacher is paying attention to you?

...no one pays much attention to you unless you misbehave?"

Goal Two—Power. *"Could it be that...*
...you want to show Mom and Dad that you are the boss?

...you are going to do only what you decide to do and not what Mom or the teacher wants you to do?

...you will do your chores only when you decide and not when someone else wants you to do them?"

Goal Three—Revenge. *"Could it be that...*

...everyone gives you a bad time so you will just get back at them?

...you want to get even?

...you feel hurt and want to hurt others?"

Goal Four—Assumed Disability. *"Could it be that...*

...no matter how hard you try, nothing comes out well so why try at all?

...whatever you do in school, it never is good enough so you give up?

...you want to do a very good job and, don't think you can, so you don't try at all? You just want to be left alone."

Reaction to Correction. Another reliable way of understanding the purpose of children's behaviors is to observe how each child reacts to our method of correction. If the child pursues goal one, the child will stop for a few minutes when the adult fusses with the child or pays attention to him/her in one way or another, and then starts the attention getting behavior again. If goal two is pursued, the child will continue the behavior even when the adult takes time and pays attention to him/her. If the child pursues goal three, the child's behavior will not only continue when the adult reprimands the child, but may actually get worse. If the goal is number four, the child will in no way react to attention or persuasion. Children's reactions to reprimand are outlined in Figure 4.2 for each of the Four Goals of Disturbing Behavior.

We are not in favor of parents disclosing the goal to the child. The reason for it is mainly that parents usually don't do it correctly and goal disclosure is effective only if done in a very definite way. Parents usually repeat the goal disclosure to the child until the child gets fed up with it and stops listening. Parents also are often accusatory in goal disclosure; therefore, we strongly recommend that the counselor disclose the goal to a child and instruct the parent to refrain from goal disclosure. However, it is helpful for the parents to understand the goal of the child's misbehavior for it enables them to avoid falling into the child's trap.

Disclosing the goal does not necessarily imply that, now knowing the purpose of his/her misbehavior, the child will stop the behavior. This will occur in some cases. But children, who understand the purpose of their behavior and continue despite it, seldom derive the same pleasure from it. As Adler said, "We spit into their soup," and Dreikurs added, "they may continue eating the soup, but it will never taste the same."

The most important aspect of helping parents to understand the purpose of misbehavior is to help them give children the feeling of being accepted. Parents also need to develop opportunities for positive contributions so that children will not resort to mistaken behavior in order to try to find a place in the group.

What the parent can do will be discussed in the various vignettes and cases dealing with various kinds of child misbehavior found throughout this volume. Several effective corrective measures for each of the four goals are listed in Figure 4.2.

Guessing the Hidden Reason

In attempting to reveal the client's private logic by guessing the hidden reason, the counselor is not trying to determine the long-range or short-term goals of the client's behavior, but is trying to elicit the client's own justification for the behavior. In other words, the "why" or client's rationale of what was said or done. The hidden reason technique has many advantages (Dreikurs, 1973). Most people who come to counseling are seeking explanations as to why they act as they do or why their children act as they do. Revealing the hidden reason of their private logic has a powerful effect. Client reaction is invariably reliable and he/she will verify that the counselor correctly guessed the exact words that were going through the client's mind at the time of the behavior or statement in question. An added advantage is that no harm is done if the counselor guesses and doesn't get a positive confirmation. Dreikurs (1973) wrote an excellent example.

A fourteen year old black girl was in violent rebellion at home and in school. While she constantly misbehaved, she always felt abused. She could only talk about what wrongs other people did to her. We asked her whether she wanted help, and she vehemently replied, "No." Then we had to ask why she shouted "No."

Here is the point where many trained students will run into difficulties. Until now they have been taught not to look for psychological understanding of goals. And here we are not concerning ourselves with any goals of the patient but only with his "logic," although it is his/her private logic. There are many psychological interpretations of the girl's reaction, and many are probably even correct. Perhaps she was pessimistic and did not think anybody could help her. Perhaps she wanted to continue her rebellion and her desire to punish others, to be defiant in order to show her independence. All these are psychological explanations, worth investigating and revealing to her. But one can be sure that none of these thoughts were on her mind when she rejected help. She, herself, could not say why she said it. Then each student in the class tried to figure out what was on her mind. After many futile suggestions, one guessed it. She was thinking, "I don't need help, the others do." Not only did she agree to that, but immediately her facial expression changed, and she became accessible and receptive. (Dreikurs, 1973, p. 30)

The client's hidden rationalization can suddenly become perceptible to him/her and result in immediate relief and encouragement that comes with feeling understood. The counselor may ask the client what he/she feels in describing the problem and what may be going through his/her mind. After listening to the client, the counselor may express his/her own feelings and how the counselor perceives the problem. In order to avoid the possibility that the client may feel accused, we suggest that the counselor put his/her suggestions in the form of a hypothesis, the same way as is done when disclosing the goal of behavior to a child.

Could it be that...?

Is it possible that...?

I am wondering if...?

The following example will further explain this technique. The first is from a Parent-Counselor Conference:

> **Problem:** Mary who is in second grade takes no interest in school. She does not work in class and she does not do her homework.
>
> Counselor: *Does Mary have any chores at home?*
>
> Mother: *You can't expect a child her age to do housework.*
>
> **Guess:** It is possible that mother has low expectations of Mary. She may feel sorry for her daughter. It also is possible that the mother feels accused by the counselor and is on the defensive.
>
> Counselor: *I hope that I haven't given you the impression that I am accusing you. It is not uncommon for some parents to feel that children Mary's age are too young to be given responsibilities in the home. However, some children, even younger than Mary, have shown themselves to be quite capable of helping with household chores.*
>
> Mother: *I don't believe in that sort of thing. Children go to school and that should be all the responsibility that they should carry. I deliberately don't ask my children to help around the house so that they may have all the time they need to do their school work.*
>
> **Comments:** Counselor's guess that this mother may feel accused seems to be confirmed. She has very strong and definite opinions and standards. She goes by her private logic. It may be difficult to help her understand the correlation between Mary's lack of training toward the acceptance of responsibilities at home and her resistance to accept responsibilities at school. The counselor is advised to go slowly with this mother; help her realize that she understands this mother and that the counselor is concerned.
>
> Counselor: *I can see that you are making every effort to help Mary with her school work.*
>
> Mother: *I try my best. I still don't know why she doesn't do any work for school. I make no demands and I give her every opportunity to have all the time she needs. She is not dumb, you know.*

Guess: Mother may be angry at Mary for defeating mother's efforts.

Counselor: *Could it be that you are somewhat angry because it seems as if Mary were defeating all of your efforts?*

Mother: *Of course, I am angry. Wouldn't you be? She has absolutely no excuse and she knows it.*

Comments: Mother's response points more toward anger than towards feeling sorry for Mary. This former guess may now be discarded. The counselor is now in a position to deal with Mother's problem of anger and frustration.

Another example of the effectiveness of revealing the hidden reason follows:

Problem: Patrick, eleven, has no interests. He stays home after school and watches television.

Father: *A kid must have something that interests him. I don't care what it is, playing with other children, ride his bike, read, just do something. It isn't natural for a kid his age not to be interested in anything.*

Guess: Patrick seems to let father down. Father may disappointed in his son; he may worry that Patrick will never become a "real" man; possibly that the father himself is a "doer" and can't tolerate inactivity. It is possible that the father is ashamed of his son. Another possibility may be that Patrick may have a sibling who is very active and who is a discouraging factor in this problem.

Counselor: *What do you do when you see Patrick in front of the television?*

Father: *I used to force him to go out and play with the boys in the neighborhood. He hated it, but I wanted him to be one of the boys and to make friends. Finally, I got tired of chasing him every day and I gave up. Even a father can do only so much.*

Comments: Our guess that this father feels let-down by his son seems confirmed. The fact that he made Patrick play with "the boys" also confirms our feelings that father may be worried about Patrick's masculinity.

Counselor: *Are you a very active person yourself?*

Father: *No, not really. I work hard and I am too tired when I come home. But he is just a kid and he should have the energy and the interest.*

Comments: We were wrong about father being an active man himself. However, he may want his son to be what he himself is not. Father may have some problems with his own male image and this may add to his worries about his son.

Counselor: *Is there anything that Patrick does or any quality that he possesses that you like?*

Father: (After some hesitation) *He has a heart of gold and he would give you the shirt off his back, but that's something . . . I don't know how to explain this. Patrick has never picked up a hammer or a tool of any kind. I have tried to get him to help whenever there is something around the house that needs fixing but it's always the same battle. I almost always have to force him.*

Comments: We now have further confirmation about father's disappointment in his male child. He may associate "a heart of gold" with femininity.

Counselor: *How is your younger son, Howard?*

Father: *These two are like day and night. Howard is always active, and always with the boys. In fact, we have just the opposite problem with him. We can't keep him in the house. But Howard is two years younger than Patrick. I don't expect of him what I expect of Patrick. Maybe I expect too much.*

Comments: This information reinforces our guess that Patrick does not live up to father's expectations. We also guessed in the right direction that a sibling may be a discouraging factor. With this knowledge, the counselor is in a better position to plan a course of action during the session.

Another example:

> **Problem:** Six year old, Paul doesn't mind his parents. He yells and he throws tantrums whenever he can't have his way.
>
> Mother: *Paul does not have this problem with his father. It's only with me that he acts up like this.*
>
> **Guess:** Mother may feel victimized; she may resent Paul's relationship with his father; she may feel that men stick together and that she, as a woman, has no chance. She also may try to manipulate the counselor to feel sorry for her and be on her side.
>
> Counselor: *Could you give me an example of a situation where you had a problem with Paul but your husband didn't?*
>
> Mother: *Like the other day, after Paul went to bed, he came out of his room and asked for an apple. He knows that he can't have anything to eat after he brushes his teeth. My husband knows this, but he got up and gave Paul an apple.*
>
> **Comments:** This statement puts an entirely different slant on the problem. It shows no indication that Paul has no problems with his father, as mother had put it. It is more of an indication that the parents play the child against each other. It is possible that this is a bad marriage. But there is some support for our guess that "men stick together" and that mother sees no chance for herself.

We do not suggest that the counselor with this family who came for family counseling should now do marriage counseling. The parents may feel unprepared for this and resent it. But the counselor may suggest that the parents seek marriage counseling. Timing is of great importance in such a situation. We suggest that such recommendation should not be made until the counselor has established rapport with the parents and has won their complete confidence.

Use of Long-Range Goals
of the Lifestyle

The Adlerian counselor will not often utilize confrontation of lifestyle goals in family counseling and should not do so unless well trained in the technique. Such confrontation is usually reserved for psychotherapy. However, the authors have found lifestyle goal confrontation helpful in very difficult families. It usually becomes obvious in such cases that an unaware goal or mistaken attitude of one of the parents profoundly influences dynamics of the family in a negative way. An illustration is

> Parents of three young sons recently came for family counseling. They all came quite willingly. The agreed upon complaint was that they were drifting apart as a family as the oldest was away at college, the second son was more enamored of spending time with his girl friend than with the family. The third son was still actively participating in family life. As lifestyle assessments were made on each of the parents, the real problem was revealed quickly. The mother was the youngest of four children and felt strongly that she had never occupied a significant place as a child in her generic family. She also felt that her own parents never fostered much of a family life, at least not as she developed an ideal concept of family life. As a result she had an unrealistic notion on what family life should be and the mistaken view that she could force everyone into her idealistic family mold. It resulted in general passive resistance and withdrawal on the part of other family members. This created a wary distance rather than closeness in the family. After considerable reeducation on how and why the mother was functioning, and some alternate and more effective ways to accomplish her common sense goals, cooperation and atmosphere in the family improved.

Shulman's Typology of Confrontations

Shulman (1971) classified several types of confrontations that are somewhat similar to revealing the hidden reason aspect of the private logic. These similarly are designed to reveal other aspects of the private logic or to promote movement or action of some kind on the part of the client. The authors have found the following useful. It is vitally important in the counseling process to first confront the client with the psychological goal of misbehavior before proceeding with a discussion of alternative behaviors.

Confrontation by Presenting Alternatives. Presenting alternatives are often an effective way of bringing a sharp focus to situations that may seem amorphous to a family. For instance, it is common experience to counsel families who came for help because a junior or senior high school student is on the verge of flunking. The counselor can confront with alternatives such as:

> *You could go back to school, ask for help, buckle down, and pass. Or, you could just drop the whole thing and forget it. Or, you might consider dropping out now and repeating the subject in summer school, or next year. Or, you might drop regular school now, enroll in the GED program, and look for a job. By presenting these alternatives the counselor confronts the client with the sharp realities of the situation and can help the client develop a plan that helps solve the current dilemma.*

Confrontation of Negative Behavior. Most counselors have experienced children and adult clients who have manipulated counseling sessions in various ways. Confrontation of the client about negative behavior is discussion about what is happening in the counseling session. A typical example is a child changing a line of discussion to avoid being found out.

> Counselor: *Mother tells me that you kick her sometimes when she doesn't give in to you. Would you discuss this with me?*
>
> Child: *We have a new car—a red Buick.*
>
> Counselor: *You changed the subject. Do you know why you did it?*
>
> Child: *I didn't hear what you said.*
>
> Counselor: *Is it possible that you felt that you have a right to get what you can and to punish those who refuse to give in to you?*
>
> Child: *Maybe.*

Counselor: *Could it be that you also realized that this behavior is no way of treating others and that you felt ashamed?*

Child: *Yes.*

Counselor: *Maybe it's good that we talked about it. Perhaps you will now ask yourself, "Must I always have my own way?" And then decide that it is not always possible, then you won't be so angry about it. What do you think?*

Child: *I won't hurt mother anymore.*

Counselor: *What about having your own way always?*

Child: *I'll think about that too.*

Time Confrontations. Confronting client(s) with a time frame question often gives sharp focus to solution of a problem. These can be either on a short-or long-term basis such as:

"You obviously take great delight in calling your mother foul names. How long do you want to continue? Perhaps you would consider giving it up this summer?"

Or, to a six-year old who takes great delight in smearing feces on the bathroom wall:

"How long do you think you want to still be doing this, until you are ten, fifteen, twenty-five?"

All of these suggestions must be done in a friendly manner without any hint that you are trying to get a change in behavior or that you are condemning the behavior. In most cases the youngster will understand that the behavior is unworthy of him/her and it ceases.

Confrontation of Feelings. As the counselor listens to the client, he/she will take special clues from feelings of his/her clients. When Adlerian counselors ask a client how he/she feels about a specific situation, it is not an idle question posed because of kindness. The emotional reaction or mood of a client in a given situation is a clue to his/her goal int he situation and is often a prelude to action. By bringing attention to the changing emotional states during the counseling session, the counselor often can bring new insights into the family dynamics as these are definite clues to the goals and intentions of various members of the family.

SYNTHESIZING INFORMATION

The counselor who has learned to look for patterns and to be alert to hidden reasons and goals knows how to look beyond what the client says so as to gain an understanding of what the statements imply. A trained and experienced counselor can understand the basic character of a seemingly complex problem after one session. These data and understanding of the problem are derived from what is heard from individual family members, or from the student and the teacher if either or both are involved. As the counselor listens, he/she observes how the individuals relate to each other, constantly questioning the underlying dynamics of the problem. The counselor may wonder who in the family is "in charge" and how this individual maintains command. He/she may question who is allied with whom and against whom and in what manner. The counselor may observe who in the parent-child relationship has to be "right" and who is stronger in his/her determination. The counselor is forming a mental picture of who feels misunderstood or abused, who feels sorry for whom, and who feels superior and triumphant in the relationship. The counselor is continuously forming hypotheses. From the fragmentary bits of information offered by each individual, the counselor attempts to plot a consistent movement—a persistent pattern in each one's emotional reaction to the problem and the possible goal that each pursues in his/her unique behavior.

To each statement of the client, to every description of feeling, thought, and action, the counselor brings to mind a series of questions:

What would have to be true for this behavior to make sense?

What would life have to be like for these thoughts and feelings to be appropriate?

How does this person perceive the situation and his/her place in it? (Powers, 1978, interview)

As the counselor listens to the client, and at the same time watches the client's facial expression, body movement, and general mannerisms, the counselor begins to speculate about the client's rationalizations for his/her feelings and for behavior. The counselor then tries to reconstruct in his/her own mind what goes on in the client's mind. The counselor may get the impression that the client gets upset each time someone shows disapproval of what the client did or said; each time he/she is not in control of a situation; whenever the client feels that he/she is not being liked; or whenever the client believes him/herself to be unable to live up to other's expectations. The counselor may notice that the client is overly concerned with orderliness and neatness or that he/she must always be "right" and "win" in an argument. The counselor also may perceive that the real problem is not with the children but with one of the parents.

The counselor must first test his guesses by obtaining additional information from the client before establishing validation of the assumptions. Even then, the counselor may still be wrong. Whenever the counselor guesses, he/she risks being wrong. Because the counselor is not concerned with "who" is right, but rather with the understanding of the situation, guessing wrong is not threatening. One can always make another guess or correct a wrong one. Nobody gets hurt in the process. Through a process of guessing and elimination the counselor can quickly reach an accurate assessment of the situation.

REFERENCES

Ansbacher, H., & Ansbacher, R. (1964). *The individual psychology of Alfred Adler.* New York: Harper & Row Publishers.

Dreikurs, R. (1957). *Psychology in the classroom.* New York: Harper & Row Publishers.

Dreikurs, R., Grunwald, B., & Pepper, F. (1982). *Maintaining sanity in the classroom, (2nd ed.).* New York: Harper & Row Publishers.

Dreikurs, R. (1973). The private logic. In H. H. Mosak (Ed.), *Alfred Adler—His influence on psychology today* (pp. 29-31). Parkridge, NJ: Noyes Press.

Powers, R. From a discussion with Bronia Grunwald, 1978, Chicago, IL.

Shulman, B. *Eight confrontation techniques.* Paper presented at the 1971 Convention of the American Society of Adlerian Psychology, Timberline Lodge, Mt. Hood, OR.

CHAPTER V

DIAGNOSTIC TECHNIQUES GATHERING SIGNIFICANT INFORMATION

Collecting many facts in order to understand the dynamics of a presented problem is not necessary. The well-trained counselor can tell with considerable accuracy why a certain problem exists after only brief communication, providing that he/she listens, not only what clients relate, but also the manner in which the problem is presented and its emotional overtones. While the counselor is cautioned not to gather information which has no direct bearing on the problem, we stress the importance of collecting basic information necessary to assess relationships within the family, how family members interact, how each responds to the others. Such information leads to an understanding of the dynamics of the situation and why the family has the problems presented.

It is important to have the facts about the family constellation—the people who live in the family, the alignments in the family, the role each member plays, how each parent responds to the individual children, how the parents perceive each of their children, and the roles that the extended family (grandparents, aunts, and uncles) play.

As the counselor listens to parents describing their problems and how they attempt to deal with them, every bit of information may be significant. The alert counselor will discern clues that point to underlying dynamics that may have contributed to the difficulties. The counselor should look for patterns in attitudes, values, and behaviors on the part of various family members. Parents may exhibit tendencies to be overambitious for their children, for domination, or overprotectiveness. One parent may resent lack of involvement in the child rearing task on the part of the spouse or feel guilty and blame him/herself for the children's problems. Some parents inadvertently create problems because of unrealistic expectations for the children. Such parents are often overly concerned with their children's school performance, thereby exacerbating the problem. Inconsistency in whatever child rearing principles are being used often contributes to the difficulties. Many mothers allow themselves to become slaves to their children and thereby lose their own self-respect and the respect of the children. As a result the parents' ability to influence their children is greatly impaired.

On the positive side, of course, the counselor may discern parental attitudes of loving concern, eagerness to learn how to be more effective, consistency, and respect for self and the children. The counselor can always be glad to detect a sense of humor in parents. The ability to laugh at oneself and parenting errors paves the way for reeducation and learning more effective ways of dealing with children.

The counselor will be alert to identify these and other prevalent patterns while systematically gathering information that will lead to correct assessment and remediation of the problems presented.

THE FAMILY CONSTELLATION AND VALUES

Alfred Adler (Ansbacher & Ansbacher, 1956) was among the first to regard the family constellation as a basis for personality determinant. He believed that in the life pattern of every child there is the imprint of the child's position in the family and that much of the child's future attitude towards life depends on this one factor. However, he stressed that one should not regard the family constellation as the "cause" for a child's personality development, but to view it as the field in which it may develop. It is from the family constellation that the child first draws conclusions about life, about his/her own worth as compared to others, and his/her feelings of belonging or not belonging. Depending on the child's interpretation of his/her position, he/she develops a unique attitude and behavior pattern which serves as a way to find a place in the group. This interpretation may make no logical sense to anybody but to the child.

Rudolf Dreikurs (1957) stated that personality and character traits develop from competition between siblings, that the competing opponents watch each other to see ways and means by which the opponent succeeds or fails. Where one sibling achieves, the other, especially the one next to this child, may give up; where one shows weakness or deficiencies, the other may succeed.

Except for Adlerians only in recent years have some behavioral psychologists probed for evidence of the possible impact of the ordinal position of children. But of all psychological orientations, Adlerian psychology has given the most attention and attributed the most significance to the family constellation. We stress the importance of understanding the psychological position each child occupies in the family in order for the counselor to understand the child's attitudes and deep convictions. With this knowledge, the counselor is in a position to help parents as well as children to understand who and why they compete and how they influence one another. Parents and children are helped to understand their own concept of the position they occupy, their own feelings of being loved or not loved as much as another sibling, and of being needed by the family. This induces them to treat others the way they expect to be treated. The counselor must exercise care to explain to the children that they do not do this knowingly. Children usually follow their feelings which, in many cases, are misleading.

There are never two children born to the same family who grow up in the same family atmosphere. Neither are there two children who are regarded or loved in the same manner by their parents. It is a myth that parents love all of their children the same. They may love each child, but each child occupies a different position in their hearts. Parents react differently to a first-born than they do to a second or third-born. Some react differently to a boy than they do to a girl, to a child that is beautiful as compared to a child that is homely, to a child that is healthy and active than to a sickly and passive child, to a child that is very intelligent as compared to one who is dull, to a child with special talents as contrasted to an average child. The counselor needs to help parents accept that this is natural, that they are not bad parents because they have different feelings toward each child. So many parents suffer from guilt feelings because they feel closer to one child or because they are more affectionate with one child than they are with the others. While parents need to be encouraged to accept this reaction to the individual children as normal, they need to be educated how to behave and what not to do that may cause permanent hurt to the other children which might result in negative behaviors.

As previously stated, no two children are born into the same family atmosphere. With the birth of each child the atmosphere changes because the parents change. They have gained experience in bringing up the first child and may now take an entirely different attitude toward the way they treat the next child. They may be more secure economically. They may have moved to a new neighborhood which has an affect on their outlook and on how they strive to rear their children. This is bound to affect the children. A new baby always affects every member in the family. If this should not happen, the new member of the family group may remain an outsider and a potential source of disturbance.

Each child achieves self-identity through the child's participation in the life of the family group. The child's participation and cooperation will depend on the conclusions the child draws from his/her experiences and the way the child views his/her position in the family. A child may feel that he/she is less loved by father than the other children are, that he/she is mother's favorite, that boys are preferred to girls, that a certain sibling is superior to him/her and, therefore, more important, or that nobody treats him/her fairly.

Characteristics which often are found in children based on their original position in the family may not always follow as described in this section but are strong possibilities. The youngest child may exhibit character traits that are mostly found in an oldest child, or an oldest child may behave in a manner which is often found in the youngest. Behavior will depend on how these children view themselves in the family group and how they try to find their places.

The Only Child

An only child is usually more sensitive to parents' rules and expectations than other children and strives to live up to them. Such children tend to measure themselves by adult standards because there are no other siblings in the family against whom the child can measure self. Only children are often more traditionally oriented, ambitious achievers, and many move into leadership roles in later life. There are a number of advantages as well as many disadvantages for the only child. These advantages include:

> Parents can usually provide more for an only child than they can for several children.

> Parents have more time for the child.

> Parents give the child more affection.

> The child will never go through the trauma of being dethroned by another child.

> The child will never be exposed to competition with siblings.

> The child may be the center of attention of the extended family—grandparents, aunts, uncles and others.

The disadvantages include the following:

> The child may be lonely.

> The child may become self-centered.

> The child may be overprotected and not allowed to lead a "normal" life and be as physically active as most other children are. The parents may tend to shield the only child from any possible physical harm.

The parents often compete for the love of the child and this may cause friction between them and establish a situation where the child can "play" one parent against the other.

The child often feels the burden of carrying the responsibility toward the parents all alone.

The child may live in fear that should anything happen to the parents he/she will remain alone in the world.

The child may have difficulties making decisions because all decisions are made for the child.

The child may have difficulties forming relationships in school because he/she has little experience relating to other children.

The child may feel a general deprivation because he/she has no brothers or sisters.

Only children may be conservative, but they also may become rebels. They either take on all the parents' values or rebel against them. They seldom take a middle course in life.

The Oldest Child

While the oldest child may exhibit a number of characteristics found in an only child, considering the fact that for some time the oldest child was an only child, the oldest child now occupies a distinctly different position than an only child. Similarities among oldest children rest in their ambitions and in being more traditionally oriented than second or third-born children. When we refer to "oldest child" it implies that there are other children in the family. The arrival of another child is almost always threatening to an oldest child. The oldest does not have to share the parents' affection and attention until arrival of the second child. We say that the coming of a second child "dethrones" the oldest. None of the younger children are as dethroned as an oldest child because they never were only children; they have always had to share parents with a sibling. One of the most noticed characteristics of an oldest child is the child's need to remain "first" and to be first in everything in order not to relinquish this position. If the child cannot succeed in being "first" through positive behavior, he/she may seek to remain "first" through negative behavior and keep the parents more occupied, more worried about him/her than the parents might be about the other children. Many feel entitled, because of their position, to receive special consideration and to occupy a special position in the family. Oldest children are often timid and oversensitive. Many of them are close to their parents. Many are serious and responsible, serving as a model for the other siblings. In this capacity, they may become very bossy. Some oldest children resent the responsibilities placed on them by their parents, like taking care of the younger sisters and brothers, having to do more household chores, and being deprived of material advantages because they must share with younger siblings. But, by and large, oldest children are "good" children who develop skills that will bring them adult approval.

The Second Born

A second child may have an uncomfortable position in life. Everyone in comparison to him/her seems big and accomplished. Generally, the second born compares self with the older sibling, often feeling inferior to the latter. A second-born child is usually a very competitive child determined to catch up if not to surpass the older brother or sister. Only recently a six-year old child, who may have surpassed her seven-year old brother, told us, "I am already six and he is only seven, that's why I can read better than he can."

A second-born child never experiences the parents' undivided attention as the first born had for some time. The child may rebel against the dominance of the first-born. In most cases, the second-born child is just the opposite from the first born. If the former is passive, the second-born is usually active. In fact, some are so active that they are considered hyperactive. If the first child is cooperative and pleasant, the second may be a behavior problem. Many parents believe that these children were just born with different personalities and temperaments. Parents need to be educated to become aware that these differences are due to competition. With this understanding, they will refrain from comparing the two and using one as a model for the other.

When a third child comes into the family, the second born changes his/her ordinal position and becomes a "squeezed" or "sandwiched-in" child. This often changes this child's entire attitude to life and to people. The child often deduces that this is unfair, may feel less loved (why would the parents have another child then?). Many become so resentful that they become rebellious and problems to their families as they feel that they have no place. They compare themselves unfavorably with the oldest, who has all the authority, and the youngest who is free of pressure and whom the parents protect. It is interesting that so many of the former Hippies were middle children. These children especially are sensitive to criticism. They consider it as being bossed. They break with traditions and often find a replacement for their family in the peer group.

The Youngest Child

A youngest child always occupies a special place in the family. How special will depend on whether the parents cling to this "last baby" and make it dependent on them more than would normally be necessary, or whether the coming of the new baby was not planned and basically not wanted. In the latter case, the youngest child may feel unwanted and never quite belonging. These children may try to ingratiate themselves through charm, obedience, and attempting to please everyone. Or, the child may withdraw, feel lonely, and remain an outsider. But these are rather rare cases. In general, the baby of the family is pampered and protected by all the family members, and, in a sense, has more than one set of parents. According to how the family reacts to the child, the youngest may conclude that staying weak and dependent is a comfortable position because he/she can put everyone in his/her service. Or, the child may want to catch up with all the "giants" in the family and becomes a serious student, a fast learner, and often the most successful of all siblings.

Youngest children are often the bosses of the family. They make demands and dictate to others. If their demands are not met, they throw tantrums. Very often, they get what they want in the end as the parents demand that older children give in to the child because he/she is still very young and "doesn't know any better." Thus, youngest children may become tyrants. On the other hand, youngest children do not have to depend on their parents to entertain them or to keep them company. Youngest children often form strong attachments to the entire family and particularly to one sibling. They also form attachments to other children in school or in the neighborhood. One may find that youngest children may feel inferior to their siblings because they are not taken seriously and not being listened to carefully.

Thus, each child, no matter what his/her position, has more than one road open and the direction the child will take can never be predicted just from the ordinal position. The child, subconsciously, decides the direction that he/she is going to follow, depending on how he/she perceives the situation.

A number of other factors affecting the child's personality development must be considered. A boy and a girl, if there are no other children, may be treated as two only children and may have many characteristics often found in only children. Similarly, when children are born six or more years apart, they may be treated as only children.

When two or more children are close in age followed by additional children after four or more years, the children should be considered as two groups. In such a constellation each child occupies the psychological position he might have had if there had been only one group. For example, in a family of five children, Steve is 16, Daniel 15, Thelma 11, Penny 9, and Mike 3. We may have three sets of children. Steve and Daniel would comprise the first set, Thelma and Penny the second, and Mike the third, occupying the position of an only child. Steve and Thelma may exhibit character traits often found in oldest children while Daniel and Penny may show personality traits of second-born children. Other important factors to consider are as follows:

A sick child which may be treated as "special."

A very beautiful or very talented child of whom the parents are very proud and who occupies a special position in the family constellation.

A child born after the death of a child.

An only girl among several boys or an only boy among many girls.

A child being particularly favored by a parent.

A very bright or a very slow or retarded child.

An oldest boy who is followed by a very speedy and successful sister.

All mentioned factors may have a strong influence on the development of the child's self-evaluation and personality and, therefore, must be carefully evaluated by the counselor. This understanding helps the counselor to remove the parents puzzlement and perturbation about the differences in their children "who grew up in the same family" and in placing the blame on hereditary factors. Parents begin to understand that, in a sense, the children did not have the same parents in terms of family atmosphere and psychological attitudes to each child. They begin to understand that each child acts, thinks, and feels in response to the world in accordance to the child's perception of his/her position and how the child compares self with the other siblings. It is encouraging to parents to realize that the child's personality development does not depend only on what parents did or failed to do, but that the child influenced the parents' behavior toward him/her as much as the parents' behavior influenced the child. Thus, parents learn to be alert and discern how each child views his/her position in the family. Parents learn to avoid showing favoritism, which they may have done before, as nothing is as painful to a child than the conviction that a sister or brother is more loved by the parents. Parents realize the importance of winning the middle child; to concentrate on this child's positive attributes, and minimize the negative ones; to refrain from overprotecting the youngest child and to stop referring to a child two years or older as the "baby." The counselor helps parents to put less pressure on an oldest child and refrain from demanding that he/she serve as a model to younger siblings and assume undue responsibilities for them. Parents are helped to understand that overemphasizing the beauty or the ugliness of a child may do much harm to both children, especially to the not-so-good looking child. Often parents tend to verbalize their feelings, "Why did you have to be born with such a large nose? I don't know whom you resemble. Nobody in the family has such big teeth." As for the beautiful children, because of being treated as "special" and bringing honor to the parents, they often grow up very self-centered, feeling entitled to special consideration, narcissistic, concentrating on being beautiful and neglecting school, feeling superior to other children, remaining friendless, and constantly worrying about the time when their beauty will fade. Many once beautiful children have nervous breakdowns as they enter middle age and are no longer considered as beautiful.

Parents and children after learning about the influence of the family constellation begin to understand what "made" them the way they are and the power they have to help one another. Children especially become aware of how and why they may discourage a sibling and learn new and more effective ways to live in harmony with others in the family.

To someone who is not acquainted with the Adlerian emphasis on the importance of examining and understanding the family constellation, our recommendations to parents may make little sense. However, as they study the family constellation and take the time and effort to observe the interrelationships among the children, they become aware of an approach which is more revealing than any they may have practiced before.

TWENTY BRIEF POINTS FOR THE COUNSELOR

Begin Every Counseling Session With a Plan. Know what you want to accomplish, the information you need to accomplish it, why you need it, and how you plan to elicit this information from the client. The counselor may divert from the plan once a session is underway, but begin with a plan.

Refrain From Aimless Conversation. One should refrain from aimless conversation and collecting unnecessary information—practicing "factophelia." Small and/or general talk is often a means of avoiding the problem situation.

> For example, *when a mother tells the counselor that her child has an eating problem, it would be utterly superfluous to know what the child wants or likes to eat in order to understand the problem. The important information needed is what mother does about it. This information would help the counselor understand how it pays off for the child to fuss over eating.*

Each Question Must Serve a Purpose. The counselor is advised to refrain from asking questions that do not apply directly to the problem. Questions should be structured in such a fashion that they flow out of the last question and lead in to the next. Example:

Mother: *Mornings are terrible. Karl doesn't ever want to get up.*

Counselor: *When does he like to get up?*

This is a superfluous question. When Karl likes to get up will not help the counselor understand why he doesn't want to get up. A question which may shed more light on the purpose of Karl's behavior would be, "What happens when he doesn't get up? What does the parent do about it?" Counselors who do not realize the importance of meaningful questions usually respond with, "I see" when there is nothing to "see" that helps understand the problem or with "Ahem," and nodding of the head. Such sessions usually become dull and the hour passes without anyone having profited from the interview.

Examine Every Bit of Information and Look for Patterns. The counselor watches for patterns of behavior or feelings. The counselor may perceive that the client gets upset each time he/she can't have his/her way, that the client is overly sensitive and feels hurt, that he/she sees all situations from an "unfair" point of view, or withdraws, or retaliates when someone disagrees. The counselor also may perceive family patterns. For instance, every member in this family yells and threatens, everyone is vindictive, distrustful, or that everyone is polite, soft spoken, and respectful of the other. What is being emphasized is that each piece of information should be evaluated from the point of view if it is a consistent part of the pattern, or if it falls outside the frame of the pattern of behavior.

Use Openended Questions. We distinguish between open-ended and closing questions. Through questioning and probing, the counselor gets the information needed to understand the underlying problem after one interview. Therefore, it is important that the counselor poses the kind of questions which lead to further information. Any question which can be answered with "yes" or "no" is a closing question. For example:

Counselor: *Does Jolie wash her hands before she comes to the table?*

Mother: *Yes.*

Comments: This finishes the conversation concerning Jolie's eating habits.

In comparison:

Counselor: *Tell me how it is when Jolie is coming to the table? Does she wash her hands on her own?*

Mother: *Are you kidding? If I weren't after her, she would not mind if her hands carried a ton of dirt. I have to tell her a hundred times to wash her hands or she won't be served.*

Comments: The counselor's open question led to much important information which the counselor would not have learned if a closing question had been asked.

Use the Stochastic Method. Various types of guessing were discussed previously. Constant use of this technique keeps the counselor "working" and to understand the problem more quickly. It helps establish a working hypothesis which leads to subsequent meaningful questions.

Distinguish Between Logical and Psychological Explanations. A client may give a perfectly logical explanation why a problem exists. For example a client may say:

"I was too tired and therefore could not control myself."

"The child is bored in this teacher's class and therefore can't do any work there."

"His/her father is too strict with him/her."

"He/she has been a nervous child ever since he/she was born."

While these explanations sound logical and might be accepted by many counselors, they do not help us understand the psychological problem. A parent may use "tiredness" as an excuse rather than admit that he/she does not bother to control himself/herself when feeling tired. Or, he/she may admit that he/she was angry because of not being in control of the child. When a mother accuses her husband of being too strict with a child, one may question if the child provokes father in order to get mother's sympathy and protection. Adlerians do not accept causes for certain behaviors. All behavior is viewed as being purposive.

Listen for "Gold Mines." Gold mines are words or phrases that imply a broader meaning, an underlying attitude, or strong feeling that influences the client's behavior. The feeling tone used by the client also is a clue to the underlying significance of the statement. What kinds of expressions are considered as gold mines? Some examples:

Counselor: *How is Simona in school?*

Parent: *She could be better* (gold mine).

Comments: Parent doesn't even answer the question but expresses disapproval and higher expectations.

Mother: *I always have to tell her not to remove the leash from the dog. If I told her once I have told her a hundred times.*

Comments: "*I always have to tell*" is the gold mine. It tells us that mother may nag, that she assumes the responsibility to remind, that she has no confidence in the child's ability to assume the responsibility without being reminded.

Parent: *You can't expect a five-year old child to have an opinion.*

Comments: "*You can't expect.*" It shows complete lack of understanding of the child and of confidence in the child's intelligence.

Parent: *I am accustomed to...*

Comments: The gold mine tells us that this parent is rigid and does not allow for any deviations.

Parent: *Jack's work in school is not bad, but it is so sloppy.*

Comments: The gold mine is the use of "but" which tells us that she is a discouraging mother who builds on negatives.

Parent: *I may as well tell you, I have a bad habit,..."*

Comments: "*I may as well tell you,*" this gold mine indicates "Go easy on me. Before you tell me what I do wrong, I'll tell you, and you will treat me with more understanding and kindness."

When a parent comes back for a follow-up, then the counselor inquires how things are going at home.

Mother: *It's better, but I don't know how long it will last.*

Comments: This is a pessimistic expectation. She also is reluctant to give the counselor the satisfaction that he/she had advised her correctly.

When the counselor recognizes a gold mine, Dreikurs suggested that he/she "start digging" because it usually leads to further important information (Grunwald, 1973). The counselor is advised to ask for specific examples and what the parent did about the situation.

Study the Family Constellation. One should study the family constellation as discussed earlier in this chapter. Make use of the information to make guesses and to understand the psychological dynamics of the problem situation.

Use the Typical Day Approach. Ask the client for a description of a "typical day" in their lives during the first interview. This will focus the session and quickly reveal specific sources of difficulty. Details of a "typical day" interview are found later in this chapter.

Avoid Power Struggles with Clients. Counselors who get into power struggles with clients often are concerned with being right. The counselor must freely admit to clients that he/she is "powerless" to "make" the client do anything and is willing to accept the client's decision. If a client resists most efforts for help over a period of time, the counselor should not hesitate to suggest that he/she may be the wrong counselor and that someone else might be of more help.

Interrupt the Client When Necessary. It is advisable to interrupt the client who goes on talking without getting to the point. We do not agree with those who believe that it is disrespectful, if not harmful, to interrupt a client. Disrespect will depend on the manner in which the counselor interrupts the client and not by the interruption as such. If the counselor is to understand the problem after the first interview, interrupting a chattering client may be necessary. It is, however, important that the interruption be done with tact and at the right moment. The counselor may say:

"Excuse me for a moment. You said something a while ago which puzzles me..."

"You said something which I did not understand. What did you mean by...?"

"Would you mind explaining what you meant by...?"

"Before we go any further, may we discuss the point you made a while ago, namely..."

"May we retract a bit? You said... May we talk about this before we go on?"

Our experience has been that the counselor's active intervention makes for a vibrant and fast moving therapeutic process, increasing the scope and depth of the counseling. It keeps the counseling process at a rapid pace and makes the dialogue more meaningful.

Pinpoint the Issue. Help the counselee understand how he/she is functioning by pinpointing the underlying issue(s) in the problem case. This major goal in counseling was previously discussed in Chapter III.

Use the Four Goals of Misbehavior. Help parents understand the child's goal of misbehavior, how to recognize it, and what to do about it (Chapter IV).

Make Specific Recommendations. Be specific when making suggestions and recommendations. Explain these in minute detail, asking the parents to articulate their understanding of the recommendations in order to check the accuracy of their perception.

Recommend Only a Few Changes at One Time. Work on the one or two items that are most troublesome at the time. The counselor should exercise care that parents are confident that they *can* be successful in implementing the recommendations. Success in dealing with one or two problems will encourage parents and they will be prepared to carry out additional changes in the future. If too many recommendations are made at one time, parents may not be able to follow through on all of them and become more discouraged.

Suggest Use of the Family Council. Teach the family the value of and how to implement the Family Council as a means to solve problems more effectively. Timing is of utmost importance in introducing this concept. It is usually better to wait until some progress has been made and the level of hostility has been reduced. Otherwise, the Family Council may furnish yet another arena for continuation of the power struggle (See Chapter VI).

Suggest That the Family Join the Local Family Education Center or Parents Study Group. Explain that these opportunities can furnish much helpful information from other parents with similar problems. Many counselors suggest appropriate materials to parents for reading and study.

Encourage the Family. Every counseling session should include items of encouragement for the family. These are described in detail in Chapter VI. In addition, the counselor should teach the family members how to encourage each other.

Plan the Next Session. This can best be done at the end of session. Record brief notes as an agenda. Ask the clients for their ideas on what they might like to include. The plan should include the time and date for the next appointment.

THE INITIAL INTERVIEW

Each counselor will eventually find his/her own structure for a first interview. However, a structured format is very helpful to the beginning family counselor. It is not suggested that the counselor follow the outline rigidly, but it will be helpful to him/her until such time that the counselor finds his/her own style. Counseling must never become rigid or mechanical. The proposed format should, therefore, not be considered by the reader as a "must" but as a possible guideline.

The interview should begin with a warm-up. Greet each member, and ask them how they feel about being in the office if counseled in the privacy of the counselor's office or how they feel about being counseled in front of an audience as is done in classes or in Family Counseling Centers. Reassure the family that their apprehension is understandable and that we will only discuss those areas that they are comfortable with and about which they are willing to talk. This gives the client some time to perceive the counselor as a human being. The client, then, usually will relax and feel more at ease.

One may say that the first step in counseling is the establishment of a proper relationship based on trust and mutual respect. It is important that the counselor "win" the client over and gain his/her confidence. The first encounter is, therefore, crucial. One of the most important steps in winning the client and gaining his/her confidence is the establishment of a common goal. This process was discussed in greater detail in Chapter III.

The next step is to assess the family constellation—the psychological position of each child in the family as discussed previously in this Chapter. However, we should like to add that the family constellation should not be regarded as the only influencing factor in the child's personality development, but should be regarded as an important, meaningful probability and the information should be used as a starting point.

The counselor needs to know the birth order of the children, their ages, and grade placement. Knowing the grade level of each child may help the counselor detect if there are any problems in this area. For instance:

If Paul, age 11, is in fifth grade and his sister, Barbara, age 9, is in the fourth grade, it immediately tells the counselor that Paul may have a school problem. He is only one year ahead of his sister but he is two years older. Usually eleven year olds should be in the sixth grade. Barbara is most likely an ambitious girl who tries to catch up with the older brother. This may be very threatening to Paul. With this observation, the counselor is in a position to set up a hypothesis and to check it out during the interview.

The counselor would want to know if there were any miscarriages or children who died. If so, it is important to learn when this occurred. The death of a child, or even a miscarriage, may seriously affect the relationship between the child born after such an event and his parents. Parents often become overprotective toward the next child. Others, again, may hold the deceased child as the perfect model and the living child must then compete with a deceased sibling. As a nine-year old boy told us, "My parents regard my dead brother, Edward, as an angel. He never did anything wrong. I can never be as good as he was."

The counselor should inquire if any of the children had or still have any serious childhood illnesses, such as polio, rheumatic fever, serious digestive problems, or if they were born with an organ inferiority, such as a speech, visual, or hearing impediment. The counselor needs to know how long the child was ill, how the parents related to the child during the illness, and how they feel about the child now. This information may shed light on the present problem, not only with the identified problem child, but with the harmony or disharmony that may exist between other siblings. A sick child, or one born with a permanent deficiency, usually receives much more attention and concern from the parents than a healthy child. The latter often resents this. Little children sometimes express the desire to become ill, also, in order to receive as much attention as their sibling. Furthermore, it may happen that the child who was, or is ill, may want to prolong the illness and resort to all kinds of misbehavior after he/she gets well in order to keep the parents occupied with him/her as they were before.

We suggest that the counselor inquire about other persons who may live with the family and the relationships they have with the children. There may be grandparents, aunts and uncles, maids, or foster children. All these people may influence the child's behavior. We are especially concerned about grandparents. Such "outsiders" may be a contributing factor to the existing problem. Grandparents often interfere with the rearing of the grandchildren as they often sabotage the efforts of parents. It was reported that one grandmother kept food in her room which she gave to a grandchild when he/she was sent away from the dinner table because of naughtiness. There are those who give the child money after parents have refused the request. This, indirectly, conveys to the child that the parents are not being fair. Grandparents usually protect the grandchild that they feel sorry for and in so doing they exacerbate the problem. Then there are parents who are still striving for the approval of their own parents. Such parents may respond to the child's misbehavior in a manner which might please the grandparents even if it is not effective. The counselor would need to help such parents free themselves from the dominance of their own parents. Dreikurs (1972) suggested that parents not fight with the grandparents, but neither should they give in. The parents may agree with grandmother, "Yes, I am a bad mother, you may be right, I will have to think about it," but the parents should act as they see fit.

The counselor now may ask the parents why they came for counseling. One may usually assume that most parents are more concerned with the behavior of one of their children than they are of the others. The counselor may ask which of the children worries the parents the most. Ask the parents to describe this child and ask for an example of a specific situation where the described behavior occurred. The counselor will understand the nature of the problem and why it exists much faster if he/she asks for specific examples. Generalities such as, "He is always fresh," "She can't sit still for one moment," or "He/she drives me up a wall," enable the counselor to pick up clues to the relationship and interaction between parent and child. Example:

Mother: *You wouldn't believe how fresh Hans can be.*

Counselor: *Give me an example of such a situation.*

Mother: *Like this morning, when I asked him not to forget to tell his teacher that he has a cold and that she should keep him in during recess. His answer was, "Mind your own business."*

Comment: From this answer, this counselor may guess that the boy resents it when mother tells him what to do. He may have been provoked by her demand "not to forget." We also may wonder if mother is constantly giving reminders.

Counselor: *And what did you do?*

Comment: Dreikurs (1972) always said that "a child's behavior makes sense only when one knows the counterpart played by the parent..., when we know how the parents react to the child's behavior." If we inquire also how the parent felt when the child provoked, we are in a fairly certain position to understand the child's purpose of his behavior—the goal (see Chapter IV).

Mother: *I slapped him across the mouth and told him that I will show him how I mind my own business. I won't allow any of my children to talk to me that way.*

Comment: From mother's comments, the counselor may guess that both mother and son are out to hurt each other. Each must revenge self for what the other is doing or saying.

Before going into depth about the behavior of one child, the counselor should find out about the other children in the family. The counselor may say:

Counselor: *May we divert for a moment and talk about the other children before we pursue the problem you have with Hans. Tell me about each of your other children. What kind of child is each of them? How do they get along with you and with the other members of the family?*

Comments: This information is important in order for the counselor to understand the dynamics of the family constellation. For instance, it may be that Timothy finds approval through cooperativeness and pleasant responses. This may be

threatening to Hans who tries to find his place through provocative behavior and by keeping his parents busy with him. He
may believe that he cannot be as good and as appreciated as his
good brother. At the very best, he can be only a poor replica of
Timothy, and he is not going to settle for that.

The counselor who does not investigate personalities and behavior of the
other children may be mislead about the nature of the "problem child."

If both parents are present, the counselor should explore how each
sees the problem as was described. If other family members are present,
they too should be asked to give a reaction on how the problem was
presented. If mother is the one who describes the problem, as in the
previous case, the counselor may ask the father, "How do you see this
problem, Mr. Smith? Do you see it the way your wife described it?" If
they disagree, the counselor may want to ascertain how each of them
handles such disagreement. An example:

Mother: *Tanya can do no wrong as far as her father is concerned. He lets her get away with murder.*

Comments: Mother may feel jealous of her husband's relationship with the daughter, and she may alienate both Tanya and her
husband with constant accusations and, perhaps, scenes.

Father: *This is nonsense and you know it. I don't stick up for
Tanya when I know that she is wrong, but I can't pick on her the
way you do. I try to be fair to all of my children. At least I try,
while you don't.*

Comments: This could develop into a marital quarrel if the
counselor does not channel the conversation back to its original
point and establish more constructive communication. This condition is not the time to go into marriage counseling. At a later
time, the counselor may suggest that the parents seek some
counseling for their own relationship.

The counselor may now inquire how things go at school; what the
parents do when a teacher complains about a child and how they are involved with homework. The counselor may get important clues if he/she
also inquires how the children behave when they are being taken shopping, visiting relatives, or friends, and playing with other children in the
neighborhood.

One should always inquire how the children get along with each other. Who gets along best and least well and with whom. This usually indicates where the competition is at its greatest. When parents complain that the children fight, the counselor should always examine what the parents do about it. The counselor also should inquire as to how the parent feels about what they do when a child cries or comes with a complaint.

The counselor determines what kind of fun the family has together and how much time each parent gives to each individual child. Children need to have a parent to themselves some of the time; it usually strengthens the relationships between each child and the parent. Especially important is that the identified problem child receive special time all to himself/herself from a parent or from both.

Now the counselor may go through a "typical day" in the life of the family. It is recommended that counselors use this typical day description because parents feel least threatened in reporting how things go during the day. It is an easy format for both the parents and the counselor to follow. It provides a comfortable way to get the session moving and usually leads to a focus on the problems. This technique should include what happens during an average day and how the parents react to each behavior or misbehavior described:

- How the children get up in the morning; if they need to be awakened and if this causes a hassle.

- How they get washed and dressed.

- How breakfast goes.

- If the children are ready in time for school.

- What happens when the child comes home from school.

- How they handle television.

- How the children behave at dinner.

- What happens when it is time to go to bed.

- If the children stay in their rooms all night, etc.

Each time the parents indicate that they have some difficulty, the counselor should go into specifics and always find out how the parents react at such times. This information enables the counselor to know the behavior pattern (goals) of the children and behavior patterns of the parents. The counselor may notice that in each situation the parent first yells, threatens, and then gives in, or that the parent gives long lectures and punishes the child that apparently causes difficulties. Some parents may do nothing but feel sorry for themselves and cry, trying to make the children feel guilty.

The counselor has now gathered enough important information for an initial session. He/she may summarize his/her observations and make recommendations at this point or see the children next. After the parents leave, the children enter. The counselor can learn a great deal about them from observation of how they enter the room, how they choose to sit, and how they send out nonverbal messages to each other and the counselor. An example of the usefulness of this technique is found in the section on interviewing children later in this chapter.

The counselor greets the children, offering to shake hands in the process of introduction. The children may be asked how they feel about being there, if they have an idea why the parents came, and why they brought them. The counselor should then tell the children what his professional role is and why the parents sought help. The counselor discusses with the children the difficulties that the parents presented. Each child should be asked how he/she perceives the problem and why they have this problem. After the discussion, the counselor should proceed to a disclosure of the child's goals using the "Could it be ...?" technique and watch for the recognition reflex.

The counselor should tell the children the recommendations he/she is going to make to the parents (or has already made) and ask the children if they have any other, perhaps more effective suggestions, on how to improve the situation. It is not unusual that children come up with better ideas than the counselor. In such a case, the counselor should congratulate the children on their good thinking and tell them that this is what he/she will now suggest to the parents. He/she should ask them if they want to sit in on the rest of the interview when the parents return or if they would prefer to wait outside. The counselor should accept their decision.

Some counselors are reluctant to include the children at this time in the counseling session. They are afraid that this would embarrass the children or that they may feel hurt and resentful. We do not share this pessimism. Furthermore, we have much confidence in the children's basic fairness and their ability to understand and respond to the situation. Most of them actually enjoy being included, listened to, and are often relieved to learn that what they considered as being bad is only because of their need for attention or that they want to have their own way.

The counselor shares his/her impressions of the children with the parents without going into details about the conversation with them. He/she tells the parents the goals that each child pursues according to his/her perception and the recognition reflexes observed as the goals were disclosed to each child. Next, the counselor then reviews the parents' account of how they handle the problems. He/she first inquires if the parents have any suggestions of how they might have handled the problems differently, more effectively, or how they intend to handle such problems in the future. It is always advisable to give parents an opportunity to solve their problems. Explain to the parents what changes the children would like to see if they made any such requests. If, however, they are still uncertain, the counselor then makes his own suggestions. The counselor should reassure the parents that, if the suggestions should not work, others can be made which also have proven effective. The parents should be helped to realize that whatever they do must be done with confidence in the children and in themselves. The moment they doubt the recommendations, they are bound to fail. Our suggestions work mainly when we believe in them. Review the recommendations with the family and make sure they are properly understood. Conclude by asking if the parents have any other special requests or questions and arrange for a followup session if needed.

THE INTERVIEW OF CHILDREN

The counselor can often make an immediate hypothesis about the children's roles and their interrelationships from the mere observation of the manner in which they enter the counselor's office and take seats. The counselor should note who enters first, who hesitates, who has to be encouraged to enter and by whom, which child pushes another out of the way in order to get to a specific seat, who is concerned about a sibling and helps him/her find a seat, or lifts the child into the chair, which child has an expression of anticipation or curiosity, and who looks sullen or angry. Each of these manifestations gives the counselor a clue on how the children relate to one another, and how they react to the situation. For example, let us follow the entrance of the three Grant children—Mildred 12, Stewart 9, and Noah 5.

When the counselor invited them to come in, Mildred went to the back and motioned with her hand for the children to enter.

Comments: We may assume that she is occupying the role of a second mother, and that she feels responsible that all should go properly when the parents are not around. She takes charge.

Stewart literally pushed Noah out of the way and ran into the room, pushing the chairs aside in order to get to the first chair. He sat down but after two seconds changed over to the next chair. Before the others had a chance to come in, he quickly switched back to the first chair. He sat smiling, looking at his siblings in a challenging way.

Comments: We may assume that Stewart's behavior may challenge and provoke the parents. He may be more self-centered than the others; he may provoke the other children through aggressive behavior. He may also doubt his place in the family, never quite sure if his behavior is accepted or if he made the right choice, disregarding how his behavior affects others, and may be regarded as a difficult child.

Noah stood at the door, looking at his sister entreatingly. When the counselor tried to take his hand, he shrugged it off and shook his head. But Mildred took Noah's hand, led him to a chair and motioned to him to sit down. Noah just stood there. When Mildred attempted to lift him into the chair, he protested and indicated that he wanted to sit in Stewart's chair. Mildred suggested that Stewart change chairs, but he refused. Noah kept pulling Mildred's hand, expecting her to do something about this situation; he was not going to sit in the chair that was left for him. He began to cry and ask for his mother. The counselor finally asked Noah to sit down because he would like to talk to all of them. Noah said that he wanted to stand and the counselor said that this was all right.

Comments: Noah seems to be the baby in the family. In spite of his five years, things may be done for him which he is very well capable of doing for himself. He is showing signs of having to have his way and of stubbornness. We may wonder if, at home, the parents or Mildred are after Stewart to give in to his little brother.

The counselor should make mental notes of his/her "guesses" and confirm them as he/she interviews the children. The tentative assumptions or guesses will enable him/her to come to the core of the problems much faster. The counselor may, after the initial "warm-up" of the session, or after a short discussion of why they came to see him/her, disclose the goal of each child's behavior to the child. It is especially important to observe if the counselor's observations concur with the impressions and assumptions made as he/she listened to the parents' description of their children. The counselor may find a discrepancy between the two in which case he/she may explain these to the parents when they return.

For instance, in the case of Noah, mother said that he was an independent, fun-loving, cooperative child. This would contradict the behavior that Noah exhibited in the counselor's office. Upon further questioning, the counselor learned that, yes, they do ask the older children to consider Noah's age and to go along with his demands. When Noah basically gets what he wants, he is very pleasant to have around. The counselor also learned that Noah refuses to ride the school bus (he goes to kindergarten) and that his mother drives him to school. Noah has no friends, which is another indication that he might antagonize children by insisting on having his way. This example illustrates how much a counselor can learn about a child although the children have not yet spoken.

The interview with the children should be friendly but brief. After introducing himself, the counselor should inquire if the children know why the parents brought them to counseling.

Stewart says, "I have a problem because I don't like to clean my room." The counselor should ask who else has this problem. In the discussion that will follow, the counselor may learn that all the others are or one of the siblings is just the opposite from Stewart and keeps his/her room very neat. This may be a clue as to why Stewart is creating problems by keeping his room messy. It is possible that he receives a great deal of attention from the parents because of this. He can put mother in to his service by letting her assume the responsibility for cleaning the room.

Whenever a child declares that he has a problem, we can quickly help the child understand the possible purpose of having this problem, by asking the child, "Why do you think this problem exists?" This question is a kind of preamble to the next step, namely revealing the goal to the child. When the child gives reasons why the problem exists, the counselor follows with his hypothesis of why (for what purpose) the problem exists. Some authorities recommend securing permission to disclose the goals to the child. Because children sometimes deny permission, the authors recommend proceeding directly to confronting the child with the goals of misbehavior. The counselor then says, "I have an idea why you may have this problem and I am going to tell you what I think. Could it be that you keep mother busy with you this way? Could it be that this way you get a lot of attention?" The child's facial expression (recognition reflex) will tell the counselor if he/she is correct. Should the child deny this possibility the counselor may go to the second goal, power, and reveal this to the child by asking, "Could it be that you don't keep your room neat because you don't want anyone to tell you what to do? Is it possible you want to show that you are the boss and that nobody can make you do anything?" The counselor should go through all four goals that children pursue when they do not cooperate as explained in the section on Confrontations in Chapter IV.

Once the counselor has guessed in the right direction, he/she is in a position to help the child find other, more effective ways to reach his/her goal. The counselor may also explain to the child what suggestions he/she will make to the parents in regard to dealing with this problem.

As suggested, the counselor should tell the children the problems that the parents presented. There are counselors who feel that this is a betrayal of the parents' confidence and therefore avoid confronting the children with the main issue. They may try in roundabout ways to deal with these problems and coax the children with questions such as, "Are you sure you have no other problems? Think a little, maybe you will remember what may be a problem to your parents? Are you afraid to tell me?" In most cases, once a child has denied having any problem, he/she will maintain his/her position and the counselor will waste the entire session getting nowhere.

The counselor should confront the child directly with the problem such as, "Your mother tells me that you don't come home from school on time. Why not?'' This question should always be asked when a child is confronted with a behavior that causes problems even though he/she does not know the answer to the question. As pointed out, this is a forerunner of the next step. "I have an idea and I will tell you what I am thinking? Could it be that...?'' as the counselor proceeds with the confrontation technique.

Another example: "Mother told me that you are fighting. Why is that?'' Counselors who inquire about who started the fight are wasting time with irrelevant questions. It is entirely insignificant who started it, but it is important for the child or children to understand the payoff there is in fighting.

It may happen that the counselor's initial guesses are wrong, and that he/she may have to shift to another direction. This should not disturb the counselor; guessing is always only a possibility. After the counselor has discussed the problems that the children enumerated and those which concern the parents, he/she would share with the children the recommendations that will be made to the parents. The counselor may say

> *"Your parents came here for help. They want very much to find a way for all of you to get along better, this means that they want to feel better also. I will suggest to them that you are big and smart children, and that you have a right to fight if you want to. They may ask you to go outside or to your rooms to fight, but they should not stop you.*
>
> *I will further suggest that the room belongs to you, Stewart. You have a right to keep it neat or messy, but your parents should not assume the responsibility for you and clean the room. In a way, this is an insult to you. Mother treats you as if you were still a baby who can't take care of himself. I think that you are capable of cleaning your room, if you so decide.*
>
> *I will also suggest that mother should stop nagging you about eating your breakfast, Bill. You can decide if you want to eat or not. Mother should let you decide and not get upset if you decide not to eat."*

These explanations should be brief, expressed in a very friendly manner, avoiding any "put downs" or shaming of the children. Again we stress that when recommendations are made to the parents, each should be done in a detailed and precise manner. This is important because so often the parents leave the counseling session without quite understanding what the counselor suggested. As a result, they carry out the recommendations in a faulty manner and often meet with failure.

In ending the session, the counselor may shake hands with the children, wish them good-luck, and express hope that when he/she meets them next time, everybody will feel happier.

The next interview is illustrative of several essential points that the counselor should remember in counseling children. Be brief, explicit, and move directly to the problem. Give each child equal treatment and deal with each in a friendly, respectful manner. Use the technique of confrontation.

The parents complained that Melvin, age 7, takes money from mother's purse or father's wallet, and sometimes brings things home from school, claiming that he found them. They also were concerned about Martha, age 9, who seemed overly sensitive and cried "at the drop of a hat."

> Counselor: *I am Steve Denner, a counselor whom your parents came to see. I believe you are Martha and you must be Melvin. How are you?*
>
> Both: *Fine, thank you.*
>
> Counselor: *How do you feel being here?*
>
> Martha: *I am a little scared and sad.*
>
> Counselor: *What about you, Melvin?*
>
> Melvin: *I am okay. Where are my parents?*
>
> Counselor: *They are in the other room and will come back after a short while. You can see them any time you want. Tell me, Martha, why are you sad?*
>
> Martha: *I don't know. Why did my parents come here?*
>
> Counselor: *Maybe you can guess. Why did they come?*

Melvin: *Mother did not tell us.*

Martha: *No, mother did not tell us and I don't know.*

Comments: It seems that these children are used to mother telling them what to do and what is going on.

Counselor: *Your parents came because they want to learn about families and what to do to make all of you happy. Do you think that this is a good reason for coming?*

Martha: *I guess so.*

Melvin: *Yes.*

Counselor: *Do you have any problems at home that your parents might want to discuss here?*

Martha: *Melvin has.*

Comment: Martha seems to elevate herself at the expense of her brother.

Melvin: *Yea.*

Counselor: *What kinds of problems do you have, Melvin?*

Melvin: *I don't know. Sometimes I fight in school.*

Martha: *You steal.*

Comment: Our assumption is confirmed.

Counselor: *What do you think, Melvin?*

Melvin: *You are probably right.*

Martha: *You mean I am right. You said, "you" and that would mean the counselor.*

Comments: Martha again puts her brother down. She has to win.

Melvin: *I don't always steal, only sometimes.*

Counselor: *I would like to ask both of you some questions. Okay?*

Melvin: *Okay.*

Counselor: *Martha, do you know why you are telling me things about Melvin which he may not like for you to tell?*

Martha: *Because he would not tell you himself.*

Counselor: *I would like to tell you what I think. Could it be that you are trying to show me how good you are by pointing out the bad things Melvin does?*

Martha: (Shrugs her shoulders) *I don't.*

Counselor: *Melvin, why do you steal?*

Melvin: *I don't know.*

Counselor: *I am sure that you don't. But I would like to guess why you do this. Could it be that you do this in order to upset your parents and then they would get angry, scold you, and you like to keep them busy with you?*

Melvin: *Maybe.*

Counselor: *I have another idea. Could it be that you like to do what you want to do and if you want to take something that doesn't belong to you, nobody can stop you?*

Melvin: (Grins) *Maybe.*

Counselor: *I have still another idea. Could it be that you feel that your parents are not being fair with you and that you want to upset them and get even with them?*

Melvin: *I don't understand what you mean.*

Counselor: *Let me see how I can explain this. Could it be that you feel that your parents get angry with you and punish you when you had done nothing wrong?*

Melvin: *No.*

Comments: The counselor did not confront Martha with her goals. It is obvious that she has to be the good girl at the expense of others. From Melvin's responses and recognition reflexes, it is obvious that he likes to get attention and be the boss. Because he is an acting-out child, the counselor did not check out goal four, but some counselors go through all four goals in each case.

Counselor: *Martha, your parents tell me that you get upset when they are displeased with you and that you cry.*

Martha: *I can't help it.*

Counselor: *May I tell you what I think? Could it be that you want to show the parents that you are their good child and that they should praise you and pay much attention to you because of it?*

Martha: *Yes.*

Counselor: *Could it be that you do only what you want to do and that you will cry when you want to and nobody is going to stop you?*

Martha: *I can't help it when I cry.*

Counselor: *Nobody is accusing you, dear child. But it might help you to understand why you cry. You think that you must always be so very good. And sometimes, you show how good you are by pointing out to others how bad Melvin is and that you would never do the things he does. What do you think?*

Martha: *I do want to be good but I don't tell on Melvin to get him into trouble. I just want him to stop doing bad things.*

Counselor: *What would happen if you did not tell anyone about what Melvin is doing?*

Martha: *I don't know.*

Counselor: *Does he ever do nice things?*

Martha: *Sometimes.*

Counselor: *Do you point them out to your parents, when Melvin does nice things?*

Martha: *Sometimes.*

Melvin: *You never do.*

Counselor: *You want very much to be good, Martha, and so does Melvin. You see, each one tries to keep the parents busy with him—you by showing how good you are, and Melvin by doing things to provoke them because he doesn't believe that he can be as good as you. But you could help him. Do you want to?*

Martha: *Yes.*

Counselor: *I thought so. Do you know how you could help him?*

Martha: *By not telling bad things about him to my parents.*

Counselor: *You see, you knew it all along and I didn't even have to tell you. I would like to ask you one more thing. Would you be willing to find out what will happen if you make a mistake or if you are not always so good? Would you want to find out?*

Martha: *No.*

Counselor: *All right. Let's leave it only with the one thing you agreed to do. That is fine.*

Is there anything you would like for me to discuss with your parents, something that they do which you don't like.

Melvin: *No.*

Martha: *I do. When Melvin comes into my room he messes it up and my father always tells me that boys are not like girls because they are messy. I wish he would not say this because then Melvin thinks he can always do it.*

Counselor: *I will discuss this with your father. Anything else you want me to tell your parents?*

Martha: *When mother takes me shopping for clothes, she never let's me chose what I like. I always have to take what she likes. It's not fair.*

Counselor: *Okay. I will discuss this with your mother. Anything else?* (No answer) *Okay, I shall now see your parents again. Do you wish to sit in with them? You don't have to.*

Melvin: *No. I'll go out and play with my tractor.*

Martha: *I would like to stay.*

Counselor: *Okay, you stay then.*

The counselor asked the parents to return. He/she explained how he/she perceived the children's goals, reported what the children had requested him/her to do and also told the parents that Martha decided not to tell anything bad about her brother. Then, he/she discussed whatever the parent's concerns were before the counselor talked with the children and made his/her recommendations.

COUNSELING FAMILY MEMBERS
TOGETHER AND SEPARATELY

One of the counselor's goals is to help the family become family centered rather than individual centered. In many cases, this can be achieved by counseling the entire family together. However, it is our experience that rapport is more easily established with the parents and with children up to age nine or ten when we see them separately. When seen together, the parents are prone to monitor the children's behavior, watching every move they make, and controlling them through eye and body movement. It is not unusual that mother does not hear the counselor's question or comments because she is too busy reprimanding a child for having his finger in his nose or mouth, for being restless, not paying attention, for a girl not having her dress pulled down, etc. The counselor often has to repeat questions because the parent was busy with the children. The children, on the other hand, often look to their parents for signs or directions on how to answer the counselor. Sometimes, they do not answer at all and then a parent takes over. The flow of the conversation is not as smooth or as effective as when the counselor sees them separately. From the way the parents describe their difficulties with the children and after talking and observing the children, the counselor will have a fairly accurate picture of how the various family members interact.

When children are not present, parents usually feel free to discuss anything that matters to them and can give the counselor their full attention. Equally, children without the parents' presence, sense that the counselor expects them to respond to all questions and with rare exceptions do so. Their answers are more spontaneous and honest and do not depend on what they think the parents would want them to say.

When older children are involved, they are usually included in the interview with the parents. Older children resent being left out in the counseling process with their parents. They often become suspicious and may, if counseled separately, sabotage the counselor's efforts. They often become noncommittal or openly show anger.

When a family has both young and older children, the older children are usually included in both interviews—the one with the parents and the other with their younger siblings.

Counseling Parents and Children Together

Basically, we follow the same steps as outlined previously in the general interviewing session. Whenever a parent describes a youngster, we ask each child to respond to this description and voice an opinion. The children are also asked to respond to the way their siblings describe them. The counselor then asks each youngster to describe the parents and we go through the same procedure. Each time a member brings up a problem, the counselor checks it out with all members and gets their input. The counselor often asks a youngster how he *feels* when the parents describe him as he has heard. This often reveals if a child thinks he/she is misunderstood by the parents. The counselor also asks the children how they would prefer for the parent to perceive them and to respond to them. Parents are asked to comment on the child's request.

The counselor is constantly stimulating a dialogue between the parents and their children. The counselor asks each how the other family members can encourage them. He also asks what each is willing to do to improve the situation. Then, the family comes to an agreement on how to handle the problem.

The following case is illustrative of a counseling session with all members of the family present.

> *The family included, father, mother, Sandra—17 and a senior in high school, Lex—16 and a junior, Helen—13 and in grade 8, and Butch—9 and in fourth grade.*

Comments: We may see this as possibly three sets of children. Sandra and Lex are close in age and may be competing with each other. Helen may feel distant to her siblings or may be close to Sandra if Lex keeps the parents busy through rebellious behavior. Butch may be the baby in the family, pampered especially by Sandra. Lex and he may be allied against the girls or Lex may resent Butch and have little to do with him.

After the initial greeting and getting acquainted, the counselor asked for the purpose of their coming. Nobody said a thing for a while but looked at each other, expecting that someone else would start the conversation.

Mother: *Since nobody is talking I will start this session by saying that we as a family are not happy. We don't communicate and the only time we talk is when we argue and fight.*

Counselor: *How do the others react to what mother said?*

Father: *I don't quite agree with my wife. We do have good times together sometimes. But, as a whole we seem divided. Everyone lives his own life and we do argue a lot. That is true.*

Counselor: *How do the others feel?*

Butch: *I agree with my parents. We do fight a lot.*

Sandra: *I would like to know why we came here and what all this talk is going to do for us? I agree that there isn't much of a family life. Thank God, it won't last much longer for me.*

Counselor: *How about you, Lex, or Helen?*

Lex: *I did not come here to talk so leave me out of this.*

Helen: *I think that it's good that we came. Maybe we can find out why we don't get along. I agree and it's okay with me.*

Counselor: *I see something very positive about you as a family. You all came and that is to your credit. Some kids refuse to come.*

Father: *I don't know if they would have come if we had not insisted. At least Sandra and Lex would not have come.*

Counselor: *Sandra and Lex, you did come and that is important, but tell me, do you always do what father tells you to do?*

Both: *No!*

Counselor: *But you did do what he wanted you to do this time and there must have been a reason. Why did you not refuse, Sandra? You don't have to answer me if you don't want to. Nobody has to, but it would help me understand your problem if you would talk. I do not sit in judgment of you, so you needn't be on guard on what you say.*

Sandra: *Well, I came because I was somewhat curious about what you do.*

Comments: She is challenging the counselor. As the session proceeds, he/she will have to confront her with the challenges and reveal the goal to her, but not yet. The counselor's immediate objective is to get the family to talk.

Counselor: *How about you, Lex, why did you come?*

Lex: *I didn't want to come but then I thought that maybe I should because I want to tell my father what I think of him. I don't ever have such a chance.*

Father: *What do you mean "to tell me what you think of me."*
What do you think of me?

Lex: *Since you ask me, and since in here you might listen, I want*
to tell you that you are a selfish, self-righteous, old-fashioned
fuddy-duddy.

Father: *Well, now you can understand what I mean when I say*
that we fight. Here is your example.

Lex: *I suppose you will start the fight, not I. Why don't you*
discuss it and find out why I feel that way?

Comments: The counselor has succeeded in getting the conversation rolling.

Counselor: *How do the others feel about what Lex said?*

Mother: *I do think that what just happened is an example of*
what goes on at home. My husband cuts off all possibilities for
communication.

Father: *Now I have heard everything, would you...*

Counselor: *Would you mind waiting until the others have com-*
mented and then you may respond. Please.

Sandra: *I don't think that Lex and Mother are quite fair to Dad*
when they say he is always at fault. Lex is always angry and he is
always accusing Dad. Not that I say that Dad is easy to get along
with. I have plenty of problems with him.

Counselor: *What about the others?*

Helen: *I can talk to him. I can't always talk to Mom, though.*
She is short tempered and she shows little understanding.

Counselor: *It would help me if each one of you told me a little*
about how you see the other members in the family. That would
really help. Would you help me with this request? Who would
start?

Lex: *I will. I already told you how I see Dad. You can't get through to him. I gave up trying. As for Mom, she tries, but she is always complaining and she always makes you feel guilty. I can't much talk to her either. As for Sandra, I really don't like her. She is stuck up and a know-it-all, and always telling you what you do wrong. I like Helen. She is nice and tries to help everyone. Butch is a pain in the neck. I wish he would grow up. I really don't have much to do with him.*

Comments: Our guesses about the characteristics of the individual children were not quite right. Helen, of all people is the one who tries to please and is the peacemaker. This may be the reaction to Lex's defiance. We were also wrong about the boys possibly uniting against the girls.

Counselor: *Who is next?*

Helen: *I also told you how I feel about Dad and about Mom. I agree with Lex somewhat that Sandra is sometimes a little mean, but not too much. Sometimes I want to talk to her but she brushes me off. Butch can be very nice when he wants to, but he fights a lot and he often behaves like he is the most important person, but I like him.*

Mother: *I think that we have very nice children and I don't want to give the impression that I don't like them or am not proud of them. But, to tell you something about each of them, well, let me see. Sandra and I have the hardest time. I would say that we disagree the most. She has her ways and there is nothing to stop her. I can talk to Lex sometimes. He is not home very much. He has his buddies and he listens to them more than to his parents. He's not a bad boy at heart. I worry about his school because I don't know if he will finish high school.*

Helen and I get along much better than she gave the impression here. Really, I don't know what she means when she says I am short-tempered. I hope she can explain this later. As for Butch. Maybe we spoil him a little. He is our last child and we may tend to baby him. He can be rather nasty and he often gives the older children a bad time.

Counselor: *Father, would you care to react now?*

Father: *I don't know how to begin. I am also curious why my wife didn't react to me; she said nothing about me. I may be a little strict and I don't say that I am always an angel, but I'm not as bad as the kids make me out to be. I am willing to listen, Lex, if you would speak to me with a civil tongue. I can't allow you to talk to me with disrespect, as you always do.*

Lex: *Well, don't ask me any more questions. I have had it now, and you may go on without me.*

Comments: Lex is again challenging the counselor. It is important that the counselor help him understand how he operates.

Counselor: *Lex, you seem to withdraw very quickly. Do you know why?*

Comments: Lex gave no answer.

Counselor: *May I tell you my impression. I may be wrong, but could it be that you don't participate unless things go your way?*

Comments: Lex does not answer.

Counselor: *Could it be that you are thinking: "That counselor is not going to make me talk; I talk when I want to."*

Lex: *You may have a point there.*

Counselor: *Lex, would you like to see changes in your family?*

Lex: *That depends.*

Counselor: *What would each of the family members have to do to encourage you?*

Lex: *They could stop bugging me.*

Counselor: *Could you give us a specific example?*

Lex: *I don't want to be told what to do at every step I take.*

Counselor: *Would you address yourself to each member and tell this person how each could make you feel happier at home?*

Lex: *Father could stop reminding me how much money I spend. It's my money.*

Counselor: *Would you care to comment, Mr. Peel?*

Father: *It's true that it is your money, but I can't stand it when you squander it, like spending a fortune for a crazy horn for your car.*

Lex: *It's my money. I earned it.*

Counselor: *Would you, Mr. Peel, be willing to let Lex decide how he spends the money he earns?*

Father: *Okay, if you say so.*

Counselor: *Not because I say so. If you want to improve the relationship, please, do not get involved in how Lex spends his money, and don't react with any anger, even inwardly, without expressing it. I know this will be hard, but it would help.*

Father: *I'll do my best. I won't interfere with how you spend your money.*

Counselor: *What could Lex do to encourage you?*

Father: *Mostly he could make me feel lots better if he'd take care of his appearance. It bothers me when he looks disheveled and dirty.*

Counselor: *How do you react to this, Lex?*

Lex: *I don't think I am dirty. I bathe but I may not comb my hair every day and I wear creased pants.*

Counselor: *What are you willing to do to encourage your father?*

Lex: *If my hair bothers you so much, okay I will comb it but I won't dress up for you or anyone.*

Counselor: *Will this do at this point?*

Father: *That will help, but not much.*

Counselor: *Is this an agreement between the two of you—what each will do?*

Father: *Agreed with me that you will wash and comb your hair.*

Lex: *Okay with me. I didn't say I'll wash because I do.*

Counselor: *What can mother do to make you feel better at home?*

The counselor goes through this procedure with each member. At the end, the family agrees on a number of things. At times, the individual members may have to give in some way. In other cases, the parents must cooperate and agree to things which they did not accept before. The counselor concentrates on one problem for each member and postpones other recommendations for the next session. It is important to give this family a chance to be successful in some area of their coexistence. This, in turn, may encourage them to make new agreements when they meet again with the counselor.

At one point, the counselor should find out why Sandra and her mother have a hard time with each other. The counselor may suggest that mother be less critical, less demanding (as pointed out by Helen), and accept that Sandra and father get along better than Sandra does with her. This may be a sore point in their relationship. Sandra may have to be confronted with comments such as:

> *"Could it be that you feel that you have a right to do as you please?"*

> *"That the others are unfair to you and you want to get even?"*

> *"Are you aware that you are much more powerful than your parents?"*

> *"Can mother make you do anything you don't want to do?"*

> *"But you can make her stay up at night and wait for you, worry about you, cry, beg you, and so forth. Now you tell me who is stronger?"*

The counselor may reveal the goal to each of the children who are causing difficulties and ask them if they are willing to do something—even one thing to change the situation. If they are not willing to change any of their activities, they may be willing not to argue and not to show disgust and contempt for their parents when the latter talk to them. That alone would help the relationship. The counselor may have to teach each how not to argue without giving in. This is only a preliminary stage. As the relationship improves somewhat—not having any nasty arguments—the counselor may go to the next step and solicit one area where each is willing to change and come to an agreement.

When a child complains that the parent treats him with distrust and with disrespect, the counselor should explore if the youngster treats the parent with trust and respect. He/she should also help each family member to see how they distrust each other and how each contributes to the problem.

Counselors should be cautious about considering children as victims of their parents. The child trains his/her parents and influences them just as much as parents influence the child. Parents and children must be confronted on what they do to each other, and both must make concessions in order to improve the relationship.

Older children often feel that talking is dangerous and that they may give themselves away and then refuse to talk. The counselor should confront the youngster with this possibility. Some examples follow:

> "Could it be that you don't talk because you are afraid that the parents won't like what you have to say and may be angry with you or even punish you?"

> "Could it be that you want to show me that nothing I say will make you talk? That you decide when and if you talk?"

> "Could it be that you have talked this over before you came and all of the kids decided not to participate in this session?"

It is better to stimulate the youngsters and even to make them angry than to be passive and just let the session go on without their participation. In their anger, they will often begin to talk about what bothers them. Keeping quiet and waiting for the reluctant adolescent to get involved in the conversation will usually not be too effective. The counselor must be a match for these cases and respond to silence and other provocations in a manner in which the reluctant participant will respond.

THE FOLLOW-UP SESSION

The suggestion is that the counselor see the family, especially the parents, for several follow-up sessions even if the parents are enthusiastic and seem to understand and accept the counselor's suggestions in the first interview. It is not easy for parents to give up a pattern of behavior which they have followed for a long time. Slipping back into old patterns is often discouraging to them. They may start doubting themselves or doubt the validity of the counselor's recommendation. They may need several sessions in order to grasp adequately the role that they play in their conflict with the children as well as understand the obstinancy with which some children provoke the parents. Children may even become worse when they sense that their parents are changing and no longer fall victims to the children's provocations as they did before.

An important point is for the counselor to review with the parents what was discussed at the previous session, what was suggested, and how the parents implemented the counselor's suggestions. The counselor is helped to understand why parents were or were not successful if they ask the parents to report in detail what the children did and how they responded to their irritation with the children. In this way, the counselor is in a position to help the parents detect a pattern of typical reactions toward the provoking child. The parent is then helped to either change this pattern entirely or to modify it, perhaps not to react as angrily, as punitively, or shock the child by doing just the opposite of what had been expected. Example:

> A mother reported that she never saw her ten-year old son so surprised as when he told her, "Kiss my a—" when she refused to allow him to go out without a coat. She replied, "With pleasure. Just let down your pants and bend over." He stared at her for a while, and then both broke out into great laughter. She told the counselor that at one time she would have slapped his mouth for such an insulting remark.

Preferably the children will attend follow-up sessions, however, it is not required. The presence of children gives both parents and children an opportunity to express feelings of appreciation if there was progress in the relationship. Children may feel more at ease expressing positive feelings toward the parents in the presence of the counselor, especially if they are not used to complimenting their parents.

Should the parents or the children, or both, complain that nothing has changed or that the home situation even got worse, the counselor must exercise great care to ascertain the specific, minute details of how the recommendations were implemented, how the children responded to the corrective measures, and what the parents did when things went wrong. The counselor may role-play a specific situation that occurred at home. In these ways, he/she is able to perceive what each is trying to do to the other, as well as to determine whether the parents really followed the recommendations that they were given at the previous session. Example:

> Seventeen-year old, Alexander asked his father if he could use the car in the evening. The father said "no" without giving any further explanation. Alexander wanted to know the reason for father's refusal. Father said that he did not have to give any reason. This made the boy very angry. He went out of the house, slamming the door and stayed out all night.

The original suggestion to this father (He and Alexander had had many fights over the use of the car.) was to discuss with his son when it would be convenient for the parent to let him have the car. They should come to some agreement which would be satisfactory to both. Alexander may have agreed to use the car once or twice a week on certain days. If the parent has been consistent, they could have avoided such an unfortunate incident as the one reported.

We find the following reasons for failure to bring about changes for the better in the family:

1. The parents talk too much at the wrong time; they still remind the children what to do and when; they continue to nag, threaten, and they still talk to the children disrespectfully.

2. One or both parents can't stop feeling sorry for a particular child and come to this child's "rescue," and in this way alienate the other children.

3. Parents are inconsistent, they follow through the counselor's recommendations when they are in a good mood or not tired, but fall back on their previous methods of disciplining the children when they are tired or don't see immediate results.

4. Parents are impatient. They don't allow sufficient time for the child to do his chores and take over for the child.

5. Parents may confront the child with his goal and do this a dozen times a day until the child becomes angry or parent-deaf.

CULTURAL DIFFERENCES

The counselor should be aware of cultural differences and values when counseling families. These differences are sometime so strongly ingrained that it is extremely difficult for some parents to accept child-rearing principles which are geared to the present democratic society. Such parents cannot believe that our techniques are effective or that they really work. Some may understand that what is suggested is correct, but still cannot follow our advice. Many parents confuse principles which are geared to the present democratic society. Such parents cannot believe that our techniques are effective or that they really work. Many parents confuse democratic principles of child rearing with permissiveness and reject them out of hand. This is an intellectual understanding to which the client has a strong emotional resistance.

Such situations call for re-education of the parents. An example of cultural differences:

> *The parents had difficulties with both children. Melita, 6 and Jarval, 3. Father was from Pakistan and mother from Yugoslavia.*

> **Problem:** *Melita dawdles and is never ready in time for school.*

> *Jarval refuses to do anything for himself. He has to be fed or he screams and throws the plate with the food on the floor. If the parents refuse him anything he demands, he throws and breaks*

things. He pulled down the drapes in one of his rages, and at another time he took a kitchen knife and cut up the bedspread.

Both children insist on sleeping with the parents. They go to their respective bedrooms, but as soon as the parents go to bed, both come running and go under the covers with their parents.

Father: *He sees nothing wrong in the children's behavior because "that's how young children are." He also believes that it is good for the children to be close to the parents at night; that it gives them a feeling of protection and security. In his own country it is not unusual for children to sleep with their parents.*

Mother *realizes that there is something wrong with the behavior of the children, especially Jarval; that something must be done to change this, but she maintains that she could never let a child cry no matter how much she realizes that it would be best to ignore it. She invariably would comfort the child and give in to the child's demands. No amount of explanation could help this mother accept our suggestions, to tell the child that he can cry and have a tantrum, but that it would not change the parents' determination not to give in. Mother always replied, "I know that you are right, but I also know that I could never do this."*

In such a case, the counselor would do better to concentrate on an area which would be easy for the parent to accept and to wait until the parents feel more comfortable with new suggestions. Once the parents meet with success in this one area, they may feel encouraged and willing to apply other suggestions made by the counselor. These parents agreed to set a time for the children to watch television. Television was always a great problem and caused many hassles. They also agreed to let the children pick out their clothes in the morning, something that was difficult for mother who was a perfectionist.

When the family came for their follow up, they reported that after a few trying days the television problem worked out satisfactorily. The children were happy to be allowed to wear what they chose. The counselor suggested that they may now want to work on Melita's eating problem. She dawdled while eating, left the table numerous times and then came back. Mother agreed to take the food away when Melita left the table. Melita, reluctantly, also agreed to this. This solved the eating problem with Melita. Gradually, the counselor was in a position to suggest other changes which the parents were more willing to follow than they were at first. In such cases the counselor must proceed very slowly and make only one recommendation for each child at a time. More recommendations might very well confuse the parents and they may completely disregard the suggestions.

It does not help to remind the parents that their culture may be different from the present democratic culture of America. However, the counselor should slowly help the parents understand that the entire family will be happier and that the children will be better adjusted if they understand the changes and accept the values of our times. This should not be misconstrued with behavior which is of a negative and destructive nature such as delinquency or crime.

We stress again the importance that the counselor's goals for the family be aligned with the parents' goals if the counselor hopes to be effective. Therefore, the counselor would do well to concentrate on one problem at a time where such alignment is possible and proceed from there.

MISCELLANEOUS FACTORS IN COUNSELING

Counselors in training often ask the following questions:

1. How does the counselor control very young children during an interview when they are disturbing the session?

The counselor does not control them; they usually control themselves. Most children become actively involved in the counseling process. However, if a child should act up, the counselor should first disclose to the child the purpose of his/her behavior. Acting out during a session is mostly associated with goals one and two. The counselor may give the child the option to stay and help either through participation or through listening. We do not insist that the child must talk. If the child refuses to stay, the counselor suggests that the child wait in another room until the interview with the rest of the family is finished. The decision is up to the child. However, the counselor appeals to the child to stay and help the parents with their problems. In the rare occasions in which a child creates such a disturbance that totally disrupts the session, the counselor should remove the child in a friendly way and talk with him/her later if possible.

2. We are often asked if very young children understand what is meant when the goal of their behavior is disclosed to them.

It is amazing how much even babies understand. They may not understand the words that are spoken to them, but by the tone of the voice of the counselor, they sense what the counselor is referring to. Babies perceive and understand much faster than they learn how to talk. Since they cannot verbalize their perception, we often assume that they do not understand what we are saying, but they often do.

The following example may illustrate this point:

> *Parents with three children came to be counseled. The oldest was a boy of seven, next came a girl of five and then came a baby of ten months. The baby kept crawling on the floor, pulling out the cord of the tape recorder that the parents had brought along to record the session. Interchangeably, the parents picked up the baby with a "no, no" and put him back on the floor next to one of them. But it did not take a minute and the baby was up to his former behavior. Finally the counselor decided to disclose to the baby the goal of his behavior. The counselor said in a friendly but firm voice, "Could it be that you want your parents to keep busy with you and keep picking you up? Could it be that you want to show us who is the boss here?" The parents and the students in class (this was done in front of a class the counselor was teaching) were astounded and even somewhat angry that the counselor would disclose a goal to such a young child. But to everyone's amazement, the child looked at the counselor and slowly crawled back to where his father sat. This baby did not disturb them for the rest of the session. Obviously the child did not understand the exact meaning of the words, but could tell from them and the tone of voice that what he did was met with disapproval. And the child responded.*

To give another example:

> *A two-year old child was a tyrant in his family and his two older sisters complained about him. When the counselor disclosed the*

goal to the child, the older siblings said that he did not under-
stand what was said to him. But when the counselor told the
sisters to stand up to him and not to give in to him as they did
before, this two-year old child, who was not supposed to under-
stand what was being discussed got up from his chair, walked
over to the counselor, pointed a finger at the counselor, and in a
clear voice said: "I don't like what you are saying and I don't
like you." And with this he walked out of the room.

These two episodes clearly exemplify how prejudiced we are against young children and how little credit we give them for their understanding and intelligence.

3. When children are left in the playroom and the counselor sees the parents alone, what should a counselor do when there is an infant that cries when the parents leave?

We suggest that the parents take the infant with them. If they hear the infant crying, they will not concentrate on the interview and the counselor cannot be effective. The parents may hold the child while they talk to the counselor.

4. Should the counselor record the session?

This question, whether the counselor should record the session, and if so, in what manner, is often raised by students. It is advisable that the counselor restrict him/herself to a minimum of writing while the interview is going on. The counselor may jot down a few basic points which he does not want to forget. The counselor, who does not have information from a formal intake done before the interview, would need to write down the names, ages, and grades of the children. He/she may also record the other people who live with the family. It is helpful if the counselor writes the names of the children on a horizontal line, leaving some space between each child. The counselor may then put down a word or phrase under each child as the child is being described by the parents.
Example:

Tess, 11, grade 6	**Lola, 8, grade 2**	**Barry, 6, grade 1**
cries easily	aggressive	quiet
sensitive	fights	affectionate

| good in school | average in school | adores Tess |
| father's favorite | complainer | wets at night |

The counselor may note the parents and others who live with the family in similar fashion and make comments as appropriate.

Mother	**Father**	**Grandmother**
critical	easy going	feels sorry for Tess
perfectionist	seems disoriented	critical of mother
very serious	has fun with	bribes children
possible problem	children	
with husband		

Some counselors find this kind of short outline helpful, but many get along well without any note taking at all during the session. It is wise for the counselor to assure each member of the family that they may see the record if they wish. This often disarms suspicious or hostile youngsters, especially teenagers. Some counselors make notes after the session. Having some notes is helpful, not only to refresh the counselor's memory before subsequent sessions, but may be helpful if it is necessary to refer a client and send a report to the new counselor.

5. How and when should a counseling series be terminated?

This question cannot be answered with a specific statement. It all depends on the problem and on the cooperation of the individual family members. But in general, Adlerian counselors do not continue with counseling for a lengthy period. Usually, if the family has many problems, no more than fifteen to twenty sessions are needed, but the average family sees improvement after two or three sessions and often even after one session. Much depends on how the family responds to the counselor's recommendations and the level of difficulty when counseling began.

6. How should sessions be spaced?

We usually see the family once a week at first. It may happen that for the first two or three weeks we see a family twice a week. As the family experiences success, there are fewer problems to solve and the counselor schedules them at longer intervals, perhaps once a month.

Eventually, sessions are not scheduled, but the family is encouraged to call on the counselor and make an appointment when they encounter a problem. A session usually lasts 45 minutes to an hour.

7. What is recommended as an office setting?

Counselors work in all kinds of settings: in the privacy of an office, at a community center, in schools, jails, and hospitals. It is helpful to have a warm, homelike atmosphere. The office does not need much furniture, but should have enough chairs to seat larger families. Since the counselor often sees parents apart from the young children, the counselor should have a room where these children can wait for their turn. It is suggested that the counselor keep toys, books, etc., for the children to occupy themselves while they wait.

REFERENCES

Ansbacher, H. L., & Ansbacher, R. (Eds.) (1956). *The individual psychology of Alfred Adler.* New York: Harper & Row Publishers.

Dreikurs, R. (1957). *Psychology in the classroom.* New York: Harper & Row Publishers.

Dreikurs, R., & Soltz, B. (1964). *Children the challenge.* New York: Hawthorn Books.

Dreikurs, R. (1972). *Coping with children's misbehavior.* New York: Hawthorn Books.

Grunwald, B. (1973). *Rudolf Dreikurs' contributions to education* in proceedings of the Rudolf Dreikurs Memorial Institute, Espinho, Lisboa, Portugal.

CHAPTER VI

CORRECTIVE MEASURES

RECOMMENDATIONS

Making suggestions and decisions is an essential part of family counseling. We do not support those who believe that the client knows best what he/she should do or in waiting until the client is "ready" to make his/her own decisions. Had the client known how to deal with the problems he/she would not have come in the first place. Adlerian counselors take a very active part in the counseling procedure both verbally and nonverbally. They guide, suggest, and try to motivate the client to apply alternative methods toward coping or solving problems. Experience seems to show that clients feel encouraged when they leave a session with something concrete on which to work.

Usually, the counselor shares conclusions about how he/she perceives the family problem after he/she has talked to both the parents and the children. He/she then invites members of the family to consider other possibilities to handle the problem. For example the counselor may say:

"As I understand the problem, Mother gets upset each time Tommy does not come home to change his clothes before he goes out to play with the other children and dirties his good clothes. The parents punish him by grounding him for the rest of the day. Tommy feels unjustly punished and it results in an argument."

Counselor: *Could this problem be handled in a way that would be more satisfactory to all of you? What might you do when this comes up again?*

Mother: *I really don't know what else to do. We can't afford to let him dirty or tear his good clothes. We have told him that he must come home and change before he goes out to play.*

Counselor: *What about you, Tommy, have you any suggestions?*

Tommy: *I am very careful. I hardly ever get my clothes dirty. When did I last dirty my clothes, Mom?*

Counselor: *How about you, Mr. Smith, do you have any suggestions?*

Mr. Smith: *I don't see why Tommy has to dress up for school in the first place. My wife feels that he has to dress up.*

Counselor: *Mrs. Smith, how do you feel about what your husband just said?*

Mother: *But why can't he come home and change? I don't see why he can't cooperate in this?*

Counselor: *You could avoid any argument if you gave Tommy the choice, to play very carefully and not dirty his clothes or wear his ordinary street clothes to school. Let him decide. How do you feel about this suggestion?*

Tommy: *I would like it fine.*

Mr. Smith: *Okay with me.*

Mother: *Two against one. I wouldn't mind if he really did not dirty his clothes, but I am willing to try it.*

Counselor: *Would you be willing to "do" it rather than to "try" it?*

Mother: *I will do it.*

The counselor may explore other possibilities and let the family members decide which one most appeals to them. The counselor must help the client realize that the suggestions have a better chance to work if the client believes in them and if the parents give the child a choice. Giving choices for the child's decisions enables him/her to consider the matter and, if consequences were to follow, to associate them with his/her own decision and not with the parents' unfair treatment or punishment.

As already stated, it is advisable that the counselor refrain from giving too many suggestions and recommendations at one time because it becomes too great a task for the parents to follow through successfully and discourages them further if they don't succeed. On the other hand, if the parent or child sees results, it encourages them, and they probably will be willing to accept additional recommendations at the next interview. Furthermore, also helpful is for the counselor and the family members to discuss the possibility that changes may take place slowly and that they should not give up if this should be the case.

The counselor should alert the parents to the fact that, when power conflicts are present, children often may find new ways to exert power when the parent has successfully withdrawn from earlier conflicts. Dreikurs referred to this phenomenon as the child's "redoubling his efforts" to control the situation (Dreikurs, 1957). This occurrence is usually temporary as the parents implement more effective methods of dealing with their children.

Finally, the importance of the parent consistency in following through on recommendations should be strongly emphasized. Consistency is probably the most vital aspect of any corrective measure undertaken. If the parent is not consistent, the child learns that the parents can still be defeated if the child only redoubles the effort. Telltale remarks by parents such as "I tried" or "I did it most of the time" will reveal inconsistent follow through to the alert counselor.

ENCOURAGEMENT

Rudolf Dreikurs (1959) often stated that "the child needs encouragement like a plant needs water." This statement may be equally applied to all participants in the human endeavor. Rolla May (1975) wrote that the great philosophers—Kierkegaard, Nietzche, Camus, and Sarte—all agreed that "courage was not the absence of despair; but the capacity to move ahead despite its presence." A thorough knowledge of the principles, skills, and techniques of encouragement can be one of the most effective ways in which the counselor may assist parents. As stated in the preface of a recent publication on the topic, "It (encouragement) is the most effective way to stimulate movement in others and to increase their feelings of worth and acceptance" (Dinkmeyer & Losoncy, 1980).

Authorities in Adlerian psychology often have indicated that children misbehave because they are discouraged. Parents are not aware of how they systematically discourage children by instilling in them the idea that they are not good enough as they are. Gradually, the children withdraw from them, feel mistreated and misunderstood, and that nothing can be expected from their parents. As the children become further discouraged, they see little hope for improvement in the relationship and increase their negative behavior. Thoughtful reflection gives rise to an important corollary—parents and other adults also do not function effectively when they are discouraged. More specifically, what is really meant is that children who misbehave, and parents who are not functioning effectively, are both psychologically discouraged. They are unable to interact positively (in the social interest) with others. Thus, the result is disruptive behavior from children and ineffective responses from parents. It follows, then, that children, especially those who misbehave, need to be encouraged (Dreikurs, 1959). McKay (1976) also pointed out that a discouraged parent cannot encourage a discouraged child. Therefore, it is essential that every counseling session include some aspects of encouragement for all members of the family. More importantly, the counselor must impress the family, particularly the parents, of the importance of and teach them techniques for encouraging each other.

The following discussion will define the principles of encouragement, explain their importance, and outline skills and techniques for implementation.

Mutual Respect

A perennial complaint from most parties to a disrupted family relationship is that there is little or no respect for each other. Children and youth generally complain that they do not feel that their parents and other adults usually respect them. If parents do not set a personal example in courtesy and considerate treatment between members of the family, how will the children learn to be courteous and respectful? More vital, how will they learn that it is important and necessary to comport themselves in a courteous and considerate manner in the larger society? It is easily discernible that children often do not respect their parents and teachers. Discourteous tone and terminology of language in the counseling session often eliminates all doubt. The counselor's first chore in such cases is to make the individual members aware of this discourtesy and to teach them to treat each other with respect. In discussing the meaning of mutual respect, Mosak (1978) gives a helpful definition and makes the important point that because Adlerian psychology is a psychology of use, then, "one demonstrates respect by regarding others and treating them as if they had equal worth." Mosak further explained that this does not mean that children are equal to parents in experience and wisdom, but that they should not be treated as idiots or as stupid just because they are children. All members of the family should have equal rights and should receive respectful treatment shown by an acceptable tone of voice and language. Sarcasm and degrading language, not only is disrespectful, but also further damages the relationship between any two persons regardless of the age or status of either party. Furthermore, respect cannot be generated on demand; it can only be earned and emanate from a relationship.

The first step in establishing an atmosphere of mutual respect in the family is to make certain that parents maintain their own self-respect. It is a dictum of life that no one will respect an individual who does not maintain his/her own self-respect. If a mother allows children to be rude and abrasive, allows them to be manipulative, is a slave to them and their foibles—she shows no respect for herself and neither will the children respect her. The mother in such a situation must be firm about what she will or will not do. She probably cannot make the youngster help with household chores, but she can refuse to wait on the child and be a servant if the youngster continues to be uncooperative. At the same time, parents must learn to be considerate of their children, their views, and their needs. Nothing can infuriate a teenager more than to be requested to do an unscheduled task when he/she is on his/her way out the door to go swimming with a friend. We believe emphatically that if family members were as considerate and diplomatic with each other as they are with their best friends, most family problems would disappear.

Counselors will find in some cases that various members of a family need to have one or two separate sessions in order to prevent the overt, hostile dialogue that shows disrespect and further disrupts the relationships. In separate sessions both children and parents can be confronted with how they are being disrespectful to other members of the family, and the counselor can usually avoid the "blame searching" syndrome in which most families engage. The age old golden rule—do unto others as you wish others to do unto you—is probably the best advice in these cases—and is familiar language that most families can understand.

Equality

Equality as a principle of encouragement in human relationships is a close corollary of mutual respect. In fact, everything stated in the preceding section on mutual respect could be appropriately repeated in discussing equality. In a sense that is what this book is all about—*developing mutual respect and equality in family relationships.*

Just what does equality mean in day to day relationships? How does a family implement equalitarian relationship effectively, given the factor of differences in knowledge and age among the various family members? Usually, the equal worth concept discussed is quite acceptable to most. Dreikurs (1972) emphasized the "equal worth" meaning of equality and pointed out that only in a democracy has this ideal emerged. The next question is how family members relate to each other if they believe that each has equal worth? Dreikurs again delineated the history and difficulties involved in developing the techniques demanded by the new democratic condition in family life, but concludes that there is no alternative. Again, Mosak (1978) is helpful as he pointed out that the adult respects children by listening to them, being friendly and courteous, accepting their rights to opinions, understanding them, and refraining from being eternally judgmental. Certainly, one of the most important techniques is to learn how to disagree without being rude, inconsiderate, and disrespectful. An example of a father being disrespectful to a son follows:

> *A sixteen year old boy told his father that it made him feel good and grown-up when people addressed him as "Mister..." The father laughed and said: "Don't think that this makes you a man and that you know much. As far as I am concerned, you are still wet behind the ears." The son withdrew, saying, "I'm sorry I told you." Such treatment of youngsters who want so desperately to be regarded and treated as young adults, often causes alienation from adults who respond as this father did. Gradually, the youngsters lose confidence in their parents, never show them respect, and tell them less and less.*

Children and youth have telltale terminology in describing parents who relate to them on an equal basis. "Mom treats me grown up," from a six-year old. "I can really talk to my Mom," from a fifteen-year old girl. Or on the contrary, "It's no use talking to my parents, nothing I say ever makes a difference," or "She treats me like a baby!" These are some of the clues which will indicate to the counselor the level of equality and mutual respect that members of the family have for each other.

Understanding as Encouragement

Few principles of encouragement are as effective as that of showing counselees that they are understood. This promotes rapport between counselors and clients of all ages. It establishes credibility. The client thinks, "Here is someone who understands me and my problems; here is someone who can help me out of my dilemma." The counselor may indicate understanding of the counselee very early in a session by making the following types of inquiries:

> *Could it be that you work very hard and that no one appreciates your effort? Could it be that you try very hard to please everyone? Could it be that other members of the family take advantage of you? Could it be that you feel that you get no help from your spouse? Could it be that you feel frustrated and angry about the situation?*

After the counselor has checked out these feelings, and the client has relaxed somewhat, the counselor proceeds to help the parents understand how unwittingly they fall to the provocations of the children, and the role that the parents play in the problem.

Having Faith as Encouragement

One of the most pernicious and unknowing ways in which parents discourage children is to indicate by word and attitude that they really don't have faith that the child will improve or accomplish the tasks that are set. The parents thus reveal their own discouragement and this is transmitted to the child. This contributes to the child's already low esteem and self-confidence. An example:

> *A father and his twelve-year old son, Norman, were counseled by one of the authors. The boy had difficulties at school and at home. He refused to help with any household chores and this caused many argumentations, especially with his mother. When the counselor finally succeeded in soliciting an agreement with Norman that he would make his own bed from now on, the father responded with "I am willing to bet with you (the counselor) that he will never do what he promised."*

Thus, many parents contribute to the child's unreliability through their own doubt in the child's sincerity. The child then lives up to the parents' expectations.

As counselors, the authors have repeatedly experienced the phenomenon that when they have confidence in the child, the child will accomplish an agreed upon task, and will live up to his/her agreement. Expectations must be kept reasonable and the parent must keep faith that the child will achieve them. Dreikurs (1959) emphasized the relationship between faith and encouragement in the following statement. "Encouragement implies your faith in the child. It communicates to him/her your belief in his/her strengths and ability, not in his/her potentiality. Unless you have faith in the child as he/she is, you cannot encourage the child."

Asking for Help as Encouragement

Most people will respond positively to a sincere plea for help. Counselors will find this particularly helpful if the request is put on a personal basis. There are many ways to request help from counselees and thus encourage them. Several suggestions follow:

> *"It is somewhat difficult to decide what to do in this problem. Could you help me by suggesting some other ways to do it?"*

OR

"Gary, I want very much to help your family, but in order to do this I need your help. Do you think that you could stop disturbing the session for the next ten minutes? That would help me very much."

OR

"You could help me better understand the problem if you would role play the situation that you just described. Assuming that I (the counselor) am your son, Tommy, would you please wake me using the same words and tone of voice that you use when you wake him the first time. Now, assuming that I do not respond, use the words and tone of voice that you use in awakening me a second time. Now, I still do not get out of bed. Show me what you do and say the third time that you awaken me."

In following such a procedure, the mother, as well as the counselor, comes to understand the escalation of annoyance, frustration, and anger and how the son can exercise power over the mother in upsetting her. The counselor will be in an improved position to help the mother because he/she will better understand the situation after the role playing incident.

Another common situation in counseling would be to ask the children to help the parents remember recommendations and to report back at the next session on what happened during the week. Children almost invariably will remember and report in specific detail, often even more effectively than the parent.

Logical Consequences as Encouragement

The opportunity for making choices and assuming responsibility is an encouraging aspect of the consequences system. Removing the superior-inferior relationship from the family dynamics that results from implementation of logical consequences is greatly encouraging. The next section will concern at some length with this theme.

Honesty as Encouragement

Often those new to Adlerian counseling express first doubt, then amazement that direct confrontation techniques almost invariably result in a friendly, understanding relationship between the counselor and the family members. This is because the counselor respects the client and his/her manner of using confrontation. The counselor is communicating that clients have the strength and ability to deal with the situation. To avoid an open and honest assessment of disruptive behavior in the family implies weakness and inability to deal with life on their part. Such an approach never fails to discourage.

Right to Decision Making as Encouragement

A very important aspect of our democratic tradition is the right to make decisions that affect us. This right can range from the choice of a five-year old of the clothes he/she will wear to kindergarten to an adult choosing where he/she wishes to live and how he/she wishes to earn a living. Parents and teachers frequently make decisions for children that the children should make for themselves. In so doing, children are not only systematically discouraged, but also deprived of numerous opportunities to learn how to direct their own lives. These examples illustrate the point.

> Parent to child: *I don't want you to wear this green sweater with your purple pants. Why don't you wear the nice gray sweater you got from Grandma?*
>
> OR
>
> *Don't spend your allowance on a gift for Jimmy. What did he ever give you for your birthday? Nothing! So don't waste any money on him.*

Critics often raise issue that children lack the knowledge and experience to solve problems. This argument usually is made to defend the adults' position of making all the decisions for the child. Discussion with children however will usually reveal which decisions they feel capable of making and which they are willing and happy to leave to others. This will vary from family to family based on past involvement of the children in decision making.

There is one magnitudious truth to be kept foremost in mind when helping families determine what decisions can be confidently left to children. The children, especially teenagers, are going to make many decisions anyway. The counselor should keep in mind that behavior is goal oriented and self-selected and that as long as this is true, adults should assist the child in making the best decision possible rather than making decisions for him/her. The counselor also should impress on youngsters that making decisions is not only their right, but that the results are also their responsibility.

Setting Goals as Encouragement

One of the many complaints that parents have about children is that they are aimless, have no goals, and do not look farther ahead than tomorrow. This complaint is sometimes accurate, and counselors can greatly encourage children, and adults as well, by helping them plan and set goals. Each counseling session should result in some goal setting and a plan for action. Much of this goal setting will be of a short term nature in the form of recommendations designed to change disruptive behavior. However, as the relationships improve the counselor should help the family set longer range goals for each member of the family as well as for the family unit.

An example of a short-term goal might be a child's acceptance of the responsibility for making his/her own bed or helping with the dishes during the next week. Another example might be the parent's agreement to refrain from nagging and reminding during the same time. Longer-range goals are usually possible only after the level of hostility has decreased and the family has established more friendly communication. A long-range goal might be planning for vacation trips or establishing a financial plan which enables individual members to make a large purchase.

Helping families set goals also often provides them with some order and pattern in their lives that has been missing. So many families lead a disordered, aimless, disorganized, day-to-day existence. This often contributes to the disruptive behavior of the children. The counselor can greatly encourage them by lending assistance in goal setting with respect to organization of the daily routine. The Family Council is probably the best vehicle by which families can set goals which are appropriate for them. This approach is fully covered in the section on Training the Child.

The counselor also can teach the family valuable and necessary communication skills as he/she leads family discussions in goal setting. The counselor should exercise care in helping families and individuals set achievable goals. Achieving goals, both short and long term, is encouraging; failing to attain them has the opposite effect.

The Right to Participate is Encouraging

As all members of society move toward equality, all members demand participatory rights. This trend has not gone unrecognized by children and youth of today. The Adlerian family counseling model provides for full participation of all family members. It provides the basic counseling structure by which the counselor can move the family toward a participatory, democratic living unit which contributes to encouragement.

Consistency as Encouragement

A serious irritant to children is inconsistency on the part of parents and teachers. All children desire parameters by which they can behave with security, i.e., know where they stand and where parents stand. However, because of many factors parents change methods, waver and wattle, feel guilty about being too harsh and become overly permissive—all of which appear as inconsistency. These many changes occur because of the parents' ignorance of how to be more effective. Children sense this insecurity and inconsistency on the part of parents and take advantage in order to get their way. Once parents adopt an approach and are consistent in the way they carry it out, children understand that no amount of nagging will upset the parents, and they will conduct themselves in a more acceptable manner. However, if parents keep children guessing with inconsistency, one can be assured that the children will keep parents guessing as to their responses.

Myths About Encouragement

A wide variety of societal myths about what constitutes encouragement are almost universally accepted and erroneously used.

A common example focuses on a child's potential. Parents are prone to say, "You have the potential, why don't you live up to it. You can do it if only you would work; a B is a pretty good grade, but if you will work a little harder you can get an A." The authors submit that all such comments are uniformly discouraging. What such statements actually convey is that the child is not achieving what he/she should, that he/she is shirking the job, and is a disappointment to the parent.

A second myth concerning encouragement is that it is encouraging to use rewards for achievements and punishments for failures. This topic will be dealt with more fully in a succeeding section; however, it suffices to state that the authors have seldom known a troubled family who experienced success with a rewards and punishment system. We seem to live in a mistake oriented society which explains why so many parents and teachers believe that children's mistakes must be specifically corrected in order to prevent further errors. One must only be reminded of the theory of purposive behavior and the four goals of misbehavior in order to understand the result of reminding children about mistakes.

Misplaced Competition

Misplaced competition is almost a scourge of our society. Competition tends to become inextricably involved with many family and educational activities on the basis that it will motivate achievement. The opposite result is usually experienced. Perhaps the highly achieving child, who has the self-confidence to compete, is motivated by competition, but the remaining members of the family or other group members will generally be discouraged by their second place status. Successful family life fundamentally depends on cooperation—not competition. Therefore, it is counter productive to develop competitive activities within the family. Recognition of the importance of developing cooperation in families has lead to a whole new movement in developing cooperative versions of competitive family games and of new non-competitive games. To those who raise the question as to how the children can best be prepared for life in a competitive society, the authors emphatically respond that developing cooperative skills is the best preparation for living and learning in a democratic world.

Discouraging Words

Parents often think that they motivate children to behave better if they issue certain admonitions prior to an activity. Corsini and Painter (1975) indicated that often the result is opposite of that intended and offer some typical examples:

> Don't get dirty.
> Be Careful.
> Let me show you how.
> If younger children can do it, so can you.

These same authors also offer examples of discouraging statements often made to children after the behavior:

> You could have done better.
> I've told you a thousand times.

When will you become responsible.
If only you would listen to me.

Encouraging Words

Counselors need to teach parents how to phrase encouraging remarks. Encouragement involves the ability to focus on the assets and strengths of children and to build their confidence and self-esteem. According to Dreikurs and Dinkmeyer (1963) the parent who encourages placed value on the child as he/she is shows faith in the child and enables him/her to have faith in him/herself, sincerely believes in the child's ability, and wins his/her confidence while building his/her self-respect. A feeling of encouragement can come from nonverbal gestures like a smile, wink, or pat on the back. Encouragement also may be shown by what is said. Reimer (1967) offers the following phrases to be used to encourage a child:

> *You do a good job.* (Children should be encouraged when they do not expect it. It is possible to point out some useful act of contribution in each child.)

> *You have certainly improved in keeping your room neat.* (Children will usually continue to try if they can see some improvement. They do not always see it because they themselves have become perfectionists. But when we point the improvement out to them, then, they see it.)

> *We like you but we don't like what you do.* (Children frequently feel disliked after having made a mistake or after misbehaving. A child should never think that he is not liked.)

> *You can help me... you are helping me...* (To feel useful is important to everyone. Children want to be helpful, but we just have to give them the opportunity.)

> *Let's try it together.* (Children who think they have to do things perfectly are often afraid to attempt something new for fear of making a mistake.)

> *So you made a mistake! So what did you learn from it? There is nothing that can be done about what has happened, but a person*

can always do something about the future. (Mistakes can teach children a great deal if they do not feel embarrassed for erring.)

Keep trying, don't give up. (A comment might help the child who wants to give up because he/she is not successful.)

I think you can straighten this thing out, but if you need help, you know where to find me. (Adults need to express confidence that children are able to and will resolve their own conflict if given a chance.)

I can understand how you feel (not sympathy, but empathy) *but I feel confident that you can handle it.*

I noticed how hard you worked at this. I really admire you for your persistence and for not giving up. (Children feel appreciated when their efforts are noticed.)

Praise and Encouragement

Many adults equate praise and encouragement; however, there is a vast difference in general usage. The counselor will need to teach most parents the difference. Praise is generally directed toward the doer in our culture. "You are such a good girl to get all A's on your report card." Such statements also carry a corollary, "Am I still a good girl if I don't get all A's?" or perhaps a more subtle hint, "I have to be perfect in order to be accepted by Mom." A more proper comment is directed at the report, "That is a great card, you must really be pleased." Or in the case of a poor report card, "What do you think about your grades? Do you want to talk about it? Could I be of any help?" These are kinds of approaches that encourage. The basic principle is to compliment the deed and the effort and to accept and support whatever the outcome.

In their attempt to encourage the child, parents frequently misuse praise. They may compliment a child when both the performance and effort are negligible or unsatisfactory. The child is usually aware of such insincerity. Such undeserved praise often reinforces the child's feeling of unworthiness and further discourages him/her. A parent or counselor can usually reverse a basically negative situation of this kind by asking the child to explain the situations which do not merit praise. Children often express their negative feelings and can be helped to choose a positive approach to improving the situation.

TRAINING THE CHILD WITH
NATURAL AND LOGICAL CONSEQUENCES
(AUTOCRATIC VS. DEMOCRATIC METHODS)

Parent Dilemma in Child Rearing

Traditional methods of punishment are no longer effective in correcting children's misbehavior, juvenile delinquency, or crime in today's world. Correcting misbehavior or rehabilitating delinquents would be easy if only the children and youth would do what the adult world instructed them to do. The current dilemma stems from the unwillingness of most people, including children and youth, to accept the autocratic, superior-inferior relationship that is the foundation of the traditional system of rewards and punishment used in the past. Women and minorities no longer accept being treated as inferior; evidence surrounds us daily. What may not be so evident to many is that children and youth also are rebelling because they are no longer willing to accept the dominance of parents, schools, or community authorities, and an inferior position in society.

It is difficult for parents to understand why children no longer positively respond to the child rearing techniques that were effective when they, the parents, were children. "Why don't the old methods work with our own children?" they often ask. The counselor must help these parents realize that they are now living in a different age and different world than when they were children, that a major change from an autocratic to a democratic ethic is evolving, and that most conditions under which people live are rapidly changing. The counselor must help parents to realize that children no longer accept the autocratic structure of the past and will fight those who try to dominate them and retaliate when punished. The days when mother could threaten the child with, "Wait until I tell your father what you did," are long past. The father was generally the ultimate boss of the family in the autocratic past, and everybody, including mother, had to do what he said. The role of who is boss, however, has been reversed in many homes. If anyone dominates, it is often the children or youth. Parents, therefore, are compelled to learn new techniques to deal with the situation—techniques that eliminate any kind of bossing or domination.

Children of today have learned, but not always consciously, that the ideal of today's life is democratic co-existence. They are aware that they have rights and will not allow themselves to be pushed around. The major problem, then, for parents, counselors, and teachers is to develop techniques to teach children the necessity of social controls, i.e., that no society can exist without order as specified in law, rules, and regulations. Natural and Logical Consequences, a system based on principles of democratic cooperation and co-living, is suggested as an effective approach for children and youth who deliberately disregard the rules of the household or of society. This is a system whereby the child can associate consequences of mistaken behaviors with his/her choices of action. For example, if a child consistently leaves his/her bicycle outside and the bicycle is stolen, the logical consequence is that he/she would have to go without a bike until such time when he/she saves enough money to buy a new one. The parents should not replace it at their expense, not scold him/her, or make him/her feel guilty. The loss of the bicycle is sufficient for him/her to learn the lesson of properly caring for the property.

Individuals must distinguish between "logical" and "natural" consequences. A natural consequence is one that comes about without anyone making an arrangement for it to occur. For instance, if a child breaks a dish and cuts his/her hand in the process, the natural consequence of the cut hand results in injury and pain. Another common example is that of a child's running on the stairs falling and injuring himself/herself. The resultant pain teaches him/her to refrain from that "mistaken" act. A natural consequence teaches rapidly. Once the child experiences a "natural consequence," the parent should refrain from adding punishment or a "logical consequence."

The major task in moving from an autocratic to a democratic family model is to replace the arbitrary authority of the parent with a structure of logical consequences in which all members of the family experience consequences if one of them disregards the rules. Such a system places responsibility for right acting squarely on each individual, including the children.

Historical Antecedents

The English philosopher and essayist, Herbert Spencer, wrote about the efficacy of natural consequences for educating children about 100 years ago. He pointed out (Spencer, 1885) that unavoidable consequences of mistaken behaviors are the best teachers. Adler (1963) later wrote of the "ironclad logic of the social order" when applying this principle to action and reaction in a social group (family, class, and so forth)

(Adler, 1963). Dreikurs and Grey (1970) pointed out that Spencer's ideas can be readily applied to daily living in the form of common sense logical consequences which may be arranged. Dreikurs (1958a) outlined the fallacies in the rewards and punishment system and several basic principles of an effective operational system of logical consequences.

> The distinction between punishment and natural consequences is equally clear. It is our experience in the Community Child Guidance Centers (5) that parents find it very difficult to understand the far-reaching and essential differences between punishment and natural or logical consequences, which form an integral part of the approach which Alfred Adler (1) suggested for the training of children. The main distinctions between the two are: Punishment is imposed upon the child for past transgressions; the consequences, which must be natural and logical to the disturbance of order, are self-evident and, therefore, come into play only as long as the child disregards order. It is order and reality by itself, not the arbitrary power of the adult, which brings about the unpleasant consequences. The child always has a choice, and thereby determines what he will experience. The parent can stand by as a friend, because he does not feel personally defeated.

Dreikurs (1958a) continued:

> If the adult becomes angry, the best natural consequence is turned into punishment. Not all these distinctive qualities are present in each case. There are situations where the distinction between a punitive approach and the application of natural consequences is not absolutely clear; but the trained educator can become sensitive to the all-important difference—and the child reacts completely differently to each of these two approaches.

> These new methods indicate the shift from an autocratic to a democratic society with the development of mutual equality and mutual respect as the basis for inter-personal relationships. We will not be able to apply them as long as we do not free ourselves from autocratic tendencies which tradition has instilled in us.

Basic Principles of Natural and Logical Consequences

Several principles for effective implementation of a logical consequences system can be inferred from the foregoing. It is important to emphasize to parents that it is not necessary that all the foregoing principles must apply in one situation in order for logical consequences to be effective. However, generally the more principles that apply to a specific case, the more likely it is to be effective in deterring future mistaken behavior. It is important to note, also, that mistaken or "bad" behavior is that which upsets or disturbs the family or other group in some way.

Principle 1. The principle of relatedness. The consequence should be directly related to the mistaken behavior. If a youngster for no excusable reason is late in getting ready to attend a ball game or movie with the family, the family should proceed without him. Missing the event is the obvious consequence. The relationship between being late and missing the event is direct, logical, and easily understood by the child. Should a child be deprived of TV because he misbehaved at a picnic on Sunday? The child will see no logical relationship and will not be motivated to improved behavior during the next public outing. It may not be easy to think of logical consequences at first, but family discussion and consulting the sample literature in the field (see bibliography) will furnish ideas for most situations.

Principle 2. The principle of meaning. The consequence should be meaningful to the child. Often punishments or consequences are applied that are meaningless to a youngster because they are outside the realm of his/her experience. For example, a five-year old would not readily understand the value of $5.00. If he/she is required to pay for something he/she deliberately breaks that costs that much or more, the experience is probably not meaningful to him/her and will not be effective. However, a child of 11 or 12 has usually had enough experience with money so that he/she would understand the sense and relationship in paying $5.00 for a lost or destroyed library book. It is essential that consequences fall within the experience of the child if they are to be meaningful and effective.

Principle 3. The principle of prior knowledge. The consequences of misbehavior should be known ahead of time. This requires that they are established in advance, preferably by agreement of all members of the family. Knowing the consequences in advance places the responsibility for the choice on the individual. Again, referring to the previous example in Principle I, the child can come home and get ready to go to the movies with the family, or he/she may choose to continue his/her play and not go—the responsibility and choice is the youngster's. This example leads to the next principle.

Principle 4. The principle of choice. The efficacy of choice is such that it often induces cooperation when an arbitrary punishment would incite hostility and rebellion. The basic system of logical consequences provides a choice for the individual as shown in the previous example. The foregoing example clearly indicates that the child has a choice. A second type of choice is often helpful, particularly when initiating the logical consequences with teenagers. This is the choice of selecting one from several possible consequences. Having three or more choices often will make a situation much more acceptable. An example:

> *Rodney wanted to invite some friends for a party. He wanted to use the living room and entered into a discussion with his mother. Mother gave him three choices: (1) he might use the living room provided that he agrees to clean it and leave it in the same condition in which he found it; (2) he might use the basement playroom where there would be less cleaning; or (3) he might hire a cleaning woman to take care of the cleaning and pay for it out of his own money.*

Principle 5. The principle of immediacy. The consequence should take place as soon as possible after the mistaken behavior occurs. Delays in applying consequences usually lead to protracted discussions, arguments, and loss of effectiveness. For example, if a baby abuses its freedom of movement by trying to crawl up the stairs or into the fireplace, the mother can immediately deprive the child of freedom by putting him/her into the playpen. Depriving the child of freedom the next day would not be effective; the child would not make the connection between the act and restriction of freedom. The principle of immediacy is less important with older children as far as effectiveness is concerned. For example, if there is a rule that clothes don't get washed unless they are placed in the hamper, it may take several days or perhaps two or three weeks for the youngsters to deplete their supply of clean clothes. They suffer the consequences of the mistake many days or weeks later and realize its effect.

Principle 6. Consequences should be of short duration. They should be changed only to a longer period of time if the child breaks the agreement. Long term consequences are seldom effective. For example, Steve and his parents agree that if he failed any subject one grading period, he would be totally restricted for the next nine-week grading period—an unreasonably punitive time. A case may be made for some restriction from evening activities in relation to study time, but the time involved must be reasonable. Needless to say, this consequence did not work even though Steve had agreed to it. Consequences will be effective in most situations when they are applied and finished in a day or two or shorter time.

Principle 7. Consequences entail action. It is especially important that the consequence involves some action rather than talking or lecturing. The less said by the parent the better. Admonitions, reminders, and threats turn the most promising of consequences into punishment in the mind of the youngster. Those consequences that can be handled with no dialogue at all will usually be the most effective. The system is doomed to failure if one of the parents must be the enforcer. If there is strong evidence of a power struggle, the consequence will be effective only if there is no dialogue whatsoever. The counselor may assist the parent in constructing the consequence and informing the children if an agreement between all cannot be reached. A discussion on the system should be held at a subsequent counseling session. Whenever possible, it is suggested that logical consequences not be applied when dealing with a power drunk child until some improvement occurs in the relationship between the parents and child.

Principle 8. Principle of participation. The more family members that participate in planning the consequences, the better. It is not absolutely necessary, but it is helpful, that all agree on the consequences arranged. It is also very helpful that the consequences apply to all members of the family. (Discussed in the section on the Family Council). Parents can model the attitudes and behaviors which they desire their children to learn if the parents are willing to cooperate with the system. An example:

> *A family with three boys came for counseling. A major problem was picking up books, toys, coats, and so forth, which were strewn around the home. The family agreed on the "deposit" system for such items that were left out after a designated evening hour. A large box was placed in the corner of the kitchen for this purpose. One of the first items that found its way to the box was the mother's purse. She was inconvenienced for a few days because her car keys, driver's license, and wallet were in the purse. However, she was a good sport and went along with the consequence, thereby showing an attitude and spirit of cooperation that were expected of the boys. She walked wherever she could and postponed other activities until she retrieved her purse and car keys.*

Principle 9. The principle of consistency. Unless the parents accept these principles and apply them consistently, they will be ineffective. The children will soon learn that they can gamble on the parent's mood, and that if they hold out long enough, the parents will give in. Consistency is vital, otherwise the system becomes a new challenge to the manipulating child or youth. Consistency also helps preclude the parents from reverting to unreasonable, arbitrary actions when they become out of patience with a misbehavior. The counselor must be alert to point out to the parent that they should not decide when or when not to invoke the system. Such action will doom the system to failure as it leads to the undermining of the principles involved.

Children and youth generally are positively responsive to the logical consequences system. They see the sense and logic to it and welcome the opportunity to take more responsibility for themselves as provided by the system. Parents are usually receptive to the logical consequences system as a way to teach youngsters more responsibility. Counselors should take care to emphasize this point.

Although some children change their behavior after a few applications of logical consequences, for others it takes a few weeks or months for the system to become generally effective. The counselor should always caution parents on this point or the approach becomes one of those recommendations that "sounds good in theory but doesn't work in practice." A sound point to make with parents is that the current disruptive household probably took several months and perhaps even years to develop, and a smoothly operating, cooperative household cannot be reasonably expected overnight.

Gradualism should be practiced in implementing the system. The counselor should ask the parents to select one or two problems that they are confident with which they can be successful. After initial experience and success, the more difficult problems can be attacked.

The counselor is well advised to teach the principles involved in implementing a system of logical consequences in the family. Counselors can experiment with various effective ways to do this. The authors regard this step as vital so that families can learn to deal with new situations as they arise on the basis of the principles without having to run to the counselor. Otherwise, every new situation that presents itself demands another solution from the counselor and leaves the family dependent on the counselor. If families understand the principles of logical consequences, they can learn to apply them in new situations.

Parents should be impressed with having an orderly, well organized household that will provide the atmosphere in which children can best learn responsibility. The system of logical consequences will greatly enhance the operation of an orderly household.

Parents should avoid using logical consequences only to entice the children and youth to cooperate. Counselors cannot overly emphasize the importance that the system of logical consequences should apply to all members of the family. Disruptive children are extremely sensitive to counseling and systems that are designed to get them to do what other techniques have failed to do. Because children generally perceive that adults can do just about as they please, parental cooperation in adhering to the system will assist greatly in encouraging children's cooperation.

When Consequences Fail

It is the experience of the authors that logical consequences fail under the following conditions:

1. When insufficient time has elapsed for a fair trial.

2. One of the parents tries to enforce the consequence, thus continuing the power struggle, when the child does not cooperate.

3. The children see the system as just another way to force them to do things that they really don't want to do.

4. The system is not applied with consistency.

Dreikurs and Grey (1970) gave several suggestions to the counselor for inquiry of the family when it is reported that logical consequences do not work. Get a specific description of the step-by-step sequence of events when it is indicated that logical consequences fail. Be certain to inquire as to what was said and done, including the tone of voice, and how everyone was feeling when the event transpired. In this way the counselor can check all the details against the original arrangement and the principles to understand where things went wrong.

THE USE OF PARADOXICAL INTENTIONS

Paradoxical therapy and counseling has become a frequently used technique in recent years, especially in family counseling and in family therapy. According to Mozdzierz, Macchtelli, Lisiccki (1976) many prominent therapists have advocated the use of this technique, among them Frankl, Wexberg, Watzlawick, Weakland, and Fisch, who developed a theory of communication and change which stresses the importance of paradoxical intervention.

Wexberg (1970) coined the term anti-suggestion to describe the technique that suggests that mistaken behavior or misbehavior should be continued by the client; it may even be increased in intensity. Frankl (1960) termed the technique as paradoxical intentions. Dreikurs (1967) stated that if the counselor could persuade a client to produce the symptom he/she is complaining of, it would often disappear. For example a client claimed that he/she could not travel by ship because of sea sickness. The counselor bet this client a certain amount of money for each time he/she became ill on the voyage. The client was determined to win the bet, but all his/her efforts to get sick were failures. Crossing the ocean was made without once becoming ill.

Although paradoxical intentions seem strange to many people, they have been in use for many years. As early as 1920, K. Dunlap began applying "negative practice" to problems such as biting one's nails, stammering, and eneursis. He would ask the patient to practice the symptom, hoping that the symptom would then disappear. Adler (1963) also prescribed symptoms. His technique is known as "reframing" in paradoxical psychotherapy.

The counselor who uses paradoxical intentions should give his/her directions in a straightforward, easy to understand way. He/she may say, "Would you be willing to try something that may be strange to you at first? I would like you to write all possible ways you could use to make mother angry." Or, "I would like you to do the following. Each time you feel neglected by your mother, do something that will make her real angry. I ask you to do it, although I don't know if you will do it because you have to prove to yourself and to others that nobody is going to tell you what to do."

Counselors are cautioned to use paradoxical intentions with great care; they must never abuse this technique nor should they expect miracles from it. It does not always work. Some clients may be shocked at such suggestions and they may even become angry. Others may regard it as some kind of joke or resent that the counselor is trying to manipulate them.

The counselor may use humor to avoid the impression that he/she is cynical, derogatory, or sarcastic. The technique is illustrated with the following examples:

> During a counseling session, the counselor noticed that one of the children was slumped over and lying on the armrest of the chair. The boy confirmed that he often lay that way in school and that it caused problems with his teachers. The counselor reassured him that it was perfectly all right for him to sit that way as long as he felt comfortable in this position. The moment the boy got permission, he sat up and remained erect during the entire time.

> A mother of four children came for counseling. She complained that one of her daughters consistently called her by derogatory names. After mother was helped to understand that the daughter's purpose in this kind of name-calling was to aggravate mother and to keep her busy, she understood the counselor's goal when he/she urged the girl to increase the frequency of the name calling. The girl objected at first, but she and the counselor agreed that she would have to call mother in this fashion a minimum of seven times a week and that mother would keep score. The girl was allowed to use her "allowables" in any form and fashion she chose—one a day or all seven in one day. The first day, the name-calling occurred three times. Mother tallied the occurrences and did not make any comment. The second day, there was only one occurrence and no further repetition. Because mother did not react as she did before, all the fun in calling her nasty names was gone. The daughter's goal to upset mother was effectively removed, and the girl stopped the provocative name-calling.

> Eight year old Mila had a temper-tantrum because she was not allowed to go into her brother's room. She screamed, threw her shoes and other objects at her mother. The mother handed the shoes back to her and asked her to throw them again but with more force. This reaction surprised the child. For a moment she did not know what to do, but after a short while she put her shoes on and walked away saying. "I won't." This was meant as punishment for her mother who gave her permission.

Paradoxical intentions should never be used as punishment or to prove the counselor's superior position in the relationship. It is intended to help the client understand the purpose of this kind of behavior, as in the case of Mila, and to help the client realize that one's behavior can often be controlled as in the case of the person who suffered from sea-sickness.

THE FAMILY COUNCIL

Two of the great needs of children is to feel belonging and to experience a sense of worth. These may be achieved if the child is exposed to such relationships and is reared in an atmosphere where these potentials can develop. Therefore, the family should work toward a cooperative atmosphere in which children and adults treat each other with respect, listen to one another, and feel free to communicate thoughts and feelings. Many families are aware of these principles but do not know how to implement them and often increase disharmony and discord in spite of good intentions. We propose that the family adopt a system of a Family Council—a system which has been tested and been proven most effective. A verbatim report of a Family Council meeting is reported in *Adlerian Counseling: Proven Concepts and Strategies* by Tom Sweeney (1981).

The Family Council is based on the following propositions:

1. All members who live in the family, including children who can understand the spoken word should attend a meeting where they discuss any problem without being criticized and without having fear of later punishment. In such an open forum meeting they discuss not only grievances, but also plans for family fun and where they conduct all family affairs—negative as well as positive.

2. The meeting should be held on a specific day and specific time which is convenient for everyone but may be changed if and when the situation requires it. Emergency meetings should be avoided whenever possible. The meeting should start on time even if some members are not present. Nobody should go after those members who habitually come late. Latecomers will soon learn that it is to their advantage to be at the meeting on time because decisions will be made without them.

3. No one should be forced to attend the meeting, but members should know that it is expedient to be present because all decisions are made by consensus and not by majority rule. Everyone has a right to veto what others propose. Thus, a member who does not attend the meeting is losing this opportunity and will be subject to obey the decisions made in the Family Council.

4. Family members set ground rules for conduct of the meeting which must be honored by everyone. Rules and guidelines differ in many families. Some prefer very simple rules while others, especially families with older children, like to follow Robert's Rules of Order, and prefer to appoint a chairperson, a secretary, and often a treasurer. Families with young children usually have a chairperson whose responsibility is primarily to recognize people who raise their hands and give them permission to speak. Some families find that feelings of "unfairness" are avoided when the chairperson calls on each member and asks each to express his/her views and to make suggestions on each item considered. If a family member prefers not to speak when called on, the chairperson goes on to the next person. This has the advantage that the chairperson does not call a favorite sibling or a parent a number of times while letting others wait to be heard. All positions should rotate in order to give each family member experience serving in the various roles.

5. The Family Council should not be concerned with the kind of language individual members choose to use, nor with grammar. If this is a problem to any of the members, it should be discussed at the following meeting, not in terms of accusation, but rather in terms of one's own problem. A father may say, "I have a problem. It may be due to my upbringing. I am working on it, but at the moment, when someone uses foul or obscene language, I get upset. I need help with this. How could you help me?" Pointing the finger at oneself and bringing this up as one's own problem usually meets with greater cooperation from the culprit. The meeting must always be regarded as a safe time, no matter how a person expresses himself/herself. The moment there is fear of saying what one thinks or wants to say, there will be less free expression and the meetings may fail.

6. Members should be allowed to speak for as long a time as necessary without being interrupted unless it is obvious that this member is trying to prevent others from talking and is dragging

out the point unnecessarily. This may anger others and they may refuse to attend. The family should then agree on a maximum time a person may talk. When a member oversteps this maximum time, the chairman should remind him to come to the point and finish. The fact is that many parents take more time to make their points than youngsters do. They take this opportunity to preach and lecture. This turns the children off, and they may decide not to attend Family Council meetings or abide by the decisions.

7. The family should decide how long each meeting should last.

8. The family should set up a list of household chores which must be attended to daily. Members are to choose the chores that they will do for this one week. At the following meeting, they may changes chores if they wish. Chores should rotate which means that parents should be included in the implementation. Nobody should be stuck with a chore he/she resents. Children may exchange chores by mutual agreement until the next meeting. All assigned chores should be written down and the list should be placed where all can easily see it. This avoids excuses of "I forgot."

9. The family should discuss and decide how to handle members who do not keep their agreements. The parents should avoid the role of enforcer.

10. Discuss topics that have nothing to do with household chores. For instance, planning the weekly family fun time, a child may want to have a party, another may need some extra money for a specific purchase, an older child may ask for times he/she may use the family car, the parents may discuss when and where they should go for their vacation, etc.

11. A relative or friend may want to visit the family. Which family member(s) should relinquish his/her room, and for how long, should be discussed and decided by the Family Council.

12. It is helpful to open every meeting with a sharing time in which each family member indicates appreciation for something another family member has done in the past week.

Parents often report that they have difficulties introducing the idea of a Family Council to their children. We suggest that this should be done at a time when all members are feeling friendly toward each other. A propitious time is often during or shortly after dinner. A parent may say to the children, "We have heard (or read) about a technique which is very helpful to parents and children in learning to get along better with each other. It is called the Family Council. It is basically based on the democratic principles where every member, regardless of age, is listened to, and given an opportunity to share in decision making. How do you feel about giving this a try? If it should prove to be ineffective, we can always discontinue. I, personally, would like to try this, how about the others?" If the children show interest, the parent should explain the goal of the Family Council and the essential points which we have enumerated.

The first meeting should start with positive feelings about the family. A parent may say something like this: "We are a family for a long time. What does each one of us like about this family? Certainly, there are many good things about each one of us. For instance, I am happy that you are my children and that mother is my wife. I always enjoy seeing you." Mother may add, "I love it when we get together and sing; I also like the way Sonny is now beginning to dress himself, the manner in which Daniel goes about keeping his clothes in order," and so forth. Every person is invited to express whatever good feelings he/she has about the family. When this is done, a parent may ask, "Where aren't we doing so well? What bugs some of you? There must be ways we can improve this condition. Who is willing to start?" When the talking gets started, the chairman takes over.

Family Council is an excellent place in which to set family goals. The counselor should be aware that it is very difficult, if not impossible, to set family goals unless all family members are in agreement. This does not imply that working on goals of individual members is of little importance. However, the individual member's goal will be met much faster and with greater assurance if it is also understood and accepted by other members of the family. Thus the individual goals become family goals. The more agreement there is among the individual family members, the easier it will be for the family to achieve its goals. Should there be conflict and disagreements, the family will do better to concentrate first on short-term goals, asking each member what he/she is willing to do just for this week and come to agreements. As the family experiences success with short-term goals, they can gradually extend them to long-range goals such as Oscar reducing his smoking by Christmas, the parents allowing Josy to stay out later in the evening after her next birthday, or Stevie walking to school with the other children when he starts first grade next fall. The main objective is to help each member understand why the problem exists, how each member contributes to it, and what each could do to improve the situation. All decisions should be reasonable so that they can be implemented with a considerable assurance of success.

We have found that some families discontinue their meetings when the relationships improve and the children become more responsible. This is a mistake in our view. It would be more advisable to have fewer meetings or meet for shorter periods of time, but the Family Council should continue, because this has become the main authority for decision making and the main avenue of communication. As family members gain experience with decision making, more difficult and complex problems can be presented for solution.

It also is suggested that some refreshments be prepared which the family could enjoy either during or after the meeting.

In conclusion, an incident which supports our strong belief in the effectiveness of the Family Council.

> *A three-year old boy, whose family had regular meetings, called the counselor. He said that the family decided that mother may hide all toys and clothes which the children leave lying around the house. He now wanted to know for how long she is allowed to hide them. The counselor asked, "Didn't you discuss this at your meetings?" The boy replied, "Oh, I didn't know that this could be discussed; I will bring it up at our next meeting."*

TRAINING THE CHILD

Children need training in how to accomplish the many daily tasks that lead to self-reliance and responsibility. A mother complained that her seven-year old daughter could not button her coat properly. We usually ask a parent who brings up a problem in this manner, "How do you know that your daughter cannot button her coat?" A common response is, "I can tell by the way she does it." When asked if she has ever shown her daughter the proper way to button her coat, dress, blouse, the mother replied, "She has eyes and can see how I do it." Mothers often assume that a child "sees" and, therefore, automatically learns how to do something. This may be the case with some children, but it is not always accurate that the child "sees," nor that even if he/she did, that he/she knows how to perform the task expected. The counselor should teach the parent that expecting a child to perform a task when the child does not know how, often undermines the child's sense of self-confidence and worthwhileness. Thus, losing faith in one's ability, the child becomes discouraged.

Children need specific training in how to do certain tasks: how to tie their shoes, button their dresses, zip up their jackets, make beds, set the tables, empty the garbage, and so forth. One should never take it for granted that the child knows how to do a task just because the child is old enough to know or has seen others do it so many times. Training the child should never take place when the parent is in a hurry, impatient, or angry. This may only discourage the child further. Also, the child may associate the task with an unpleasant experience. Training should take place when mother is calm, when she has enough time, and when the child is in the right disposition. The mother may then say, "Let's practice how to button a coat, how to make a bed," and so forth. Once the child has mastered the task, he/she is expected to assume this responsibility for himself/herself and receive assistance only in extreme, unforeseen situations.

Parents should give recognition for mere trying or for the slightest improvement in doing the task. Many parents, however, don't believe in showing appreciation for a task poorly or only half done. They wait until the child has completely mastered the task. This is a mistake for it may convey to the child that what he/she is doing, no matter how hard he/she tries, is not good enough and not acceptable. This is discouraging, and he/she may show resistance in trying or learning these myriad, but necessary routine tasks of life. These routine tasks can become battlegrounds between parent and child and cause serious disruptions in the relationship.

COMPARING SIBLINGS

Parents frequently compare one child with another, unaware of damage such comparison may bring. Even during a counseling session, a parent may comment on how easy it is to bring up Carmen and how difficult it is to rear Kimberly. Parents often comment, "I just can't understand this; after all, both kids have the same parents and the same upbringing. Why are they so different?"

These parents need to understand the dynamics of the family constellation (discussed in Chapter V); the competition that usually is taking place between siblings, and how parents add to the problem with this kind of comparison of the two children. The more that parents praise one of their children, the more threatening it may be to the other, especially the sibling closest in age to the child praised. With few exceptions, the criticized child will avoid emulating the sibling and actually develop in the opposite direction. The child does not believe that he/she can be as good as the sibling, nor as loved by the parents as the child of which they are so proud. The child, wanting to have a place and be noticed, may actually provoke the parents through antisocial behavior, either to keep them busy with him/her or to get even for an injustice. For this is how such children often perceive the situation.

It is strongly suggested that parents refrain from comparing their children and instead, encourage each to develop his/her own individuality and not try to be like somebody else. Some specific areas of comparison to avoid include the following:

> 1. Avoid comparing report cards or having general discussions of school progress. The child who does well may bask in the approval, but the sibling who performs at average or below levels, has inferiorities emphasized.

> 2. A second major area in which comparisons must be avoided is that of intelligence. Most adults have friends or close relatives who have spent much of their lives thinking that they were "dumb" because their parents openly referred to a sibling as the "bright" one and the other as "he/she's all right, too," type of child. Often one child will be more active than another in school and community sports or other activities. Similar comparisons should be avoided.

> 3. Parents should avoid bragging about children's successes and popularity. The mere fact of not saying anything about the child who does not enjoy similar successes is often enough to result in deep seated inferiority feelings in the child.

4. Mothers often compare the difficulties or the lack of difficulties they had at the birth of their individual children and in the early months and years of a baby's life. "John was such an easy baby to care for," or "Mike was difficult from the day he was born" are the types of comparative statements that all parents should avoid.

5. Counselors also should caution parents to avoid comparisons of children's attractiveness, or lack of it, or resemblance to one of the parents or other relative if there is any critical element involved. For example, if two boys are compared to grandfather and Uncle Carl, and Uncle Carl is regarded as "ugly" while grandfather is generally regarded as handsome, the boy compared to Uncle Carl may very well resent it and have some resulting inferiority feelings that could be avoided. Certainly, a fond motherly introduction such as, "This is Lisa—my little ugly duckling," should be avoided at all costs.

GIVING DIRECTIONS—BE SPECIFIC

The child needs, understands, and usually accepts directions given by the parent providing the instructions are clear and specific. So often these directions are vague and the child either does not understand them or chooses not to understand them. Some examples follow:

Instead of telling the child that he/she may go out and play for a little while, it would be preferable for the parents to say: *"It's three o'clock now; I expect you back at 3:20."* A little while may be an hour's time or longer for the child.

Instead of saying, *"You may cut yourself a piece of the pie,"* it would be better to tell the child, *"You may cut yourself a piece of the pie no wider than three of your fingers."*

"You may spend a quarter on something you like" rather than, *"You may spend some money, but not too much, on something you like."*

Such explicit directions reduce misunderstandings and arguments. Whenever possible one should give young children one instruction at a time. Such instructions should be simple and easy for the child to understand and to follow. It may help if the instruction is repeated in order to make sure that the child has heard and understands what is expected.

> *"Please go to the bathroom, and wash your hands, and then join us in the dining room."*

And when this is done,

> *"Would you please put the napkin next to each plate on the side where the fork is now laying. Okay? Now, tell me what it is I asked you to do?"*

When the child completes the assignment, the parent may now proceed to give an additional task to the child. In this way, the child is more apt to meet with success which encourages him/her to enjoy being helpful. Often children do a poor job because there were too many instructions and the child got them mixed up or forgot some of them. A four-year old girl told the counselor, *"I get mixed up when mother tells me to do so many things."*

As children develop and mature, the need for detailed, specific directions is reduced. Parents at all times should avoid giving instructions when they are not needed.

CONSISTENCY

Consistency is a hallmark of a well-ordered household. Occasionally, for very special reasons, the routine might be modified; however, it will be almost impossible to maintain routine unless it is carried out consistently. When parents inquire about making exceptions, the counselor may say, "Oh yes, feel free to make exceptions—twice a year—on the Fourth of July and Christmas." Parents will get the point. A typical example of inconsistency follows:

> The family discussed and agreed that there will be no television watching in the morning on week days. Mother finds seven-year

old Edgar half dressed, watching a cartoon on TV. She angrily turns off the apparatus. Edgar: *"Oh, gee, mother, just today, please let me watch only a few minutes and I promise I will then turn it off."* Mother: *"Okay, but remember, only a few minutes."*

Such inconsistency encourages children to gamble on the parent's mood. The child is always hopeful that, if he/she nags or begs, the parent will give in. However, we must caution parents never to become rigid and disregard special situations. It may happen that something very special is shown on TV in the morning before the children leave for school. If this is discussed and all are clear about what may be regarded as "special" (perhaps important news: the appearance of a star that the children admire especially or a space shot), the children may have to agree to get up a few minutes earlier and watch for just a few minutes. It must be understood and agreed upon that this is a special situation and will not apply to everyday living.

Families most often depart from order and routine during the summer months. It seems reasonable to modify household routines for summer vacations, but to completely depart from scheduled and family household tasks because it is summer leads to confusion and difficulties. Because the departure from routine usually does not apply to the parents, the children learn that they are privileged individuals. Dad must go to work (and maybe Mom, too). Mom also has to continue to manage the household, but the children often are excused from normal responsibilities. Such inconsistencies usually undo the positive steps that have already been achieved in training the children to be positive, cooperative contributors to the well-being of the family.

MISCELLANEOUS CORRECTIVE MEASURES

Several other problems of parent/child relationships can be improved by various alternative corrective measures. The areas to be included in the miscellaneous corrective measures are avoiding talking too much, withdrawing from the power struggle, establishing order and routine in the household, avoiding threats, and having fun with your children.

Talking Too Much

Parents often talk too much, especially mothers. Lecturing, explaining, reminding, scolding, and other techniques are notoriously ineffective as corrective measures for children's misbehavior. Action not words is the dictum for effectiveness. Children learn to turn their parents off very early in life in the same way that college students learn to tune out a boring lecture and churchgoers daydream their way through a dull sermon. An example:

> A six-year old child was chatting with his/her family counselor one day and made the following appropriate comment about mothers and teachers talking too much, *"Kids learn not to listen to everything they hear."*

Another example:

> A child said, *"Mother, why is it that every time I ask a simple question, you give me such a long and complicated answer."*

The major reason that so many parents talk so much is that they don't know what else to do. One of the counselor's tasks is to provide the parent with more effective techniques to replace lecturing, yelling, and punishing.

Withdrawing From the Power Struggle

In most disrupted families the counselor will need to explain to the parents how to recognize when they are in a power struggle with the child and how to get out of it. This first step must be accomplished before many of the other techniques will be effective. The following example illustrates a typical power struggle.

> Mother to child who is watching a television program. She shuts off the TV.
>
> Mother: *No television until your homework is done.*
>
> Child: *I've done it already.*
>
> Mother: *When did you do it? Show it to me.*

Child: *I did it in school.* (He switches on the television.) (Mother turns it off; he turns it on. She smacks him one.)

Mother: *When I say the TV is off, it stays off. You better get this through your head, now show me your homework.*

After helping the parent to understand how he/she is involved in power struggles, the authors have found it helpful to explain why the children will win. Children and youth will almost always win these battles for two major reasons. One, they can spend most of their time plotting strategy while parents are involved in fulfilling the many other responsibilities of their lives. Two, the kids don't always fight fair. The parents' only recourse is to withdraw from the battle and the battleground. There is a strong advantage for parents in withdrawal as it is something parents can do and not something that they are trying to make the children do.

Establish Order and Routine in the Household

Dreikurs (1958b) repeatedly emphasized that the parents' first responsibility as parents was to maintain an orderly household. If there is not orderly routine and set of expectations for behavior in the home, how can one expect children to learn that they must conform to the expectations of the school, community, and society in general? If there is not a daily household schedule, for example, and family members can take care of their responsibilities when the notion strikes them, children will most likely have little compunction about approaching school tasks with the same attitude.

Routine usually enhances feelings of security in all family members. It prevents many kinds of problems from arising simply because a well managed household schedule precludes them. A well planned household routine also will provide more time in which the family can engage in the many more enjoyable activities available to them.

Establishing a family routine also will help to avoid chaos and argumentation. Preferably, the daily routine should be discussed in the Family Council and agreed on. The planned routine should include the following elements:

1. Time for getting up in the morning and going to bed at night.

2. Time when meals are served.

3. Time to do homework and chores.

4. Time to watch television.

5. Days and time to take showers or baths.

6. Time for children to be home from school.

7. Time for practicing an instrument or sport.

8. Day and time to place soiled clothes in the designated place for washing.

9. Time for care and feeding of pets.

10. Time for parents and children to have fun together.

11. Time and length for social telephone conversations.

12. Day and time to bring home a friend for play and/or a meal.

Such planning does not imply rigidity; it is advised for families where there exists no planning and where everyone comes and goes as he/she pleases.

Avoiding Threats

Parents often are not aware of the self-defeating patterns they use in attempting to change a child's behavior. They often yell, insult, criticize, bribe, and threaten without results. Threats almost always invite a repetition of the behavior forbidden by the parent which angers them even more. Often, when a parent tells the child, "You do this once more and I will punish you in the worst way," what the child heard was just the first words, "do this once more." The threat of punishment usually goes unheeded. Children of parents who threaten "If I catch you again, I will . . ." become more careful in their actions and avoid being caught. An example:

> Twelve-year old Yoko told the counselor that he must do his homework the moment he comes home from school. He hates doing homework immediately after he comes home, but he found a solution which has worked for him. He hides his books

under the porch and tells his mother that the teacher asked the students to leave the books in class on the days she gives no homework.

Another child told the counselor that he/she hits his/her brother hard because his/her mother threatens to punish him/her only when he/she really hurts his/her brother. He/she added, "Mother said she will not mix into our fights unless I hit too hard, so I hit hard."

From these examples we can see how quickly children pick up parents' attitudes and behavior patterns. They know exactly what to do when they want to get the parents angry and involved.

Having Fun with Your Children

It is amazing to learn how many families seldom do anything that is of a fun nature except go on vacation once a year or watch television. Such households are often grim and joyless. The children, wanting some diversion, may actually start a fight or do something to provoke the parent just to break the monotony. While the counselor should discourage giving the child negative attention, it is recommended that the children should, yes must, get attention from the parents—attention that is positive.

Many adults do not recall their parents ever being less than serious, never just playing or being silly, etc. This is a pity. Children love to see their parents laugh, be funny, and step out of their roles as the "all-knowing" adults with serious demeanor.

Some parents concentrate only on family fun—on "togetherness"—yet children have a need to have a parent to himself/herself on a regular basis. We strongly recommend that each parent spend some scheduled time with each child (just the two of them) each week. Frequency can decrease, and the length of time spent can increase as children grow older. It is not just a matter of insuring that children enjoy life but that they are important enough for their parents to set aside time for them. Thus, a sense of belonging and security is developed.

The counselor may furnish specific suggestions, if needed, to parents on what to do or say when spending time with the children alone. The following should prove helpful.

1. The counselor should suggest that parents ask their children, in addition to having fun times with the entire family, if they wish to have individual time with each of the parents. These times should be scheduled, or they generally will occur only when everyone has nothing else to do.

2. The quality, rather than the quantity of time is important.

3. It is preferable to give the child a choice of what he/she wants to do as long as it is reasonable.

4. Suggestions of things that the parent and child might do together (for short periods of time):

- listen to child's favorite record with the child,
- make funny faces—see who can make the funniest,
- dress up in old clothes—pretend to be characters of some kind,
- go to nearby place that child chooses,
- play a game of the child's choosing,
- talk about anything that the child wants to talk about,
- engage in a sport that the child wants to play in the house or yard,
- go for a bike ride, roller skating, or other sport that each can do,
- sing or dance, or
- go for a ride in the car or take a walk together.

The list could be endless. The important factor for the counselor is to impress the parent that the time spent should be the child's time and spent in activities of his/her choosing insofar as they are reasonable.

HELPFUL "DO'S" & "DON'TS" FOR PARENTS

Many of the following recommendations in this section are explained more fully elsewhere in this volume. They are summarized here for the counselor's convenient reference in selecting recommendations to make to the parents. The proposed "Don'ts" automatically indicate the

"Do's." While these suggestions are applicable to most situations, counselors should caution parents not to become rigid in their application. There are always exceptions to rules and one must use sound judgment in decisions.

1. *Don't get involved in your children's fights.* You may notice that they fight less when you are not home. Children usually fight in order to keep you busy with them. Ask the children to fight somewhere out of earshot or remove yourself to a place where you cannot hear them. A good place is the bathroom. When they stop bickering, come out and go about your chores. Say nothing to the children. They will get the message.

2. *Don't protect the child you consider "weak."* This child must learn to solve his/her own problems and find ways to get along with his/her siblings. Often this child deliberately provokes other children so that the parent comes to protect him/her. This only increases the rivalry between the children.

3. *Don't interfere with the way your spouse disciplines the children.* Such interference is resented by the spouse and shows a lack of respect for the other's judgment. Furthermore, the child soon learns to play one parent against the other. When the child complains to you, tell the child to find ways to get along. Make sure the child knows that you will not get involved.

4. *Don't talk too much.* Children become "parent-deaf" when parents deliver long lectures to them. While you don't talk, you must act. For instance, if the child disregards your instructions not to use a sharp knife, and if you see the child use one, just take it away without saying anything.

5. *Don't feel sorry or pity for the child.* The child may start feeling sorry for himself/herself and expect special consideration. Pity is discouraging. It implies that you have no faith in the child's ability to handle his/her problem intelligently. It leads to inferiority feelings. Tell the child that you realize when a task is difficult, but you have confidence in his/her ability to handle it. Show empathy and understanding.

6. *Don't set unreasonable goals for your child.* Your own high standards may be a discouraging factor. The child may feel that he/she cannot live up to your expectations and may give up. Show appreciation for the efforts even if the child doesn't accomplish much.

7. *Don't criticize.* Nobody improves because of criticism. Build on the positive instead of the negative. Encourage the child not to give up and not to be ashamed if he/she makes mistakes.

8. *Don't encourage the child to tattle on other members of the family or on his/her friends.* Your child learns to elevate himself/herself at the expense of others in these situations. Tell the child that you don't appreciate tattling.

9. *Don't do for the child anything the child can do, unless you are in a very great hurry.* By taking over you undermine the child's self-reliance. It also may teach the child that his/her importance lies in having someone serve him/her.

10. *Don't use arbitrary corporal punishment.* Instead, use natural and logical consequences. The child will respond favorably if he/she sees the connection of the consequences to what he/she did. Always give the child a choice before you apply a consequence. Tell the child, "You have the choice to behave yourself when you go shopping with me or to stay home while I go shopping." Remember that logical consequences do not work when the child is in a power contest with you. In such a case, you must first change the relationship you have with the child before you can apply any consequences effectively.

11. *Don't force the child to obey.* This does not motivate the child from within. The child may become conditioned to obey only when under pressure. Discuss the situation with the child and come to an agreement. Such an agreement should include a logical consequence in case the child breaks the agreement.

12. *Don't create a relationship in which the child feels loved only when praised.* Refrain from praising too often. The child may become praise-oriented and believe that he/she is "bad" when you do not praise him/her. It is preferable to say, "I like what you did; that's a neat job," than to say, "That's great!" or "That's the best I've ever seen."

13. *Don't equate "good" and "bad" with achievement.* The child may feel that you accept him/her on condition as when he/she is finishing a meal, when practicing the piano, or when qualifying for the Honor Roll.

14. *Don't allow the child to dictate to you.* This shows disrespect for yourself. This trains the child to give orders and expect others to obey them.

15. *Don't constantly remind the child what to do.* You reinforce the child's goal to keep you busy with him/her. Tell the child once or twice what you expect of him/her, and if he/she chooses not to listen, follow through with a logical consequence. Remember, action and not words!

16. *Don't run to school to protect your child from teacher or other children.* You convey to the child that the teacher is against him/her or is a bad teacher. This only increases the antagonism that is between them. The same holds true for his/her difficulties with other children. Tell the child that he/she should think of ways to improve the relationship and that you have confidence that he/she will find a solution. Offer to discuss the problem and help the child in a reasonable way, but that it is his/her responsibility to solve the problem.

17. *Don't cook special food for the child except for special occasions.* The child may become a problem eater. Some children may refuse to eat what you prepared in order to punish you or to force you to give in to them. Tell the child that he/she may eat or not; it is up to him/her. If he/she refuses to eat, make sure that he/she knows that there is nothing to eat until the next meal. No snacks. It is important that you use this advice in a kindly and consistent manner.

18. *Don't demand that the child stop reading or watching a television program the moment you ask him/her to do something.* Give the child a few minutes to finish the paragraph or to stop watching when the commercials come on. Don't treat your child the way we treat dogs who obey on command.

19. *Don't be permissive.* The child will not know the limits and may learn to manipulate you so that you give in. Be consistent. Once you say "no," stick to it. Only in extreme situations do we give in to the child. We then openly admit that we have erred in our judgment of the situation.

20. *Don't pay the child for doing routine household chores.* We pay servants. In paying the child for being helpful to the family, we deprive the child of the pleasure in making contributions. The child may further develop the attitude that you must pay him/her each time he/she does something to help. Give the child an allowance regardless of what he/she does or does not do. An allowance is given out of consideration for the child's needs and not as payment for something the child naturally should do. Do not use the allowance as a reward or a punishment.

21. *Don't give preferential treatment to one child.* It violates the principles of equality and breeds the feeling of unfairness and resentment.

22. *Don't talk down to the child.* Always be respectful and treat the child with the same consideration as you would an adult.

23. *Don't refuse the child if he/she wants to help you.* Don't tell the child that he/she is too little, that he/she doesn't know how, that his/her help makes more work for you, and so forth. You discourage the child from enjoyment of being helpful and making a contribution. You make the child feel inadequate and inferior. The child may become discouraged and give up trying to help. The child may later refuse to accept responsibilities when you expect it of him/her.

24. *Don't call your child humiliating names.* It may contribute to an inferiority feeling and it teaches the child to use similar methods in dealing with others. Remember that the child patterns himself/herself after you and that most behavior is "caught" rather than "taught."

25. *Don't compare children.* Comparing a child to a sibling or another child favorably or unfavorably adds to the problem and to the competition of children.

26. *Don't neglect your own physical appearance if you want your child to be concerned with physical appearance.* Children do not understand double standards.

27. *Don't be overly persistent.* Persistence may lead to the child's conviction that if he/she insists and nags long enough, he/she will get his/her way.

28. *Don't disregard standards and order.* Children who do not learn order and a certain amount of routine at home may have difficulties adjusting to school.

29. *Don't remove yourself from the child no matter what the child does.* Remove yourself only from the child's behavior. The child should always feel loved by you, although you may convey to the child that you don't like what he/she is doing.

30. *Don't be unkind when you remain firm in dealing with the child.*

31. *Don't lie to the child, and never ask a child to use a lie in order to help you out or in order to save money.* Example: "Answer the phone for me, and if it is Mrs. Brown, tell her I am not home." Or, "Tell the conductor that you are only ten; you look younger than your age. We can save half of the bus fare that way." Or, write phony excuses for the child when he/she misses school. The child learns that a lie at the right time may be very expedient, and he/she may lie when it serves him/her.

32. *Don't forbid your child to bring home his/her friends because they mess up the house or because they are too loud.* The child will not develop a feeling of being an equal member of the family. It also may prevent the child from developing social interest. Speak to your child's friends and ask them to, please, not make a mess but to enjoy themselves.

33. *Don't plan a party for your child without discussing with him/her what kind of party it should be, who should be invited, how he/she wants the room to be decorated, etc.*

34. *Don't make promises unless you can keep them.* By breaking your promise, you teach your child that promises must not be taken seriously.

35. *Don't tell your son that boys don't cry, that boys don't play with dolls, and if they do, they are sissies, and so forth.* It may hurt his image as a male child if he enjoys these activities. Provide your son with activities and opportunities for his masculine development without mentioning to him why you do it.

36. *Don't tell your daughter that she is cute when she shows tomboyish behavior.* She may conclude that boys are more appreciated and valued and may have difficulties accepting herself as a girl.

37. *Don't be overprotective.* As for instance, not allowing your child to go on a school field trip because something may happen, or having the child take the city bus or to walk just a few blocks although he/she is perfectly capable of walking alone. You instill in the child a fear of taking any risks, and you deprive him/her of new experiences and feeling independent.

38. *Don't sit with the child and force him/her to do homework.* By forcing the child, you assume the responsibility for the homework. School should be the child's responsibility. This is not to say that you should not

take a few minutes to explain to the child something he/she does not understand and doesn't know how to do. Children whose parents sit with them and help them to do their homework often don't work in class unless the teacher sits with them.

39. *Don't praise the child and then finish with a "but," such as "I like that you did your bed, but next time remember to tuck in the corners of the blanket."* At a later time, you may teach your child how to make a bed in the proper way. When you put a "but" in your praise, you convey to the child that nothing he/she does is good enough and he/she may give up.

40. *Don't throw away your child's school papers and drawings that he/she brings home without first discussing it with him/her.* It shows disrespect for the child's rights and reinforces the child's feelings that he/she is not an equal member of the home with equal rights. You, certainly, would disapprove if the child were to throw away your things without first being consulted.

41. *Don't be ashamed to admit to the child that you made a mistake.* Parents who don't ever admit mistakes convey to the child that they too must never make mistakes.

42. *Don't brag about how you outsmarted another person.* The child may deduct that it is perfectly acceptable to use any means in order to come out the winner.

43. *Don't be afraid to leave the child with a competent baby sitter.* The child may become overly dependent on your presence and may fear strangers.

44. *Don't be afraid to ask the child to advise you in some matter.* This helps the child feel that you trust his/her judgment and that you value it.

45. *Don't play "I don't know" games when you are sure that the child took something that doesn't belong to him/her.* Such as, "I wonder who took a dollar out of my purse," when you know that the child did it.

46. *Don't snoop around in your child's drawers and pockets.* You show disrespect for his property and teach him/her to hide things from you more carefully. The child may resent you for it if he/she finds out.

47. *Don't ever eaves-drop when your child is on the telephone.* It shows disrespect and disregard for his/her right to privacy.

48. *Don't fail to schedule time to play with your children.* Children and parents have a better relationship when the parents play with them and enjoy this activity. You should take a few minutes every day to listen to your children and to do something with them that is fun.

49. *Don't make all decisions by yourself.* Establish a Family Council where all of the family members plan and decide.

50. *Don't watch television for hours, yet insist that your child should not waste time in front of the tube.* This may require sacrifices on your part.

51. *Don't serve meals to the child when the child comes to the table dirty and disheveled.* You either ask him/her to leave the table and wash or go hungry until the next meal.

52. *Don't use sarcasm with children.* They do not understand it and are no match for you. They may resent it.

53. *Don't ask your spouse to handle the discipline.* Use natural and logical consequences. The child should experience consequences as soon as possible and not later after he/she has forgotten the misbehavior.

54. *Don't withhold love from the child.* Be affectionate and tell the child at frequent intervals that you love him/her. But don't smother him/her with love.

55. *Don't use profanity and then expect that your child should never use four-letter words.* Always keep in mind that most young children hold you as the model of what a person should be.

56. *Don't punish or shame your child if he/she should use profanity.* Either ignore it or discuss during the Family Council that you have difficulties with this kind of language and that you need help. Your child will be more concerned with coming to your aid. You may, if the child continues using profanity, appeal to him/her to cut down on it, or agree to use it three times a day. Gradually, you reduce the number of times he/she may indulge in such behavior. Show appreciation if you notice that the child made an effort.

57. *Don't drink or smoke and then expect that your adolescent child should not indulge or enjoy what you enjoy.* Again, you may ask the child to reduce the activity. You will encounter less resistance and resentment.

58. *Don't yell at children or at anyone.* Parents who yell usually have children who yell.

59. *Don't expect your child to be a reader unless you set an example.*

REFERENCES

Adler, A., (1963). *The problem child.* New York: Capricorn Books, G. P. Putman's Sons.

Corsini, R. J., & Painter, G. (1975). *The practical parent.* New York: Harper & Row, Publishers, pp. 29-30.

Dinkmeyer, D., & Dreikurs, R. (1963). *Encouraging children to learn.* Englewood Cliffs, N.J.: Prentice-Hall.

Dinkmeyer, D., & Losoncy, L. E. (1980). *The encouragement book.* Englewood Cliffs, N.J.: Prentice-Hall.

Dreikurs, R. (1957). *Psychology in the classroom.* New York: Harper & Row, Publishers.

Dreikurs, R. (1958a). The cultural implications of reward and punishment. *The International Journal of Social Psychiatry,* Vol. IV, No. 3.

Dreikurs, R. (1958b). *The challenge of parenthood, Revised Edition.* New York: Hawthorn Books, Inc., pp. 58-70.

Dreikurs, R., et. al. (1959). *Adlerian family counseling.* Eugene, OR: University Press, University of Oregon.

Dreikurs, R. (1967). *Psychodynamics, psychotherapy, and counseling.* Chicago, Illinois: Alfred Adler Institute of Chicago.

Dreikurs, R. (November 1972). The realization of equality in the home. *The individual psychologist,* Vol. IX, No. 2, pp. 45-46.

Dreikurs, R. & Grey, L. (1970). *A parent's guide to child discipline*. New York: Hawthorn Books, Inc.

Frankl, V. (1960). Paradoxical intentions: A therapeutic technique. *American journal of psychotherapy, Vol. 14*, pp. 520-525.

May, R. (1975). *The courage to create*. New York: Bantam.

McKay, G. (1976). *The basics of encouragement*. Coral Springs, FL: CMTI Press.

Mosak, H. H. (September 1978). Mutual respect in the classroom: A functional definition. *The individual psychologist, Vol. XV, No. 3*, pp. 12-14.

Mozdzierz, G.J., Macchtelli, Frank J., & Lisiccki, Joseph (November 1976). The paradox in adlerian psychotherapy. *Journal of Individual Psychology, Vol. 32, No. 2*, pp. 169-183.

Reimer, C. (1967). Some words of encouragement. In Vicki Soltz (Ed.) *Study Group Leader's Manual*. Chicago, IL: Alfred Adler Institute.

Spencer, H. (1885). *Education—intellectual, moral, and physical*. New York: Alden Publishing Company.

Sweeney, T. J. (1981). *Adlerian couseling: Proven concepts and strategies*. Muncie, IN: Accelerated Development.

CHAPTER **VII**

WORKING WITH
SPECIFIC PROBLEMS

In these short vignettes we have described some concrete suggestions for improving relationships between parents and their children in a variety of problem situations. The counselor should understand that these specific problem situations were selected because they are common. The suggested solutions have been tested and found successful by the co-authors and other Adlerian counselors for many years. The counselor may recommend these solutions to parents with confidence. The solutions are based on sound theoretical principles which have been explained throughout this book. This does not imply that the counselor should slavishly follow every suggestion, but within this framework these principles and close variations, will furnish effective solutions.

The main purpose in describing these specific problems and solutions is to help counselors and parents become aware of how children manipulate adults. Once parents are aware and sensitive to these provocations, they will have greater understanding and learn how to deal with various problems more effectively. The aim of the counselor is to help parents and children to become independent and to solve such problems without assistance from the counselor.

SIBLING FIGHTING

One of the most frequent complaints of parents is the fighting that goes on between children. Although some parents still believe that fighting between siblings is a natural phenomenon—that all children fight and eventually grow out of it—the majority of them claim that they can't stand this constant screaming and hitting and hope to get a solution to the problem from the counselor. The counselor's own feelings about children's fights is of great importance. If the counselor advises parents to stay out of the fights and allows the children to settle their own problems, often the counselor feels responsible for the well-being of the children and especially for the child that may be hurt.

Let us first examine why children fight and how most parents deal with the problem. Some children fight in order to get *attention* from one or both parents. This is usually a sure way of keeping parents involved. This is especially the case when parents give little positive attention to a child. For instance, a mother told us that as a child, she would take the blame for the misbehavior of her siblings in order to get punished by her father. She said that this was the only time he paid attention to her and that "this was better than being ignored."

Some children use fighting as a means to demonstrate their *power* over the siblings and over the parents, especially if they are continually stopping the children from fighting. There are parents who will allow the children almost any activity as long as they get along and don't fight. If the child is in a power contest with the parents, then fighting is an opportunity to show the parents who is boss.

Other children fight in order to hurt the parents. These children operate on goal three—*revenge*. If they feel that the parents are unfair to them, that they are being hurt by them unjustly, and if they sense that fighting and hurting a sibling will be painful to the parents, they will use this method to get even. Children in goal four—assumed disability—never fight. They are in a passive state, and if they fought, they would not be in goal four.

In many households children pattern themselves after their parents. If the parents often fight with each other or with other people, then fighting may become a family pattern. Parents often consider their own fighting as natural or unavoidable; however, they expect and demand that their children refrain from fighting. Because they usually love their children and are sincerely concerned about preventing an individual child from getting hurt, parents get involved in the entanglement. In the process they often protect one of the children, usually the youngest one or the child who is physically weak. Older children often complain that the parents ask them to be understanding and to allow the younger sibling to have his/her way because he/she is still little and doesn't know any better. The older ones resent this and are often determined to get even with this younger child. They may do this in very subtle ways. If the parents come to this child's protection, the youngest feels triumphant and is encouraged to continue his ways of annoying the older sibling. Parents do not realize how they contribute in this way to the development of competition and fighting of the children. A typical example follows.

> *A couple with three children came for counseling, Cybil nine, Maggie six, and Oscar four. The parents were mostly concerned about the children's fights. They said that the fighting goes on all the time when the children are together. The parents admitted that they always try to stop the fight, that they try to find out who started the fight and why, etc. Mostly it ends with protection of Oscar because he is too little to fight with his older sisters. When the counselor suggested that this was not necessary because interfering in the fight only intensifies it and it prevents Oscar from learning how to stand up to his sisters, the parents categorically refused to accept such advice. At the same moment, Oscar kicked Maggie in the shin. She in turn started hitting her brother. Oscar began to scream, looking at his mother for help. The parents had witnessed the incident. Still, mother*

> *got up and picked up Oscar, setting him in her lap saying, "That was not nice what you did. Mother will have to hold you now so that you can't hurt anybody." Oscar snuggled up, feeling triumphant. Maggie cried; while Cybil, with tears in her eyes, told the counselor that "this is always going on in our home. He is never punished as we are, no matter what he does."*

Parents are often oblivious to the provocation of the "good" child. The misbehavior of this child—the manner in which he/she provokes his/her siblings—through kicking under the table, hissing nasty names, pinching behind the back, etc.—comes out during the counseling session where the parents usually listen more attentively to the older children. At home these children complain, but nobody listens to them as the parents are more involved with the protection of the "baby."

Some parents believe that boys are fighters by nature and condone it although they would prefer that there be no fighting. They definitely do not approve when the boys hit girls. This double standard creates friction in a family of boys and girls. In such families we often find that the girls take advantage of their privileged position and provoke their brothers and often get into fights with boys in school or on the playground. The case of Juliana as described in *Maintaining Sanity in the Classroom* by Dreikurs, Grunwald, and Pepper (1982) is an excellent example of such a situation. (Italics added to designate example.)

> *Juliana constantly complained to the teacher that some boy hit her and demanded that the teacher punish this boy because "boys are not supposed to hit girls." The teacher had observed that Juliana provoked the boys on the playground; she interfered with their ball playing and even caught the ball and threw it over the fence. Once she snatched a boy's cap off his head and threw it over the school fence. The boy was enraged and hit her. Juliana ran crying to the teacher, demanding that she punish the boy. When the teacher told her that she saw the entire incident and that Juliana had provoked the boy, the girl replied: "Just the same, my mother told my brothers that they must never hit a girl, and that no nice boy should. I will report this to my mother." (pp. 291-292)*

Here we deal with some basic values of parents. The counselor would have to go slowly and carefully not to indicate disrespect for their values and, at the same time, help them see how this belief teaches their daughter to feel safe and even justified in provoking boys. Consideration should be mutual, and the emphasis should be that no one hurts another for no good reason. There should be no difference if this be a boy or a girl. The emphasis should be on developing social interest.

There are children who often fight for the sheer excitement when they are bored. We find this to be true in children who have not been trained to develop interests in activities and to be able to entertain themselves. Although, in the final analysis, this kind of fighting is to get parents involved and create a "tumult." Such children do not mind being scolded or even punished in the process.

The counselor can help the parents feel less guilty by assuring them that most parents protect the younger child by coming to his/her defense. However, their belief that the child is too young and not capable of protecting himself/herself is often misleading. This false impression should be corrected and replaced with confidence in the younger child's ability to learn to stay out of fights or to handle them on his/her own. This is not to say that we suggest to parents that they should never show concern or come to the defense of a younger or physically weaker child. Parents are advised to be on the alert and assess the situation carefully and, whenever possible, to remove themselves from the fighting. We also suggest that parents remove any dangerous object that a child may use in a fight. The parents should tell the children that it is all right to fight if they so desire, but only if they fight with their hands.

It is possible that a child may end up with a bloody nose, a scratch, or other small injury. Basically, siblings do not want to hurt each other seriously (there are exceptions), and rarely will a child get badly hurt. When the child comes to the parents showing his scratch, etc., the parent may say, "I'm sorry you got hurt. Would you care to wash your wound? I suggest that we put on some disinfectant. You will find it in the medicine chest, but if you want me to, I'll go with you and show it to you." The parent may even wash the wound and apply the disinfectant. But no further fuss should be made over this issue. In time, if the parents stay out of the fighting, the child will learn how to exist with his/her siblings without fighting.

It is difficult for parents to resist their immediate impulse to stop the fight or to protect one of the children. But if the counselor succeeds in helping the parent recognize the purpose behind fighting and how the parents' involvement reinforces the child's erroneous concept about how to get attention, the parents will exercise greater restraint in following their first impulse and involving themselves in their children's fights.

We do not disapprove of children's fighting if they so desire. We support strongly, however, that fights may interfere with the parents' rights not to be disturbed. Parents may tell the children, "You may fight, if you wish, but not where I can hear you. You may go to the garage or outside or any place that is out of earshot and fight to your heart's content. You are not allowed to come back until you have finished with the fight." Should the children refuse, and if they are too big to be removed bodily, the parent may have to leave and go into another room, preferably the bathroom, or even go out for a walk or drive.

The counselor should explain to parents that at first fighting may even get worse and that children will test them to the utmost in order to keep the parents involved. An example:

> *The counselor asked eight year old Amelia if she thought that her parents would follow the counselor's advice and stay out of the fights between her and her sister. Amelia said, "NO!" The counselor asked, "What makes you think so?" and Amelia replied, "Because we will fight even more and harder and they will go nuts. They will start yelling and breaking up the fight, especially my father."*

Both parents broke out in uncontrollable laughter and the father remarked, "She sure knows her old man." Such a response from the parent not only reinforces the child's determination to test the situation, but actually conveys to the child that what she is doing is regarded as "cute." We may be sure that the child will keep up her fights with her sister unless the parents decide to follow the counselor's advice.

Corsini and Painter (1975) suggested the following solutions to parents who want to stop their children's fighting:

> 1. *Bear it*—Just be quiet and let the children have their fight. Say nothing. Sooner or later they will stop.

> 2. *Beat it*—Don't be an audience. Go into the bathroom or some other place. When the quarrel is over, you simply come back in silence.

> 3. *Boot them out*—Put all offenders out of the room into the yard or street. However, you must do this precisely in this manner:

> You say to them: *"If you are going to fight, you must go outside. When you are through come back in."* Don't say it again. If they do not go out, put them out in complete silence.

We suggest the following to the child that claims that he/she doesn't like to fight:

Tell your brother/sister that today you are in no mood to fight. But, perhaps you will be in the mood some other day. You will then tell them that today you feel like fighting. Or set up an appointment for the day and hour when you will want to fight, like Thursday at 4:15 p.m.

This is a helpful technique when the atmosphere during the counseling session has become tense because of the children's fighting. Everyone sees the humor in the situation which ends in laughter.

We hope that the point has been effectively made that the best way to help a family whose children fight is for the parents to stay out of any involvement. If the parents consistently refuse to become involved, the fights diminish and usually stop. Perhaps even more importantly, when parents stay out of children's fights, golden opportunities are provided for the children to develop skills and knowledge needed to solve their own problems.

DAWDLING

Young children can keep their mother busy for hours by refusing to dress or dawdling in the process. Mother coaxes, scolds, promises a reward if the child is dressed within a given time and finally ends up by dressing the child. Often this is done in anger and resentment. There are several things that a mother can do to train the child to get dressed and be ready on time.

1. Talk to the child and tell the child that you expect him/her to be dressed by a given time.

2. Tell the child that breakfast will be served at a certain time and that it will be up to him/her to be ready for breakfast or not. If the child chooses not to be ready, he/she will have to go without breakfast.

3. If a child is transported by a school bus, the mother should inform the child that she will put the child's clothes in a shopping bag in case the child should not be ready in time, and that he/she may then dress in the bus or at school.

4. Assure the child that you will notify the teacher that the child may come in his/her pajamas and that the teacher will then handle it.

5. If the child is old enough, he/she will have to walk to school no matter how late. The school can exact the consequences for being late.

6. If the child is not old enough to cross boulevards, the mother may take the child beyond danger then say good-bye and let the child continue the rest of the way alone.

If the parent stays calm during the process, but is firm and consistent, the child usually dresses long before it is necessary. Rarely will they go to the other extreme. The parent should always show appreciation and give encouragement when the child starts dressing by himself/herself and is ready on time.

Other types of dawdling might include being late to bed, late coming to the table, and not coming directly home from school. Parents can find solutions similar to those found previously and can learn to deal with these problems in more effective ways. Implementing the principles of logical consequences, especially taking action without words, is an effective solution to dawdling problems.

TEMPER TANTRUMS

A trend in recent years has been to encourage people to express anger and hostility because it was "DAMAGING FOR THEM TO REPRESS IT." We do not support this point of view. It is contrary to the basic theory that all behavior is purposive in nature, i.e., anger, hostility, and other emotions serve a purpose or goal for the individual. There are times when we encourage people not to hold back their anger, but only under certain circumstances. For instance, when a child attempts to do something and is really trying hard but does not succeed, it is understandable that the child may feel frustrated and angry. In such a case, we show understanding and sympathy, yet, at the same time, help the child realize that his/her anger will not solve the problem. On the contrary, anger will make the child tense and less effective. We encourage the child to calm down, to consider other possibilities in order to deal with the task, and maybe even lend a helping hand.

The temper tantrums discussed are those which the child uses to show power and to force the parent to give in to his/her demands. Children who display temper tantrums are often great actors. They are ingenious in the manner in which they blackmail the parents to let them have their way. They yell and scream, throw themselves on the floor and kick, bang their heads against the floor or the wall, break things, hold their breath, threaten to run away, or even to kill themselves unless the parent gives in. Parents are often frightened by such strong displays of emotion and in desperation give in to the child. Some parents try to divert the child's behavior. Some parents punish the child or try to force him/her to get up and to go to his/her room. This almost always ends in a power struggle. Again the child wins if only by the sheer fact that he/she has again succeeded in getting the parents so angry that they resort to force and punishment. An example:

> *A five-year old boy told us that when he throws a temper tantrum his mother forces him to get up and to go to his room, "but she always gets kicked and scratched by me."*

Nobody throws a temper tantrum when alone. Tantrums always need an audience. An example:

> *When we asked a four-year old girl why she does not cry and kick when she is in her room, but always starts screaming and throwing herself on the floor the moment she comes into the room where her parents are, she replied, "but how can they see me when I am in my room?"*

The most effective method, when a child throws a temper tantrum, is to remove the audience. We invariably tell parents to walk away, giving the child permission to throw himself/herself around and to scream to his/her heart's content. Rarely will the child carry on to a point where he/she hurts himself/herself. But it may happen and if the parents get upset and frightened, the child has them where he/she wants them. The child may hurt himself/herself once, but if the parents remain calm and unimpressed, the child will rarely repeat such a performance. These are "normal" children who try to force their parents to give in to them. When a child often becomes violent and consistently hurts himself/herself, it is suggested that the parents see a psychiatrist or psychologist. In rare cases such a child may need some medication for a while. The family counselor needs to use his/her own judgment, but all in all, we caution counselors and parents not to fall for the temper tantrums trick.

Parents who ignore a child's tantrum should make no mention of it when the child calms down, but talk to the child as though nothing had happened. Should the child repeat the procedure, the parents also should repeat their procedure and walk away. If the parents are consistent, the child will not continue a practice which does not pay off. Hugh Allred (1968) puts it this way:

> "Withdrawal from the misbehavior is similar to a sailing ship riding out a storm. Rather than putting up more sails, the sailors take them down to lessen the effects of the wind."

LYING AND STEALING

Most children lie at least occasionally, and some steal from time to time. This is often a most distressing problem to families. The first thing that the counselor must remember is to ascertain the mistaken goal level of the child in performing such "bad" acts. Some children lie in order to escape actual or probable punishment; others may lie or steal in order to feel powerful and put something over on someone else (particularly an adult), and many very young children lie because their fantasies run away with them. These children usually are not aware that they are not telling the truth. Then, there are children who lie and steal in order to get even with parents to whom being truthful is extremely important. Such an important moral posture is often the parent's Achille's heel and furnishes an area in which a revengeful child may gain his/her goal—hurting parents. Children may often steal to get attention, especially when convinced that they must do something really bad in order for the parents to get involved with them. Stealing, especially shoplifting, creates excitement and, if successful, gives the child a feeling of superiority of having outsmarted the adult world. The adolescent may regard stealing as an act of revenge against a society that he/she regards as hostile.

What constitutes effective action on the part of the counselor? First, the counselor must recognize the goal oriented nature of the behavior and ascertain the particular misbehaving goal. Second, the counselor should educate the parents to the various factors that influence children and youth to lie and steal and what part the parents inadvertently have played in this act. The counselor would have to make absolutely certain that he/she remains nonjudgmental and exercises no moral judgments. A frank discussion with the child is in order which might include enough historical information to reveal how he/she came to believe that lying or stealing paid off. Such a discussion should include the standard confrontation in order to accurately ascertain the goal level of the behavior and reveal this understanding of the client to him/her. An indirect approach in discussing many of these factors is often helpful. The counselor may say, "Some kids get into shoplifting in order to get their parents interested in them again," or "I knew a kid once who would shoplift because he liked to prove that he could put things over on people." In a case of lying, the counselor may say, "I can see that it may have been useful to tell lies and help you stay out of trouble. One can always tell a big enough story to show everyone what a big shot one is. What about you? Do any of these reasons for lying or stealing fit you?"

Finally, the counselor needs to get the parents and child or youth to agree on how such future acts such as lying or stealing will be handled. Parents are not doing their children a favor by trying to ignore or deal with such problems in other than a straightfoward manner. If a teenager is involved in a household burglary and the parents learn of it, authorities should be notified. If a child "lifts" some comic books from the supermarket shelf, the parent should march the child back to the supermarket manager to "fess up" and pay.

If a parent knows for certain that a child took money from a purse (and the parent should be absolutely certain), the child should be approached directly as follows:

> *"Danny, I know that you took a dollar from my purse. You must return it. Do you have any suggestions as to how you might pay it back?"* If the child has no suggestions, the parent may tell the child that he/she will deduct the money from the child's allowance or take it from savings. The parent might also add that if such behavior is repeated, then an interest charge will be added for the child's use of the money.

Parents often are not aware of how they unknowingly teach their children to lie when it seems expedient and how difficult situations can be avoided by so doing. Examples are (also see previous chapters)

1. Writing untrue excuses for the child when a child chooses not to go to school.

2. Telling the child to answer the telephone and tell whomever is calling that the parent is not home.

3. Suggesting that a child lie about his/her age in order to save money at the movies or to get a job.

4. Instructing a child to deny something that he/she did in order to stay out of trouble.

5. Lying to a child when the parent broke a promise to them.

6. Bragging on how the parent cheated a merchant or cheated on his/her income tax.

7. The parent not admitting that he/she made a mistake when the child knows very well that the parent did.

WETTERS AND SOILERS

One of the most perplexing problems that family counselors encounter is that of enuresis, or bed wetting, wetting during the day, and soiling after the usual age of effective toilet training. In most cases such problems are an outgrowth of a bad relationship between the parent and child. Counselors and parents are put off the track because bed wetting takes place when the child is asleep and parents refrain from placing responsibility for such behavior on a sleeping child. Most adults do not understand how children will deliberately soil except in situations where they have no control over the function. Daytime wetting or soiling usually indicates a more serious level of difficulty because the child has chosen to use his/her mistaken behavior openly. In such cases, however, it is vital to adhere firmly to the basic Adlerian principles that are germane to such behavior.

One of the first approaches in problems of wetting and soiling is for the counselor to suggest a thorough physical examination by a medical doctor. The authors firmly believe that the possibilities of physical abnormality should be investigated, and if no cause exists, rule it out. Allergies also can have a marked affect on bladder retention and these also should be checked. Dairy products and artificial food and beverage additives sometimes have marked affect on bladder retention. If no pathology problem is discovered, the counselor can confidently proceed on the basis of the dynamics involved and recommend corrective measures. The counselor should caution the parent to keep these medical examinations as routine as possible so as not to create undue anxieties for the child that may relate to the problem. Ruling out physical causes also will help in convincing the parents that the problem is behavioral in nature.

The first basic principle of behavior to be considered is that all human behavior is purposive. The child does not wet or soil without a subconscious purpose. First, the counselor can make suggestions only after the psychological goal is identified. Second, one must take into consideration that the acting out child may strive for one set of purposes when awake and alert, but toward another goal when asleep. Third, Adler (Ansbacher & Ansbacher, 1964) maintained that the meaning of the function of the various bodily organs can be explained by the law of movement. Bodily movement and the functioning of organs is often more accurate in expressing the real intentions and goals of the child than the reason that a child might give for his/her behavior. Thus, "a child who behaves obediently but wets the bed at night thereby manifests clearly his/her opinion not to wish to submit to the prescribed culture" (Ansbacher & Ansbacher, 1964). It also can be assumed that the movement expressed by bed wetting generally is directed toward the mother (Adler, 1963). The particular goal may vary from child to child, but in many other cases, other symptoms will be found, especially in pampered children. Fourth, Adler (Ansbacher & Ansbacher, 1964) also pointed out in a discussion of habit disorders that children often develop an attitude or action that is directly opposite of what the parents want. For example, if a parent is overly concerned with proper eating habits, an eating problem frequently develops. If a parent is overly concerned with bathroom habits particularly with daily bowel movements, the child often will develop some irregularity with respect to this function. It may be constipation, soiling ("I couldn't get to the bathroom fast enough"), or withholding. Fifth, it is essential to respect the child's right to soil but to place the responsibility for the behavior where it belongs—on the child. It also is imperative that the counselor discuss the problem frankly and openly and with the same attitude and manner that is utilized in discussing any other problem. It is essential that we have faith in and respect for the child's capacity to cope with his/her own problems.

Dreikurs and Grey (1970) reiterated and expanded Adler's view that pampered children often develop unsatisfactory toilet habits. They indicate that children who bed wet, wet during the day, or soil, do so for a variety of purposes. Very small children generally wet or soil to get undue attention. This is most often accurate when an oldest child, who has already been toilet trained, is pushed out of the crib by the second born. The child may see the extra attention that the parents give the baby in changing diapers and mistakenly assumes that soiling again is a way to restore his/her own importance in the family. Such mistaken behavior usually has the opposite effect. If, however, such behaviors are not effective in attaining the child's goals, the child gradually gives them up. Bobby is an example.

One of the counselors offered to take care of her friend's family while the latter took a two weeks vacation with her husband. One of the friend's children, Bobby, four, wet the bed at night. His mother would take him to the toilet each evening before he retired, and around two at night, one of the parents would get up to take him to the bathroom.

When the counselor took charge of the family, she told Bobby that she will not wake him at night and that whether he wets or not would be up to him.

Bobby wet the first two nights. The counselor made no issue of it but told him that he could change his own bed if he wanted to. He did not and it remained wet. After the third night, Bobby stopped wetting until the day his parents returned. That same night, he wet as before.

It was difficult to convince the parents that Bobby enjoyed the attention they gave him, even after they learned that he kept perfectly dry for eleven days. We find that we have to work with parents who stubbornly cling to the belief that "logical consequences" and "ignoring" has no value.

Counselors should be alert to the fact that parents will often revert to old practices if they do not see immediate results from the recommendations. Parents must be cautioned to exercise consistency in following the counselor's suggestions.

Some children may use wetting and soiling as a way to rebel and exert power and domination over the parent. Few behaviors can be more frustrating and dominant than persistent wetting and soiling. The mother usually must wash extra bed clothes and personal clothing; schedules of normal activities often are modified, and there is always the persistent nagging notion that the child will wet or soil and the parent cannot prevent it. The following example is a clear indication how children may wet or soil or not wet or soil according to how advantageous it is for them.

The case also demonstrates how ingenious and logical children can think when it suits their purpose.

> *Orna, age five. The parents brought Orna for counseling because of bed wetting and wetting and soiling during the day. The problem was immediate as father was to attend a month long meeting in Europe and the family was to accompany him. The time for departure was at hand and the counselor was able to see them only three times prior to departure. The sessions revealed that Orna wished to keep her mother involved with her and that basically she could control her mother and get even (revenge level) with mother for giving birth to little brother. With the baby's birth Orna lost her special position. Orna and the counselor discussed, and she readily agreed that it was going to be very inconvenient to wet and soil on the trip. They also discussed that it might even be embarrassing and uncomfortable to be wet and smelly especially on airplanes and trains where it would be difficult to clean up and wash dirty panties. The counselor assured her that he didn't want to deprive her of wetting or soiling but was only really concerned with her well-being on the trip. Orna suggested, then, that she wouldn't wet or soil during the day while they were gone. She wasn't too sure what would happen at night, but it was agreed not to worry. Meanwhile, the usual recommendations were made, and the parents rather eagerly began implementing them. Several weeks later mother called to say that they had returned from Europe, that everything had gone well—only one accident—but that the wetting and soiling had begun again when they had returned. When asked about this in a counseling session, Orna remarked, "but that wasn't in the agreement," i.e., to stop wetting and soiling after they returned home.*

It is the experience of the authors that children most often are operating on the revenge level when misbehaving by wetting and soiling. In counseling sessions with many such children, it is often revealed that such children usually think that bed wetting is a good way to get back at people (usually the mother). Such children are also often from families with strong social and moral values which ordinarily preclude a "getting even" attitude among family members. They are often children who wish to be very good and can therefore safeguard their good intentions by wetting only at night.

Ineffective Solutions

Although it may seem to be negative to list so-called solutions that are not effective, these are so universally but mistakenly applied that the counselor should emphatically advise the parents to cease and desist these measures. No amount of nagging, scolding, reminding, or ridicule is helpful. In fact, these activities play into the child's goals and serve to emphasize that his/her mistaken behavior is indeed effective. Restricting water input after dinner, insisting on urination just prior to bedtime, getting the child up at night, and any manner of rewards or punishments are all equally ineffective. In fact, these methods may exacerbate the problem. Parents are further discouraging the child if they assume responsibilities for the child rather than effectively encouraging the child and respecting and showing the faith that the child can solve the problem.

Parents often inquire about the effectiveness of commercial devices used to control or cure bedwetting. Some devices involve tying the genitals of male children for the night. Another suggested gadget is a device that triggers a buzzer or light on the first impact of moisture from urination that awakes the child so he/she can go to the bathroom, to mention only two. The authors question such devices in principle because they indicate that the child cannot solve the problem on his/her own and may develop a dependency on external forces to solve a problem which is basically an internal goal oriented problem. The use of such devices also may lead parents to rely on the devices and relieve them of the responsibility for improving relationships within the family that are necessary to solve the problem.

Such mistaken behaviors as wetting and soiling primarily indicate a disturbed relationship between the child and the parents. The disturbed relationship is most often between the child and the mother, but not always so. The counselor's first responsibility, then, is to seek ways to improve relationships within the family and to develop a more encouraging atmosphere in which all can relate more effectively. In addition to the various counseling techniques described previously, the counselor can advise and assist in the following way:

1. Strongly advise the parent to downgrade the importance of not wetting or soiling. The less fuss the better. (Dreikurs & Soltz, 1964).

2. Refrain from nagging, reminding, questioning, and/or ridiculing. The more detached that the parent can be from the problem the better.

3. Teach the child to care for self. Clean self, change the bed clothes, wash the soiled laundry, if old enough, and so forth. Such activities will encourage the child as he/she takes more responsibility for self.

4. Indicate that it is the child's problem to solve and that you as counselor or parent have full confidence that the child will change his/her habit.

5. It is not unusual that children who wet consistently at home never wet when they go visiting. Leave decisions as to participation in activities up to the child. The child can decide if he/she wishes to go to Grandma's house, stay over with a friend, or go to camp. The parent should refrain from raising the issue of bedwetting when such plans are discussed.

6. Do not praise or reward for dry nights. This violates the basic principle that it is the child's problem and that there should be no reward for doing the proper expected thing. It is in order to show appreciation for the child's efforts to solve the problem.

The use of principles of paradoxical intentions as an approach to the problem of wetting and soiling has had a somewhat limited but successful effect. When using paradoxical intentions, we encourage the client to get worse rather than to get better. This technique is used with clients who must always prove that they are right and do not cooperate. It also works for those who cannot produce the usual symptoms once they consciously attempt to produce them. We believe that if the reason or goal of the misbehavior (symptom of bed wetting) is changed (Mozdzierz, Macchitelli, & Lisiccki, 1976) or diverted, that the child will give up the misbehavior because it no longer helps him/her gain his/her true purpose, i.e., upset mother in some way. It should be emphasized that the use of this technique is unique and should be used in conjunction with the usual methods of improving relationships and atmosphere within the family and encouragement techniques that mitigate the child's perceived need for negative behaviors. It also is emphasized that the counselor must be on very friendly terms with the child so that humor (Mozdzierz, et al, 1976) can be inserted in the situation. Gentle fun can be poked at the situation and the child can be convinced that the counselor is definitely willing to rely completely on the child to solve the problem.

The counselor's task in using this approach is to substitute another reason or goal for the child's wetting or soiling and thus induce him/her to stop fighting the problem. Thus, several successful cases in using anti-suggestion began with a frank, but friendly discussion between counselor and the youngster. These discussions include the usual confrontations as to the goals of the behavior. The counselor may then suggest that the child continue as long as he/she wishes as it is really his/her decision when to stop. The counselor offers to make a wager with the client in a meaningful way depending on the age and experience of the child. The counselor may say, "I'll bet you a dime, or ice cream bar, or lollypop, each time that you can wet the bed." Ask the child to keep accurate records and tell him/her that you will settle up at the next session. The child's goal in wetting is now changed from bugging mother to proving that he/she can do it. End the session with a review of what mother is no longer going to do about this problem, as outlined in the foregoing section, and that it will be strictly the child's own business as to what will happen. We should keep such agreements on a light, humorous level. We also want to point out that this approach should not be confused with our basic beliefs about rewards.

DISRESPECTFUL SPEECH—MOUTHING OFF

Many parents often complain that their children are sarcastic, sometimes profane, and speak disrespectfully to them. These are symptoms of a seriously disturbed relationship between parent and child. Such situations often characterize the relationship between teenagers and their parents. This is a difficult problem to attack directly. The counselor's first goal is to try to improve the family relationships which usually will alleviate the disrespectful speech. However, there are some effective approaches to work on this problem in a direct way. These are illustrated in the following examples.

> *Mother was complaining that her fifteen year old son, Irve, is fresh and she is having a hard time with him. Because Irve was present at the counseling session, the counselor asked them to re-enact a recent problem. Irve felt somewhat sheepish in the process, but the following transpired.*

Mother to fifteen year old son.

Mother: *Where are you going?*

Son: *Out.*

Mother: *Where "out"?*

Son: *I said, "out" isn't that enough?*

Mother: *Don't be fresh. I demand to know where you are going.*

Son: *Tough! I don't have to report to you each time I go out, and if you don't like it, it's your tough luck.*

Neither of them saw the part they played in the problem. Irve accused mother of snooping, that she controlled every minute of his life, while mother accused Irve of being "fresh" and disobedient. The counselor prevailed upon this mother to refrain from demanding that Irve tell her where he was going each time he left the house. He was old enough to come and go during the day without having to account for each step. Evenings, however, the parents should know his where-abouts and they should have an agreement as to the time of his return.

Another example. *This took place in the counseling office. The family consisted of both parents, their daughters, Ida, 14, and Ermeline, 11. Father complained that Ida was wearing blue jeans that were too tight and that it looked indecent.*

Ida: *You're a dirty old man, or you would not have such dirty thoughts.*

Father (To counselor): *If we were home and if she would give me such an answer, I would slap her mouth.*

Ida: *I know, that's why I don't tell you how I feel when you talk to me like this at home. But I feel this way and I wanted you to know.*

Father (To counselor): *Are you going to say something to her about this?*

Counselor: *If you mean if I am going to scold her, no. But I would appreciate if you, Ida, would discuss wearing tight blue jeans with your father in a way that might establish better communication. Only if you wish. Also, it might help if you were to discuss how you feel when your father threatens you.*

Ida: *All the kids wear tight pants. Nobody thinks that there is anything wrong with it. My father is always critical of my tight pants, and he makes me feel like I am bad or something. I hate him when he threatens me. I am not doing anything that other kids don't do.*

Counselor: *Talk to your father and tell him what you have just told me.*

Ida: *I don't know if I can; it's not the same when I talk to you.*

Counselor: *Go ahead and try. It might help.*

Ida (To her father): *I don't do anything bad. Why do you make me feel like I am bad? All the kids wear tight pants, and nobody says anything in school. I don't want to be different. Can't you understand?*

Father: *I understand that a kid doesn't want to be different from the other kids. I do understand, but I can't for the life of me, see you in those tight blue jeans without feeling annoyed. It just goes against my feeling of decency.*

Ida: *Well, then don't look. You only see what you want to see.*

Counselor: *Can we work this out to everybody's satisfaction? Is there anything you could suggest, Ida? Both of you?*

Ida: *The only thing I could do is not to wear these pants when I am at home, but I will wear them when I go out. It won't be easy to change all the time, but I will do it.*

Counselor: *Will this help you, Mr. . . .?*

Father: *It will help some. I don't like for her to run around in those pants, but, as I said, it will help some.*

Counselor: *Can we agree on this for the time being?*

Ida (Looking at her father): *I agree.*

Father: *Okay, I can see I am not going to win.*

Counselor: *Can we also agree that you, Mr. . . , will not say anything to Ida to make her feel uncomfortable or angry?*

Father: *Okay, I will keep my mouth shut.*

Counselor: *I know you don't feel too comfortable with this arrangement, but let's wait and see what will happen if you two do not argue.*

Father: *Okay, I hope you are right. I'll keep my mouth shut as long as I don't see her in those pants.*

When the counselor and the family met again, Ida was wearing corduroy pants which were not as tight as the pants she wore the first time. Father said that she had kept the agreement and that he did not see her much in her tight blue jeans, but he knew that she wore them when she went out. This was the best that could be accomplished.

The counselor should again be reminded that disrespectful language and tone of voice are symptoms of disrupted relationships and that he/she must use his/her skill and usual methods in improving the situation. This will usually include impressing the parents that they must treat children in a respectful manner if they expect children to respect them.

THE WHINING CHILD

Many young children whine in order to get their parents' attention. This usually stops as the child grows older, but until then it is often very annoying to parents. Often, parents give in to the child just to get rid of him/her. They know that this is a bad practice, but they can't stand the whining. However, even if they give in to the child, they almost always accompany this with a little lecture: "Stop that whining; I can't stand it. You're driving me crazy. How often have I asked you not to whine?" This kind of preaching barely is heard by the child, and rarely does it change the child's behavior.

We suggest that the parent ignore such behavior. If the parent can't stand it, then we suggest that the parent remove himself/herself to a place where the child can't follow. As in fighting, we suggest the bathroom.

A very effective way of dealing with a whining child is the use of shock treatment. Instead of asking the child to stop the whining we suggest to the parents to ask that the child whine whenever the child talks. A mother of a five-year old boy who whined when he asked for something, reported that each time the boy talked to her without whining, she reminded him to whine. She told him that she got so used to his whining that she missed it when he stopped. This stopped the whining completely. Once this practice was discontinued, the mother made no mention of it.

The counselor can only suggest, but the final decision rests with the parents. It is always helpful to make the parents aware that a particular recommendation may not work. In such a case, the counselor will make a different suggestion when the family comes for a follow-up session. Often parents think of new ways along the line of our basic beliefs, which are effective. For instance, one little girl whined and nagged her mother to do something with her; the child said that she did not know what to do and that she was bored. The mother ignored her. After a time of whining and nagging, the child said to her mother: "I know what to do, I will go into my room and listen to my records." The mother said, "Fine," and made no further issue out of this. We can see from this example that the child often solves his/her own problem if we don't get involved, don't talk or scold, but simply pay no attention to the child's whining.

CHILDREN DISTURBING
WHILE PARENT IS DRIVING

When children misbehave in the car and disregard an appeal to stay in their seats and lower their voices, the parent should pull to the curb, stop the car, and wait until the children settle down. The parent should refrain from threats, admonitions, or lectures. Take action—not lectures. If the children resume their misbehavior once the car is back onto the road, it is most effective to turn the car around and return home saying absolutely nothing. If the children ask why they returned home, the parent may say, "It's no fun and it is dangerous to drive when you carry on in the car the way you did. I refuse to drive under such circumstances." No amount of pleading that they will be good and behave should change the parent's decision at that time. However, in a day or so, the parent may say to the children: "I have to go shopping. You are welcome to come along under the condition that you behave in the car. You don't have to come with me, but if you do, this will have to be the agreement. What do you want to do?" Should the children accept the conditions, but not keep the agreement, the parent should turn around as before, but the parents should then go without the children for a week or two before asking them again what they intend to do. Parents who cannot leave their children at home should plan to have someone supervise them on shopping days or go shopping in the evening when the spouse is home. Parents can always find a solution to this problem. We have rarely had an experience where this approach on the part of the parent did not work.

Young children have a more difficult time in remaining calm on a long trip. It is suggested that parents provide games for them to play in the car, take along cassettes with tapes of music or stories the children enjoy, or stop the car more often to let the children exercise for a while before continuing.

TELEVISION

A major intrusion on modern day family life is television. The many negative influences of television on family life go largely unrecognized. Family counseling programs and parent education programs should recognize this problem and work toward effective solutions. If the counselor truly wants to promote some movement or change in the dynamics of intrafamily relationships, he/she must help the family bring some sanity to television viewing habits.

Some negative impacts of TV viewing are commonly known. Many parents are concerned that children don't read enough because of television. That is true, and the cumulative, negative effect on reading ability after hundreds and thousands of hours of viewing television is dramatic. There is much concern about the impact of violence on TV on children's behavior (Comstock, 1978). Research on this question can now be considered definitive (Bradway, 1982). Much youth crime is reported which indicates that the idea for the criminal behavior came from a television show. There is periodic concern about TV advertising on foods and toys directed at children. Most parents are pressured by their children to buy what is advertised on TV regardless of the merit of the product. However, the authors have other concerns of a different nature about the negative influences of television on family life, i.e., robbing family of interactive time.

One of the insidious things that children learn from television is that they can be, and are entitled to be, entertained with little or no effort of their own. All they have to do is turn on the set and thus become passive observers with no requirement to use their intelligence. The authors believe that this is a major reason why so many youngsters are bored in school; children are pampered and exhibit a "taking" attitude toward life as contrasted with a more cooperative "giving" attitude. The development of the latter is necessary for harmonious family living and developing cooperative skills required in all aspects of life.

Kindergarten and first-grade teachers of the nation face a major problem as they welcome new students each autumn who were reared on a diet of television where they are passive receptors to entertainment. No wonder that so many children are disappointed and find school dull in comparison. Even more important, however, the child on entering school must begin to *actively interact* in the educative process, but the thousands of hours logged as a *passive receptor* do not prepare the student for the active interactive role.

> *A twelve year old boy who spent most of his free time watching TV was brought to the counselor because his reading test indicated that he was reading at level three. When the counselor talked to him, she became aware of this boy's tremendous knowledge, especially in the politics of the Far East. She learned that he likes to read books and articles dealing with this subject. She was somewhat perplexed because the test indicated that he read at level three, and she asked him about it. The boy replied: "Oh, you go by the test. You see, I only read a paragraph of the test, and it bored me to tears; so I never finished reading this test." He either did not answer some of the questions, or he gave random answers.*

We can see here a case of a child, who was constantly entertained and had developed little or no frustration level when he could not get what he wanted. Such children take the attitude of "you either play the game my way, or I don't play." The interesting and unbelievable thing is that neither the teacher nor the school psychologist were aware of this boy's actual reading ability and his problem.

What is reasonable for the counselor as he/she attempts to help the family? Obviously, the counselor cannot often expect the family to turn off the TV and keep it off. (That has been instituted in extremely serious situations for profound positive effects.) More acceptable approaches need to be made. The counselor could unhesitatingly recommend a number of guidelines to parents for effectively dealing with the television problem.

- Parents should prepare a list of children's programs to which there is no objection to children's viewing.

- Agree on the amount of time and time of day that can be devoted to TV viewing on both school days and weekends.

- Allow the children to choose the programs that they view in agreement with the previous two guidelines.

- Assure children that the plan can be re-evaluated after a week or two, thus, allowing for flexibility in choice of programs.

- Should children disagree on the program to be viewed at a certain time, each child may watch his/her favorite program while the other does homework or other household chores.

- Exceptions to the foregoing may be made for very special programs, such as space shots at Cape Kennedy, Super Bowl, an outstanding drama, or concert. Care must be exercised that programs not be routinely categorized as "special" in order to circumvent the system outlined.

- Agree on consequences to be followed if the guidelines are not followed:

> (a) If a child chooses to view longer than the allotted time, he/she would forfeit viewing the next day.

> (b) If frequent disregards are made of the guidelines, all TV viewing would be discontinued for an agreed length of time. One week is suggested.

Some parents may take exception to the system as outlined because they may feel that it penalizes other members of the family rather than the culprits. The counselors should then indicate to parents that they must make a choice between their own convenience and that of properly rearing their children. In addition, if all the children are placed in the same boat, it brings pressure on them to help solve the problem.

Some parents have solved this problem by withdrawing to their bedroom or den where they can watch television without the presence of the children; however, parents need to understand that their own TV viewing habits have a great influence on their children. The parent who has the TV set on all day and watches most hours during the day and night, such as mothers who watch TV while preparing a meal, will have difficulty in implementing the suggestions given. Children do not understand such double standards. They model their behavior after their parents and do not understand that what may be acceptable for the parents is not acceptable for the child. Although it is difficult to make positive progress on the TV problem in many families, the potential gain in improvement of relationships within the family is well worth the effort.

SHARING RESPONSIBILITIES

Two important factors are to be considered when telling parents how to teach their children effectively to perform various responsibilities around the home. One is the practical factor of getting the household chores accomplished, and this is an increasing logistical problem as both parents work outside the home or in single parent families. But more important is the factor of furnishing opportunities for children to learn to be needed and useful to contribute to the welfare of the group, and to achieve acceptance as a "giving" member.

Many parents still sincerely believe that children should not be burdened with household responsibilities. Later, they will have many years when they must assume full responsibility. Parents say, "Let them enjoy their childhood; it comes only once. I prefer seeing them play than working around the house. Besides, I don't mind doing the household work, this is my job as a mother and a wife." A number of times, we have had fathers who actually resented that their children did anything in the house. They said that they "don't believe in child labor." Then, there are parents who strongly support the belief that school work is enough work for their children and that they expect nothing more from them. However, the authors hold strongly to the conviction that everyone who lives in the household should contribute to the care of the household.

Without the help of the counselor, some parents can never draw the correlation between the children's acceptance of responsibilities in the home and those they have to accept outside the home; they are bringing up their children to be on the receiving end of life, demanding special consideration from life and from people without feeling that they should give anything in return. These children rarely feel that they are full-fledged members of the family; they merely are residing in the home and expect that they should be catered to. Also, such children may come to believe that they are important only as long as they are being served.

Delegating responsibilities to children should begin at a very young age. This helps children feel that they are a part of the family, that they are being useful and needed, it brings them closer to the family. Most parents underestimate what even very young children can do to contribute to the family enterprise. A helpful guide to expectations can be found in Appendix B. The suggestions given in Sharing Responsibilities have been tested and found to be realistic with proper training.

ORDERLINESS

Parents, especially the mother, frequently complain, that children are untidy and careless about where they leave their belongings and consistently leave the house in a state of untidiness. Before any suggestions are made regarding a state of untidiness or littering, the counselor should make certain that children have special places for their property. This does not necessarily require a special closet or drawer space. Boxes, cartons, shelves, and so forth, may be designated for the various objects.

All members in the family must be considerate and must cooperate in regard to commonly shared rooms. Nobody should have the right to mess up any room that also is shared by other members of the family, such as the living room, dining room, kitchen, bathroom, or any other room that all members use. Children pattern themselves after their parents. If a father or a mother disregards this rule and leaves personal belongings in shared rooms, then the children will see nothing wrong in leaving their toys or clothing all over the house. Parents often do not realize that they set a poor example for the children. It often happens that father leaves his shoes in the living room or throws his coat on a chair, that mother leaves her gloves, hat, or other garment lying around in a room that is not exclusively her own. All must understand and agree that they must respect the rights of other members. The only area each may keep in disorder is his/her own personal room if the person so desires.

What could parents do when the child disregards the rules and continues messing common areas? The counselor can suggest the "deposit box" concept which works as follows:

> The parents should first discuss this procedure with the child and encourage the child to make a commitment to keep all personal belongings in his/her room or his/her corner of the room if the child shares a room with other children. The parent should then give the child the choice. In case the child does not keep the commitment, the parent will pick up any object that the child leaves lying around and put it away so that the child cannot find it. The child may soon find himself/herself without underwear, clothes, toys, and so forth. After a week of deprivation, the parent may ask the child to consider the situation and decide what he/she wants to do. The child should in no way be made uncomfortable or ashamed for having changed his/her mind. If the child agrees that from now on he/she will take care of his/her belongings, but again not keep the commitment, the parents should repeat the logical consequence but this time for more than a week.

Families are encouraged to work out variations of the deposit box system to fit their own situations. This way of dealing with such a problem works only if parents are consistent, do not argue with the child or remind him/her what will happen. If there is concern about what other relatives or the neighbors will think of the dirty clothes that the child wears, parents must decide on the priority. What is more important—to avoid a hassle and train the child properly, or to please other people who might judge the parents?

Many arguments and much unhappiness could be avoided if the parents would be less strict about how a youngster keeps his own room as long as the child respects common areas. Parents who have trained their child since early childhood to accept the responsibility for his/her own belongings and, who did not wait "until the child is old enough" to take care of his/her property, do not usually have this problem. If they do, it usually shows up when the child enters the teen years and does not want to be bothered with cleaning his/her room, or uses this as a means to rebel against the parents.

We have seen mothers train their infants to put their things away. One example that was observed. The mother held a tiny child, put a toy and a crayon into the child's hand and carried the child to the place where the object was to be deposited. The mother said, "Put the crayon in this drawer (the mother opened the drawer) and put the toy on this shelf." The mother thanked the child for his/her effort, and the child enjoyed the feeling of being useful. When children are trained in this manner, when it is done in the spirit of fun and of appreciation, the mother will seldom have problems with tidiness later on.

Mothers need to take time out for training the child—what to do and how to do it. At first, the mother may offer to help the child with cleaning the room, with making of the bed, and so forth, but as soon as the child knows what to do the mother should leave the responsibility to the child.

EATING PROBLEMS

An interesting fact is that children in non-Western cultures rarely present eating problems. Problems that many parents encounter with their children at mealtime are the result of their own attitudes and their own over-concern with observing what their children eat, how much they eat, and how they eat. In other words, eating problems usually depend on the importance the parent places on eating. Parents who are less concerned and who make no issue over whether a child eats or not, have comparatively few problems in that area unless a child suffers from some pathological disturbance which affects the appetite and food intake. Normal children who are served at regular times, who are not watched, nagged, and forced, usually eat without difficulty.

Children who realize the parent's preoccupation with eating habits will often utilize this opportunity to keep parents worried in order to force them to serve only the kinds of food the children prefer. And so it happens that in Western culture children are often literally undernourished because they live on a diet of hamburgers, hot dogs, potato chips, and various kinds of carbonated beverages. Parents who are tired of the hassle at mealtime often take the children to a fast food restaurant or serve prepared foods which are less than nutritious. Doing so is not only less of a hassle with the children, but less work for the mother.

Children often tell counselors that they will get what they want if they refuse to eat what mother prepares. Others admit that they eat the meal only if they are promised a double portion of dessert. Parents frequently fall for this manipulation because they are afraid that the child will suffer if they don't give in.

Good results may be expected from these children once the parents discuss mealtime with them and tell the children that whether they eat or not will be up to them but that no other food will be served if they refuse to eat. The children would then have to wait until the next meal is served. Furthermore, the child must know that he/she cannot go to the refrigerator and prepare a sandwich or any other substitute. Some parents actually put locks on the refrigerator and food cabinets until such time when this is not necessary.

It is suggested that parents who have children with eating problems should stock little food in the refrigerator or on the shelves. This may require that the mother will have to shop almost daily which is not convenient, but a few weeks of this kind of sacrifice on her part is bound to bear fruit. The counselor can assure the mother that it is definitely worth the trouble.

Others have had good results with the following technique. Let's say that Elsa refuses to eat potatoes. We suggest that the parent should do the serving rather than have the child serve himself/herself. When the parent serves food to Elsa, he/she may say, "I know that you don't like potatoes, so I won't serve them to you" and pass her up. Elsa may be surprised at this kind of treatment but at first, she actually may respond with "good," and however she will not like being ignored. The second or third day, she may either respond the same way or say nothing. After a few days of this procedure, Elsa cannot hold out any longer and is apt to announce, "I have changed my mind, I want some potatoes." The parent should make no further issue of this, serve Elsa, and tell her that whenever she changes her mind again, mother will be only too glad to accommodate her. The next day, the parent may ask the child, "potatoes or not?" Then, serve or skip her as Elsa requests. No further discussion should follow. This approach is something in the order of Adler's "spitting into the soup." It takes all the fun out of the child's capricious behavior because nobody makes an issue of it.

Proper eating habits should be established the moment the child begins to hold his/her own spoon. This may already have happened in infancy. When the mother realizes that the child is making a game out of eating, she should give the child the choice to finish the meal or to wait until the next meal. She should tell the child, "If you throw the food on the table or floor, or if you dawdle, then I'll have to take it away and you will have to wait until your next meal." The moment the child continues his/her antics the mother should silently remove the food and excuse the child from the table. No amount of crying, threatening, or pleading should change mother's warning. If she is not consistent, the child will always play on her mood and use his/her obnoxious behavior until mother gives in.

Some children take hours to finish a meal. Parents often refer to them as "needing hours to finish." When we examine what is going on while the child is eating, we find that in most cases the child gets up from the table several times in order to play or watch a television program for a few minutes, go to the bathroom and stay there for some time, or just sit in front of the dinner without eating. In all this time, the mother coaxes, reminds, scolds, threatens, begs, and often bribes the child to finish eating. How much more attention and fun can this child have? Such power that he/she can wield over the parent!

We almost never find a naturally "slow eater." The child may be somewhat slower than the other members in the family, but this is a matter of just a few minutes. Any child that requires more than an extra hour to consume a meal is doing it for a definite "goodie," that of keeping mother busy. We suggest that parents should first discuss this matter with the child, allow a few extra minutes to finish eating, give him/her the choice to finish or to leave the table, and tell him/her that no food will be served until the next meal. The parent should remove the plate in the event that the child dawdles again.

It is important, however, that parents do not feel sorry for the child or feel guilty for "depriving" the child of a meal. If the child comes later and complains of hunger, the parent should be friendly, acknowledge that "Yes, you must be hungry, but you will have to wait until the next meal." No snacks should be allowed to carry the child over until time for the next regular meal. This technique can be effective only if the parents believe in what they are doing and trust that the child, if really hungry, will eat the regular meal served.

Hunger and eating is a natural process and need not be treated otherwise. Some parents make a game of eating in an effort to distract or manipulate the child from the actual eating process while enjoying the game that is being played. For instance, mothers may say, "I imagine your mouth is a garage, and the spoon is a big Buick getting into the garage to park. Open the garage door wide, and here comes the Buick; now close the door; swallow the Buick, and make room for the next car." The child gets so involved in the game that he/she doesn't become aware of what he/she is eating. Another common eating game attempts to make a pleaser out of the child. "Come, eat one spoonful for Daddy, one for Mother, and one for Grandmother." This, again, detracts from the natural development of the pleasure of eating. A third game, "Let's feed each other; you feed me one spoon, and I'll feed you one." Thus, the poor mother is forced to ruin her own eating pleasure. Such games should never be used by the parent. These examples are given to assist the counselor in helping parents to avoid the frequent traps that detract from proper training in eating habits.

GETTING UP IN THE MORNING

One of the frequent complaints of parents is the child's reluctance to get up in the morning and to get ready for school. The mother or the father usually wakes the child a number of times, getting more impatient each time, and finally pulls the blankets off the child and forces him/her out of bed. This is one of the easiest problems with which to deal. We suggest that parents give the child an alarm clock, teach him/her how to set it (or if the child is very young, to set it themselves), and how to turn it off when it rings. We find that even kindergarten children can learn how to use the alarm clock and respond positively to it. Children are usually glad to assume such a responsibility.

The problem is more often with the parents than with the child. The parents, whose child put them into service and who have awakened the child for years (going through the same struggle each day), insist that the child will simply ignore the alarm and continue sleeping, or just remain in bed, and ultimately be late for school. This may happen the first day or in some cases for a couple of days; but, we have seldom found children who do not assume the responsibility of getting up and ready on their own once they realize that the game is over and that the parents will not assume the responsibility. In most cases, the child wants to go to school and is not happy at home under these circumstances. The child may try to force the parents back into his/her service by not going to school. It is important that the parent make no issue out of the school problem, but tell the child that as far as the parents are concerned the child IS in school. This means that the child is confined to his/her room and that the parents will ignore him/her. If the child normally stays in school for lunch, he/she should be given a packed lunch which may be eaten in his/her room. The school should be notified of the child's behavior and given permission to apply whatever consequences the school considers necessary. It must be remembered that the child's reluctance to get up and his/her defiance is not directed against the school, only against the parent who now refuses to let himself/herself be used.

Adolescents are especially prone to act "mother-deaf" when they are awakened in the morning. There are those who assume the responsibility and are no problem to the parents, but others who refuse to get up are often big problems to the parent who awakens them. Mostly, these are youngsters who have been awakened by a parent for as long as they have been going to school. They consider this as the parents' holy duty and resent it when the parent suddenly refuses to serve them. But, if the parents are consistent in not waking them and in not fighting with them, they will reluctantly assume the responsiblity for getting up by themselves.

What does the parent do with the child who is not awakened and who is then late and misses the school bus? This is often the case. If it is acceptable that getting up by himself/herself and getting to school on time is the child's responsibility, then the child may miss the bus. This is a natural consequence and, therefore, need not be followed by a logical consequence. But what is a parent to do in such a case? This depends on the age of the child. If the child is old enough to walk, it is suggested the parents let him/her walk or ride his/her bike. Let the teacher then apply the consequences of being late or of missing some school work. If the child is too young to walk by himself/herself, allow the child to miss school that day. However, the child would then have to stay in his/her room as discussed previously. In some cases, especially with older children, a taxi could be called, but let the child pay for it out of his/her savings or allowance.

BEDTIME

Children love to stay up in the evening and be part of the adult world. Few children go to bed early without putting up some kind of fuss. Parents often tell us that the time between the children's retiring and their actual falling asleep is the worst part of the parents' day. As one mother said, "I am exhausted by the time they fall asleep. My husband and I don't have a moment's peace until then."

Invariably, parents get into a power-struggle with the child that refuses to go to bed. The youngster comes out a dozen times asking for a glass of water, wanting to go to the bathroom, wanting to kiss the parents "good-night" once more, etc.

There are a number of things that the parents can do to prevent such hassles.

1. Discuss with the children the time they should be in their rooms or in the part of the room where they sleep if they don't have a room of their own.

2. While they must honor the agreement about the time they have to retire to their respective rooms, it should be up to the child when they go to bed (difficult for some parents to accept). Most children go to bed very soon once they get no attention from the parents.

3. Tell children that you will read a story or discuss something with them that they want to talk about when they are in bed and set a time after which you are not available.

4. Let them go to the bathroom before retiring.

5. Prepare a glass of water near their beds.

6. Should they come out of the bedroom and make demands, ignore them or pretend you don't hear them.

7. Should they come to where the parents are, take the child firmly by the hand and escort him/her back to the bedroom. This procedure may have to be repeated several times in one evening. But we reassure the parents that it won't go on for long.

8. Refrain from checking up whether the child has gone to sleep or not.

VISITING PARENTS AT NIGHT

When children have bad nightmares or when they are frightened at night, they often want to be close to their parents for reassurance. The child should be permitted to stay with parents for a few minutes. They should comfort the child, telling him/her that this was only a bad dream and that there is no danger and, therefore, no reason to continue being frightened. They should ask the child to return to his/her room, or, if the child is very small, escort the child to his/her room, tuck the child in, say "good-night," and leave.

It is a bad practice to allow children to join the parents in their bedroom at night. Children should be told that parents need privacy; they need to be comfortable in bed, and the children must not disturb them during the night. Should the child ignore the parents' request and continue coming into their bed at night, the parents should insist that the child return to his/her room immediately. If the child resists, one of the parents should take the child by the hand and escort him/her back to his/her room.

In extreme cases, we suggest that the parents lock their bedroom door at night, and ignore the child's knocking, pounding, or kicking the door. Some children fall asleep in front of the parents' bedroom door. But invariably give up this kind of behavior if the parent remains firm and consistent.

HOMEWORK

Children spend many hours in school where they are, for the most part, regimented, where they have to do as they are told, and where they often feel bored. The child, having spent six to seven hours in school dreams of getting out and playing or doing something of his/her own choice. Few, unfortunately, can fulfill this dream. No sooner do they come home when the parents often start asking about homework and demanding that the child "get the homework out of the way before going out to play." This means that the child has to continue "being in school" all over again. No wonder that many resent doing homework and often don't do it in spite of staying inside and pretending. It may increase the child's dislike of school. The parent, checking on what the child is doing or not doing, often becomes angry, sits down with the child, trying to force him/her to do the homework, and often a battle ensues. To a great degree, this situation can be traced to the school where teachers demand that parents see to it that their child does the homework. Children who do homework under pressure rarely learn anything from it. Teachers, who have taken the trouble to check this, will attest to this fact. The child returns perfectly done assignments but when asked to do the same work at school he/she is unable to do it, thus revealing that parents have probably completed the assignment.

Counselors should insist that homework is the child's responsibility and that the parent should stay out of it. Children who rely on their parents to sit with them while they do their homework will usually not work in school unless the teacher also sits with them. Homework may easily become a nightly battleground on which the child continually defeats the parent. The child should have a designated time in which he/she agrees to do homework. The parent may help in situations when the child does not understand a problem, but this should take a few minutes, and the parent should then remove himself/herself the moment the child understands what to do. If the child does not do the homework, the teacher should then apply logical consequences as he/she considers proper. The child should be told of this consequence and the parent should not interfere with what the teacher does. In the final analysis, if the child knows what the consequences are and still does not do the assignment, the consequences were of his/her own choice.

Children, who have not performed well in school for several years are usually so far behind that they often cannot do the work that the teacher assigns. The children who fall into this category are usually too proud to admit that they don't know how to do the work and cover it up by misbehaving or saying that they hate the work, that they are too tired, or that they will do it later. The counselor should explain to the child why he/she cannot do the work, helping the child not to feel ashamed, and not to regard himself/herself as stupid because the other children do understand. The counselor may say to the child:

> *"You haven't worked in a long time; so it is only natural that you should not understand how to do this advanced work. Don't compare yourself with children who know what to do. They have worked systematically through all the grades. That doesn't mean that they are smarter than you are. You fell behind, that's all. You could catch up with your class if you wanted to do a little extra work. If you do, I will suggest to your parents to get you a tutor who will come to your house and start with you from where you have left off, from where you feel comfortable with the subject, and gradually you will catch up."*

If the child agrees, the counselor should make this suggestion to the parents. The best tutors and those with whom younger children work most readily are older students who know the subject. Children often learn from other children what they refuse to learn from adults because they are not in a power-struggle with another child. Many youngsters are only too eager to earn some extra money and are willing to do the tutoring. Parents should ask the teacher to recommend a student, making sure that they get a youngster who really knows the subject and who is serious.

Some children do poorly in school and refuse to do their homework when they have a sibling who is a very good student and an "eager beaver." In such a case, the family needs to be helped with their ways of handling the "good kid" and what they do that discourages the child who is having difficulties. The child needs to be helped to understand why he/she is refusing to cooperate with school and why he/she refuses to do homework. The child needs to be helped to understand why he/she allows the sibling to gain so much power over him/her and to control his/her life. The parents and the teacher need to set lower standards for such children, at least at the beginnning, and in this way make it possible for the child to experience some success.

ALLOWANCES

An allowance should be given to the child without any strings attached. Parents should give the child an allowance to indicate their understanding of the need to have some money and learn how to handle it. The child should be allowed to spend this money in any form and fashion chosen without having to account to the parents for the way it was spent. A specific day should be set up for the child to receive the allowance, and if the child chooses to spend the money on the first day, no amount of pleading should change the parent's consistency in giving the allowance on the day agreed upon. Borrowing in advance is discouraged as it tends to defeat the purpose of training the child to properly manage his/her money. Occasionally, the child may borrow in advance from his/her allowance if this is in agreement. Parents must then subtract this amount from the regular allowance when it is given to the child.

One should not confuse the child's allowance with money the child gets for a specific purpose, such as buying his/her school lunch, bus fare, and so forth. Nor should we confuse this with money paid to the child for doing special work for parents for which they would normally hire somebody, such as washing windows, mowing the lawn, or washing the car.

The single mother often has a greater problem than other parents when it concerns the amount of allowance that can be given to their children if she does not get substantial child-support. What can the mother do in such a situation? The entire family must discuss the financial situation and decide what they can afford under the circumstances and come to an agreement. It is important that mother honor this agreement and not give the child the agreed upon allowances according to mother's whims. If she does, the child will learn not to take mother's agreements seriously in any situation and may cease to be concerned with what is and what is not fair. If there are older children, they should look for part-time jobs in order to lighten mother's financial burden. Children, who are twelve and older, may do baby-sitting, help other families with the household chores, get a paper-route, tutor younger children, clean neighbor's yards, mow other people's yards, rake leaves in fall, and so forth, to earn money.

SPENDING LUNCH MONEY ON CANDY

Some parents take the position that what the child does with his/her lunch money is the child's choice. So, if the child fills himself/herself with candy instead of buying lunch in school, it is the child's choice and the parents should respect it. The authors do not support such an attitude on the part of the parent. Lunch money is for one purpose only—namely for buying lunch and should not be confused with the allowance which he/she can spend as he/she wishes. The child who buys candy instead of lunch should be given the following choices.

1. Buy the lunch in school.

2. Take a lunch from home.

3. Parents may prepay the lunch at school (in which case the child does not handle the lunch money).

4. Go without lunch altogether.

The child should have the choice and no further issue should be made. Should the child agree to buy his/her lunch, but breaks the agreement and buys candy, the parent should discontinue giving the child lunch money, and he/she can take a lunch from home or go without.

CHILDREN'S FEARS

Most children will have some fears of the unknown, unfamiliar encounters which frighten them, but the degree of their fears will depend on how the parents respond to the child's expression of those fears. Parents should not ignore the child's fears but investigate what frightens the child, and if there is no real reason to be afraid, help the child realize that he/she was unreasonably frightened. When parents notice that a child is using fears in order to be unduly served and keep them preoccupied, they should tell the child that there is no cause for fear and remove themselves. When parents feel sorry for the child and excuse the behavior "because he/she is only a child," the child's demand for attention is reinforced. For example:

Six year old Ken refused to go into any unlit room in the evening even though he knew where the light switch was located. He would stand by the door and whimper that he was afraid and would ask someone to turn the light on for him. Thus, he trained everyone, including his three year old sister, to switch the light on for him and secure undue service for himself. The parents mentioned this problem incidentally as they were discussing another of Ken's problems. They saw nothing wrong in Ken's fear of unlit rooms. However, as the counselor discussed Ken's relationship with the parents and siblings, she realized that Ken used every imaginable trick to keep everyone occupied with him. He couldn't butter his bread; he couldn't put on his shoes claiming that he mixed up the right from the left; he couldn't carry his lunchbox because it hurt his hand. Everyone had to help him. The parents were oblivious of this pattern and delegated responsibilities to their older children regarding Ken's needs.

The counselor explained that, by doing things for Ken that he could well do for himself, they showed disrespect for his ability and contributed to his way of exploiting them. They unknowingly were preventing him from growing up and becoming self-reliant. The counselor appealed to the siblings to stop serving Ken in this way and to refrain from teasing or mocking him. The parents were advised to give Ken the opportunities to do things for himself and to become independent. They could tell Ken whenever he pleads for assistance, "I know this is difficult for you, but as long as we do it for you, you will never learn to do it for yourself."

The foregoing example clearly indicates that a certain symptom or behavior cannot be understood in isolation from the general behavior pattern of the child. Since a child does not waste energy on something that does not pay off, it is necessary to investigate the purpose of the child's fears and how his use of fears fits into the general pattern of his behavior.

Another example:

> *Once we worked with a five year old boy who insisted that his mother should lie down with him until he fell asleep because the devil came to see him every evening. He would not allow his father or any other member to come to stay with him until he fell asleep. It had to be mother. Of course, mother worried that the boy was developing guilt feelings and was fantasizing about being punished by the devil. It was difficult to persuade her to leave the boy alone for a few days and see what would happen. The counselor told the child that obviously the devil liked him or why would he visit him every evening? The counselor then suggested that the boy make friends with the devil and enjoy the visit. She explained that this was not possible if mother was in the room with him, and that she would not come from now on. He and the devil would have to work this out somehow. It took three days of crying and pleading before the boy stopped complaining about the devil. He fell asleep without anyone having to sit with him.*

Children are not born with fears of the dark, of being alone, or fearing an animal. These fears are often instilled in them by others who are the ones who are afraid and unknowingly teach the child fear in play or in misguided teasing. Some fears are accidentally produced, such as being caught in a fire, being bitten by a dog or other animal, frightened by a severe storm, and so forth. Such fears are not to be confused with those the child uses in order to keep parents busy with him. Parents should show understanding and reassure the child that no harm will come to him/her and that the parents will attend to the wound or take the child to a doctor. They should explain to the child how storms develop and what lightning and thunder means. They should give the child important instructions about where to stand and what to do during a storm. They should teach the child to quickly find the telephone numbers of the fire department, emergency aid, and so forth. These fears will soon leave the child if the parents don't dwell on them and if they don't show great anxieties.

Parents should be discouraged from keeping a light burning at night. Darkness is a natural part of the twenty-four hour day. Children must learn to accept darkness as natural and not to fear it. As a rule, children learn more quickly to accept the dark if exposed to it in early infancy.

LEAVING CHILDREN WITH A BABY-SITTER

Some parents never leave their child in care of another person with the exception, perhaps, of a grandmother who is a familiar person to the child. These parents never consider leaving the child with a baby-sitter—a stranger. It is usually not so much the child's fear as fear on the part of the parents who are constantly anticipating danger or who want to shield the child from any and all possible distress. Such parents contribute to the child's fear of people as well as to the child's demands that the parents should always be available to them. This kind of demand may continue until the child is much older and able to remain home without any supervision.

An example:

> Maxine was left with a baby-sitter for the first time when she was nine years old. She cried and carried on, but the parents had to go out that evening. Maxine made such a scene, threatened to do all sorts of damage, that the parents could not enjoy the time away from home. They called the house every half hour to reassure themselves that the girl was unhurt and hopefully calm. But the child had such terrible tantrums and tried to use physical violence on her baby-sitter, that the parents felt that they had to come home.

The previous incident is what brought the parents to the counselor. They took Maxine's tyrannical behavior as natural for a young child, as something she would out-grow in time. They now realized that her behavior, not only during the time they were away, but in general, left much to be desired. The counselor had to help the parents to "let go" of the girl; to provide opportunities for her to depend on herself, to encourage her toward independence, and not to allow her to tyrannize them. It was very difficult for these parents to follow through on the counselor's suggestions because Maxine was such a willful and strong child. She did not give in easily but carried on her tyrannical behavior for weeks. It is really to the credit of these parents that they held out in spite of tremendous difficulties. But eventually Maxine began to do more and more things for herself. She was now left with baby-sitters once or twice a week, and no amount of screaming or hitting did her any good. Today, two years later, the parents have few problems with their daughter. Maxine herself is now a baby-sitter for a neighbor, warning the parents of the baby not to pay attention when the baby cries but to leave the house. Quite a change from two years ago.

DEALING WITH PROVOCATIONS

Children often provoke a parent to a point where the parent loses all control, punishes the child severely, and then feels guilty for having gone too far with the anger. What happens in such cases is that the parent tries to bribe the child to forgive and to forget the incident. The following case will illustrate this:

Mother: *There are times when Butch makes me so angry that I literally see red. I could kill him at such a time.*

Counselor: *When did he last provoke you like this?*

Mother: *The other day when he cut himself a big piece of cake right after I had explicitly told him that this cake was for dessert when we were having company. I had just told him that he could have a piece of a cake that was already cut, but he went straight to the cake he was not supposed to have.*

Counselor: *What did you do?*

Mother: *I shouldn't have done what I did, but I just couldn't help myself. I was so furious that I shook.*

Counselor: *What did you do?*

Mother: *I was holding a soup-ladle in my hand, and I just hit him with it, and I hit and hit until I caught myself.*

Counselor: *And then what happened?*

Mother: *I felt terrible. I could have killed him the way I was hitting.*

Counselor: *What did you do now?*

Mother: *I started crying and I put my arms around him and told him that I love him and that I could not help what I did because he made me so angry.*

Counselor: *And then?*

Mother: *I offered him another piece of cake. Since it was cut already, it didn't matter any more.*

Counselor: *You mean you gave him a piece of the cake that you wanted to reserve for the company?*

Mother: *That's right.*

Counselor: *How did you feel?*

Mother: *I felt much better when he ate the cake, and he said that it didn't hurt any more.*

Comments: This mother is reinforcing her son's behavior, namely to manipulate the situation so that in the end, mother will feel guilty, and then she will let him have his way. Mostly, the child knows very well what he is doing and why. This is confirmed when the counselor talked to Butch.

Counselor: *Butch, how do you and mother get along?*

Butch: *Fine.*

Counselor: *Do you ever make her angry?*

Butch: *Sometimes.*

Counselor: *How do you make her angry?*

Butch: *I just do. I do something that she doesn't like and then she gets angry.*

Counselor: *Can you remember the incident with the cake that mother made for the company that was coming to your house. What happened?*

Butch: *Well, she said that I couldn't have any cake, but I went and cut myself a piece.*

Counselor: *What did you think would happen when you cut yourself a piece of the cake you were told to leave alone?*

Butch: *I knew that she would get very mad.*

Counselor: *Did you think she was going to punish you?*

Butch: *Ahem. I knew that she would punish me.*

Counselor: *You mean that you do not care if you will be punished?*

Butch: *You see, when she gets very mad and punishes me real hard, then she feels bad and then she lets me have what I want.*

Counselor: *Is this the reason you provoked her? Did you want her to get so mad that she would punish you because then she would make it up to you? Did I understand you right?*

Butch: *That's right.*

Counselor: *Does this happen often?*

Butch: *Not too often, only when I want something real bad. Then I behave real nasty, and then she gets real mad, and then I get what I want.*

Comments: From Butch's answers, we can see how skillfully he handles his mother; he knows exactly what to do in order to get his way. It is mother who does not know what to do with Butch, as she is no match for him. Mother must be helped not to react on first impulses but apply a natural consequence without giving the child the power to upset her. But, should she punish, not to feel guilty, and not to make up to the child for her guilt feelings. She should be reassured that she may now and then let her feelings get the better of her, and then she does the wrong thing. However, she should be advised to first reflect and learn from her mistakes. It will then happen less frequently. Under no circumstances should the counselor add to mother's guilty feelings. She needs reassurance and encouragement.

PROBLEMS IN COMMUNICATION

Parents often complain that they cannot communicate with their children. The children often show no interest or may even indicate resentment when the parents converse with them. As one father put it:

"Every time I try to talk to my daughter, she makes faces showing impatience. She almost makes me feel guilty for taking her

time; she waits for the first chance to get away. Gradually, I stopped talking to her except occasionally when it concerns something very important. I don't seem to know how to talk to her."

Children often complain that what the parents refer to as "talking" usually consists of lectures, scoldings, shaming and threats. This is not communication and it usually makes children feel rebellious. One adolescent summarized his feelings when he said:

"It is not that I feel that my parents don't love me or that they don't want the best for me; it is just the way they go about it. They show no respect for my ability to make an intelligent decision or to assume ability for my decisions. My father thinks that when he tells me that my thinking is immature and that I don't understand what I am doing, that I will be able to decide for myself when I am older but, that in the meantime, he feels responsible for my decisions and actions. He says that I will appreciate it some day and thank him for it. What he does not understand is that it only turns me off and that I then become more stubborn to do things my way. I get so provoked that I deliberately do things to aggravate him."

It is a fact that most parents are inclined to give lectures, that they berate a point, hoping that the child will respond the way that the parent wishes. This too, only annoys the youngster who then stops listening.

Parents often inquire how things went in school, did the child finish his/her work, and does he/she have any homework, and so forth. The following conversation took place between a mother and her ten year old son when the counselor role played the incident.

Mother: *Oh, you're home already. I didn't expect you for another five minutes. What happened?* (Without waiting for a reply) *Wash your hands, and come to the table.*

Henrik: *I ain't hungry, Mom.*

Mother: *Never mind. You'll get hungry as you eat. Anyway, I want you to eat now so that you can go to your homework. The sooner you start, the sooner you'll be done.*

Henrik: *I told you that I ain't hungry. Stop nagging me. I know what to do.*

Mother: *Yeah, you know like you always know and wait till the last moment. Now you do as I say. Eat your lunch and finish your homework, and then you may go out to play. I don't want to hear any further arguments from you.*

Henrik: *Can't I just have a few minutes to myself? Gosh, Mom, you're really mean, and I don't like you when you order me around like that.*

Mother: *I did not ask you to like me, just to obey me. I still know what is best for you, and as I said, I want no further arguments from you. I hope I made my point clear.*

It was obvious that Henrik resented his mother, hated his homework, felt utterly hopeless, and may have retaliated in some way. Mostly children do not do their homework under such circumstances, or if they do it, they do a careless job. There was no communication between these two people; no give and take, no enjoyment in their conversation. This mother took no time to talk to her child about his day away from home, his experiences and feelings, what she did that morning, etc. She might have suggested lunch, but accepted Henrik's decision not to eat. She may have asked him if he preferred getting his homework out of the way, or if he'd rather relax for a while and then do the homework. She might have shown understanding for his disdain for his homework and suggested that he go out and play for a while before he goes back to school work.

Since parents are often not aware of what they do that turns children off, they need some guidance from the counselor. Parents sincerely believe that criticism or shaming the child will spur the child on to do better. But we know that criticism only puts people on the defensive. Few people listen to any possible validity of the criticism; all they do is defend themselves. Parents often use the same methods of criticism, punishment, shaming, nagging, and so forth, for many years with their children; yet they seem completely unaware of this fact and continue making the same mistakes. One father, who beat his nine year old son almost daily, could not accept the counselor's suggestion that he stop this practice and change the relationship with his son. The father said: "I do not believe that a child will change unless you punish him for the things he does wrong. You have to beat the fear of God into him to understand that he must obey or that he will be punished." It took the counselor some time to help this parent realize that nine years of daily punishment had not changed his son. On the contrary, he became worse, using this way of getting even with his cruel father. When the counselor invited both father and son to say one good thing about the other, neither could come up with an answer. They both expected the worst of the other, and both lived up to this expectation. What suggestions might a counselor give to this father? The counselor would concentrate on a change in their relationship—one in which they would start trusting each other. The counselor might make the following suggestions to the father as a variety of ways in which the relationship with the boy could be changed:

—Stop using corporal punishment.

—Select those transgressions that are of a minor nature and postpone their solution.

—Allow the son to make as many decisions for himself as possible.

—Take the boy for a walk, a ride, for lunch, etc., where they can converse with each other and perhaps develop some mutual interests.

—Allow the son to help the father with various tasks.

—Play ball or any other game with the son. Take him to a sports event or other event that they would both enjoy.

—Discuss with the son the importance of schooling, but not in a personal, critical way.

—Plan a weekly, pleasant time together without any other member of the family.

The counselor should take care in instructing parents that their first duty in improving communications with their children is to create or provide many opportunities where the parents and the children enjoy each other. In creating these opportunities the parent must be respectful of the child's comments, learn to listen, and refrain from negative comments. Such an attitude on the part of the parent will encourage the child to open discussion. The parent cannot expect such an approach to be effective every time, but it will open the doors to improved communication if the parent is persistent.

BIBLIOGRAPHY

Adler, A. (1963). *The problem child.* New York, NY: Capricorn Books, G. P. Putman's Sons.

Allred, G. H. (1968). *Mission for mother's—Guiding the child.* Provo, UT: Bookcraft Publishers.

Ansbacher, H. & Ansbacher, R. (1964). *The individual psychology of Alfred Adler.* New York: Harper & Row.

Bradway, W. (1982). *The influence of TV violence on children's behavior.* Unpublished Master's Thesis. The Adler-Dreikures Institute of Human Relations, Bowie State College, Maryland.

Comstock, G. (1978). "Television and human behavior." Columbia Press.

Corsini, R., & Painter, J. (1975). *The practical parent.* New York: Harper & Row Publishers.

Dreikurs, R., & Grey, L. (1970). *A parent's guide to child discipline.* New York: Hawthorn Books.

Dreikurs, R., Grunwald, B., & Pepper, F. (1982). *Maintaining sanity in the classroom, 2nd Edition.* New York: Harper & Row, Publishers.

Dreikurs, R. & Soltz, V. (1964). *Children: The challenge.* New York: Hawthorn Books.

Mozdzierz, G., Macchitelli, F., & Lisiccki, J. (November 1976). The paradox in psychotherapy. *Journal of Individual Psychology, 32,* (2), 169-183.

Sonstegard, M., & Sonnenshein, M. F. (1977). *The allowance: Wages for wee folk.* Chicago, IL: Adam Press.

CHAPTER

COUNSELING
ADOLESCENTS

The adolescent's problems become intensified in our highly in-
dustrialized, complex society which has systematically excluded children
from learning many skills, both technical and human, that are needed in
order for them to function effectively as adults. Families generally rely
on authoritarian methods of child-rearing and most educational settings
also are authoritarian. Children and youth have become almost totally
excluded from the workplace. They find few opportunities to contribute
to decision making whereby responsibilities may be learned. Thus,

children are ill equipped to participate in a democratic society as they strive for maturity and independence. Rebellion is the order of the day and parents, teachers, counselors, and other adults often are bankrupt in techniques for dealing effectively with this rebellion. Bankruptcy of adults in working with alienated youth is matched by tremendous discouragement among youth as they strive to find a place in today's world.

HELPING PARENTS UNDERSTAND TEENAGERS

The teenage years are commonly approached with fear and trembling by most parents. It is as though an alarm bell would start ringing and warn parents to be on the alert for trouble with their adolescent children. Parents now increase rather than decrease their vigilance and their demands. They demand to know where the youngster is going and with whom, where the parents can reach the youth, and when he/she must be home. This usually increases the youngster's rebellion and the frustration of the parents.

With few exceptions, nobody listens to young people. They generally have no outlet for rebellion except for their dress, their language, their behavior, and their failures. They generally feel that they have no influence on their own lives—in the family, school, or community. They don't trust adults, because they don't think that they will be understood and certainly don't think that adults can help them. Youth see little wrong with their behavior and see only what adults are doing to them. Many youth believe that they have the right to do as they please. This belief is a great factor when they come for counseling. They come because they are "made" to come and not because they believe that "the shrink" can help them. Youth often resent counseling because they regard this as interference with their rights. They also fear that the counselor will want to change them and they resist such expectations.

Parents are not aware of how they systematically discourage children by instilling in them the idea that they are not good enough as they are. Gradually, children withdraw from parents. Many young people feel mistreated and misunderstood and that there is nothing they can expect from their parents. They see no hope for an improvement in the relationship. To avoid unpleasant confrontation by parents, many begin to lie. Often people refer to this state as the "breakdown of communication." Dreikurs (1982), in discussing this belief, felt that this was an unfortunate term. He saw no breaking down in the communication between parents and children because each communicated to the other what he/she wanted and what he/she intended to do. For instance, if parents and children would agree, there could be no fight, neither physical nor verbal. But, if both agree to fight, one can say in a sense, that there is cooperation or there would be no fight. People always communicate their feelings to others and it is then up to the other to respond to them or not. The moment the other person responds, he/she establishes communication. When a discussion ends because one party claims, "I can't communicate with him," it really means, "I must have my way and others must agree with me, or I don't play the game."

The counselor needs to help both parents and children understand this principle, how each contributes to the bad situation, and how each of them reacts to the other in a way that adds fuel to the fire. It is unfortunate that counselors often side with adolescents without investigating their manner of communication with parents or teachers. Counselors need to help youth understand that in defiance they usually try to defeat parents in order to feel superior and powerful. Parents often feel that they are being left out in the process of counseling, that their feelings are being ignored, and that they are being victimized, especially when the counselor does not get them involved in the counseling of their adolescent children.

In the majority of cases involving an adolescent who has problems, at least one parent is using authoritarian methods to subdue and control the youngster. We also have found that if parents previously have pampered the youth, they now become alarmed at their lack of influence and decide to "clamp down before it is too late." If parents used a little power before, they now attempt to increase the power. It is likely that a power struggle ensues in either case.

For adults to give up their values and beliefs is not easy. The counselor needs to help them investigate thoroughly what it is that the adolescent does that threatens parents. Too often, parents are overly concerned with being in command and having control. They often are afraid to give up this role because of lack of faith that the teenager will act responsibly.

Many adolescents escape their families by substituting their peer group and accepting the values of this group, believing that they are now free and have their own opinions about life and about values. Allied with the peer group, youngsters feel more powerful and are better fortified to resist their masters. They do not realize that they now have as little freedom as before. All they did was to change the frame of reference because they now follow the demands of the peer group blindly and unquestioningly rather than the demands of the parents. The counselor should confront them with this fact and help them realize that what they now believe and do is not freedom but a dependency on the reference group. This may become an obstacle to their development and to their happiness. At the same time, the counselor must help youth understand that adults alone cannot be held responsible for what ails youth. Teenagers must realize the roles that they play in the predicament and that they must assume some responsibility for themselves. It is within their power to change many things they dislike. However, these changes will not happen through rebellious behavior. The counselor would need to help youth realize how superior they feel when they defeat adults. One may give them credit for how skillful they are in doing this defeat. Teenagers often claim that adults force them to do this or that, but is this really true? Can anyone force them to do what they don't want to do? Can a parent or a teacher force them to listen in class, to study, to come home on time, or to talk to their parents respectfully? The counselor should lead youth to understand such situations through skillful dialogue. At the same time, parents must be helped to talk to their children with respect and with confidence. Parents don't realize how often they demand respect from their children without giving respect in return; how they talk down to children and youth and how they humiliate them. The following example clearly illustrates this point.

Father to a seventeen year old son.

Father: *Don't you think that you should earn some money? You are old enough. At your age, I already helped support the family. I was already a man, responsible and caring for others, while you are selfish, caring only for yourself. All you want is to have a good time and you don't care at whose expense.*

Son: *Lay off, will you?*

Father: *Don't you tell me what to do. As your father and your supporter I still have some rights. If you don't like it, you can move out.*

Son: *We have gone over this dozens of times and I am sick and tired of hearing your threats. I will move out in time, and then you will never have to bother with me again. Just leave me alone for one more year.*

Father: *Like hell I will. You think I'll stand by and let you bum around for another year, then you are mistaken. You find a job soon or I will cut you off from your allowance. You are forgetting that I am still the boss in my own house. I won't stand for having a bum for a son.*

Son: *I am not forgetting. You don't let me forget. But if you are going to stop giving me my allowance, you will be sorry. I will find a way to exist without your G.D. allowance.*

This dialogue is typical for many discussions between parents and their teenage children. The counselor must help such family members understand what each does to the other; how each provokes the other to talk and feel as these two people felt and talked. When we role played this situation, asking each to consider how he might handle the problem more constructively, showing understanding and being encouraging, the following resulted. (We role-played the same situation several times.)

Father: *I need your help in a certain matter. I am short of money and it is a hardship for me to give you the allowance I now give you. Maybe you have a suggestion.*

Son: *Not offhand. Maybe you could give me less money. I would have to figure out how much I need.*

Father: *Do you think you could get some part-time work. I don't mean for you to spend much time on the job and neglect school. I know jobs are hard to get, but maybe you know of something.*

Son: *I am not sure, but I will look around. I hope I can find something. In the meantime, I will manage with less money. Don't worry, Dad.*

Father: *Thanks, son. It was not easy for me to talk to you about it. I was afraid you might misunderstand, but I see I had nothing to fear. Thanks a lot.*

When the two came for the following session, they reported that they had actually worked out the problem the way it was discussed in the counselor's office, and that the son had found a part-time job.

Parents should encourage responsibility. Most teenagers are fully capable in thinking through such problems as the hour for coming home in the evening, sharing the use of the family car, helping with household chores, and many other responsibilities. They also should be allowed to bring home their friends without having to ask permission of their parents. This situation is not to imply that they may invite friends for a meal without checking it out with mother first. Unfortunately, parents often get involved in their adolescents' choice of friends and often make demands that the teenager discontinue the relationship. The more pressure put on the youngster, the more the latter is determined to defeat the parents. Example:

> Hilda who is a junior in high school invited her boyfriend, Hank, to join her Sunday morning when the family goes to church.

> Mother: I am sorry, Hank, but you can't come along with us. You should go with your own family.

> Hilda: But why? I asked him to come.

> Mother: You are only 16 and at your age a girl goes with her family. Now, Hank, you run along. Hilda will see you soon.

> Hilda: I am not going with you. You can go without me. I won't let you treat my friends this way, especially since I have invited him.

This incident upset the entire family. Nobody enjoyed the Sunday spirit which normally was a pleasant one. It took the counselor several sessions to win back Hilda's acceptance of joining the family on Sunday when they went to church. Mother finally agreed that Hilda had a right to go to church with whomever she pleased—with or without the family.

Once rules are established, parents should be firm and consistent in carrying them through. Parents often are afraid what their adolescent child might do if they refuse the youngster's request and therefore give in to him/her although this breaks their agreement. Once a rule has been established, parents must enforce it even at the risk that their child may suffer unpleasant consequences. Only in situations where danger is involved should parents change an agreed upon rule without consent of the youngster. Inconsistent parents send out confusing messages to their children and the children take advantage of this inconsistency or get even with their parents who do not go along with their demands. An example:

> *A sixteen year old boy demanded that his father let him have the car because he had promised his girlfriend to take her to a party. The parents needed the car themselves, but seeing their son's agitation, let him have it for the evening although they had agreed that the boy might have the car only on certain days. This was not the agreed upon day.*

> *The next evening, the boy wanted the car again, but the parents refused to let him have it as they saw no real need for it. The boy raved and threatened but the parents refused to be intimidated. The son left the house and was supposed to take a city bus. After a few hours the police called. They had caught the boy in a stolen car. When the father came to the police station, his son told him, "I told you that I might do this if you don't let me have the car. So don't say that I did not warn you."*

Because of the inconsistency of the parents, this youngster felt justified in taking what the parents refused to give him. This example is one that many counselors encounter when parents submit to children because of fear of the child's retaliation if he/she does not have his/her way.

Some parents at times must summon up their courage and let the defiant youngster take consequences which are of an extreme nature. They may let the police and the court handle the situation such as placing a child in a foster home or with other relatives. Such action will be discussed in detail in the section on Juvenile Delinquency.

A COUNSELING SESSION WITH A TEENAGER

The following case illustrates a counseling session with an adolescent who came without his family. (Transcribed from a tape of a counseling session by Dr. Rudolf Dreikurs, November 1969, with permission of Mrs. Dreikurs.)

Family constellation:

Alan, 17, senior is the client. Poor student, has a police record.

Nellie, six years older, is in college, a good student, motherly and bossy.

Dorothea, two years older, finished high school, and works in an office. Does not get along with mother but is close to father.

Phillip is four years younger, good in school, gets along with the girls, but is not close to anyone. He and Alan argue and fight.

Grandmother lives with the family. Alan is her favorite child.

Counselor: *How do you feel about being here, Alan?*

Alan: *I don't care.*

Counselor: *Good. At least you are not against it. How can I help you?*

Alan: *I don't know.*

Counselor: *What problems do you have?*

Alan: *Mainly with my parents.*

Counselor: *What about your parents?*

Alan: (Laughs). *What about them? You mean what is wrong with them? Everything.*

Counselor: *Give me an example of what is wrong with them.*

Alan: *You want an example. All right, here is an example. Like when I know that I am right and they try to tell me that I am wrong when I know that I am right.*

Counselor: *Give me an example.*

Alan: *I thought I did.*

Counselor: *You gave me no example which tells me how they are wrong or not. Can you tell me an incident with your parents which was a problem to you?*

Alan: *Like the other day. I needed five bucks, so I asked my dad and he tells me "Go jump in the lake." Just like that.*

Counselor: *So what did you do?*

Alan: *Nothing. What could I do?*

Counselor: *What did you do, Alan? Did you just walk away without saying anything?*

Alan: *I told him that some day he will come begging to me, and that I will remember how he treated me.*

Counselor: *How did you get even with him? Did you punish him? Did you do anything to upset him besides telling him what you just told me?*

Alan: *I stopped talking to him. I just did not answer him when he talked to me.*

Counselor: *So now you are angry at each other, and each tries to punish the other.*

Alan: *I guess so.*

Counselor: *Would you like to have a better relationship with your father?*

Alan: *I really don't know. Maybe not.*

Counselor: *Alan, can you recall when you first started having difficulties with your father? How old were you?*

Alan: *Oh, he and I have never gotten along as far as I can remember. We were never, what you would call father and son. I mean closeness between a father and a son. I never felt that we understood each other.*

Counselor: *How about your mother? Do you get along with her?*

Alan: *Oh, we get along fine when she doesn't bug me.*

Counselor: *How was it with her when you were a kid. Did you get along with her then?*

Alan: *We got along fine. I always felt close to her. I still do, but she wants me to be the same as I was then, like she doesn't realize that I am seventeen. But we get along all right.*

Counselor: *When you were a kid, and when you and father had arguments, how did mother react to it? Can you recall?*

Alan: *Yes, she was upset. She cried sometimes. She would try to make me feel less angry and to understand that father worked hard, that he loved me, like mothers always do.*

Counselor: *Did she ever try to protect you from father?*

Alan: *Oh, sure. She used to stand in front of me when he tried to hit me, and sometimes she would get it. But that's a long time ago and I don't see the purpose of talking about it now.*

Counselor: *I hope that you will see the purpose as we continue this conversation. Tell me, did mother protect the other children from father the way she protected you?*

Alan: *She didn't have to.*

Counselor: *Could you explain this. Why didn't she have to?*

Alan: *Well, for one, my two sisters are older and they are girls. I don't know, I think father didn't think that girls should be hit, or something. My brother was younger. I don't know why, but it seems that he always had it in against me. My father, I mean.*

Counselor: *When he punished you, did you tell mother? Did you go to her for protection?*

Alan: *I told her, but I did not go to her for protection.*

Counselor: *Was there anyone else in the family who felt sorry for you?*

Alan: *My grandmother, sometimes.*

Counselor: *How did mother get along with your two sisters?*

Alan: *Well, she and Nellie got along better, but she and Dorothea never hit it off. I don't know why but they were always arguing. They still do.*

Counselor: *Would you say that you are mother's favorite child?*

Alan: *I don't know but I guess so.*

Counselor: *Are you possibly also grandmother's favorite child?*

Alan: *I think so.*

Counselor: *Could you tell me, I mean, would you tell me how your parents get along?*

Alan: *They fight a lot. It's not easy to get along with my Dad, let me tell you that.*

Counselor: *How do you get along with Dorothea?*

Alan: *Dorothea? I have nothing to do with her.*

Counselor: *Let me guess. I would imagine that she and father get along quite well.*

Alan: *I think so, but I thought that you would want to talk to me about my problems.*

Counselor: *I am, Alan. I would like for you to put yourself into your father's skin for a moment. Could you do that? How do you think he must feel?*

Alan: *I don't know, and frankly I don't care.*

Counselor: *Here you are, mother's favorite, always her coming to your protection; conveying to your father that he is wrong, and that you count for more than he does. I am only guessing, but could it be that father feels that he plays second fiddle in the family?*

Alan: *Well, if it's so, that is his problem.*

Counselor: *Yes, but if this matters to you, you could help him. You also could help improve the relationship between Dorothea and mother. Do you know why your father and Dorothea are close?*

Alan: *I don't know. I have never given it any thought.*

Counselor: *Right. It seems to me that they had to unite against their common enemy. Do you know what I mean? Try to understand the situation.*

Alan: *You mean that Mom and I are the common enemy.*

Counselor: *What do you think?*

Alan: *I really don't know.*

Counselor: *Could it be that you don't want to know? That you would rather not know?*

Alan: *How does all this help me?*

Counselor: *It can only help you if you would be concerned about the bad relationship you have with father. If you would be willing to do something about it, something constructive instead of wanting to get even with him. If can understand how you must feel when father tells you, "Go jump into the lake." I don't defend him for it. All I am saying is that you could change his relationship. But you tell me that you don't want to. Do you know why?*

Alan: *Because it's too late now.*

Counselor: *I am not so sure of it. Could it be that you don't want to change it because you enjoy defeating your father, hurting him, and you enjoy it when mother makes him feel that he is no good?*

Alan: (Long silence). *I can't deny that I rather like it.*

Counselor: *Am I right?*

Alan: *Yes, I like to see him squirm. After all he does to me, why not?*

Counselor: *If you enjoy it then you have no problem. You are then getting what you want. But I am not so sure that you truly believe deep in your heart that you don't want a better relationship with your father. You want to hurt him, yes. You both want to hurt each other. You see, Alan, it's very hard for a husband to feel that he doesn't count, that his son means more to his wife. Perhaps if you understood this, you would be first to change the relationship.*

Alan: *Why should I be first? Why not he?*

Counselor: *Because it is you who came to me and not he. In any case, in a bad relationship each one must watch what he is doing and not what the other is doing. We can only change ourselves, Alan. As you change toward father, he is bound to change toward you.*

Alan: *What do you want me to do?*

Counselor: *I am not telling you what to do. I may suggest what you could do, and the rest is up to you.*

Alan: *What?*

Counselor: *You might start with looking friendlier at him, with greeting him, with talking to him and not giving him nasty answers, or with thanking him for something he does for you. I am sure you could find opportunities to help him feel better about you. By the way, did anything happen the day or the previous day before you asked father for money?*

Alan: *Yes, something did happen.*

Counselor: *Would you mind telling me what happened?*

Alan: *Well, I guess I did a foolish thing, but this does not mean that I should be insulted. I made a mistake and I admitted it.*

Counselor: *You are not telling me what you did.*

Alan: *I needed some money and I took it from a box where Dad saves silver dollars. I did not use the money and I was going to put it back. I told Dad that I was going to put it back.*

Counselor: *Is this the only time when you took money without asking him or your mother?*

Alan: *No.*

Counselor: *Are there other things you did that provoked him?*

Alan: *You know how it is with boys my age. We do things like everybody does things like that.*

Counselor: *You are avoiding answering my question.*

Alan: *Because you wouldn't understand.*

Counselor: *I don't think that this is the reason. Could it be that you are embarrassed to tell me.*

Alan: *Yes and no.*

Counselor: *You see, Alan, I don't need to know what you did. This is not the issue. The issue is that you seem to resent when others disapprove of what you do, no matter what it is you do. Could it be that you feel, "Nobody is going to tell me what to do?"*

Alan: (No answer.)

Counselor: *As long as you depend so much on always having your way and on punishing those who try to stop you, you are bound to run into problems. This has a lot to do with the way you were brought up. You have a very special position in your family constellation. You are the firstborn boy, and the family fussed a lot over you at first. But you then had to share your position with a brother who came right on your heels. Maybe mother felt sorry for you and protected you. This is how children develop the feeling that they must win in every situation otherwise, they think that they don't count for much. I hope you can now understand why this conversation was necessary if I was going to help you.*

Alan: *I do understand it better, yes.*

Counselor: *I think we will finish with this. Think about what we discussed here. It may help you more than you can realize at this moment. Good bye, Alan. I enjoyed talking with you.*

Alan: *Good bye. I enjoyed it also.*

Comments: In this interview, we can see how Dreikurs focused not only on revealing the goal to Alan, but on helping him understand how he happened to think and act as he did. It should be mentioned that the relationship between Alan and his father improved, and with this improvement, the general atmosphere in the home improved also.

COUNSELING THE DEFIANT ADOLESCENT

Counseling the adolescent is probably the most difficult task for most counselors. Most adolescents who need counseling fight all authority especially the "shrink" as most children call people who are in the psychologically helping professions. Defeating the counselor becomes a badge of honor. This is partly reinforced when the youngster is forced by school authorities, parents, or courts to go into counseling. Such a youngster is then determined to show that "nobody is going to make me," and either refuses to answer the counselor's questions, participate in the discussion, or behaves in a most provocative manner so that the counselor may refuse to work with him/her.

With such adolescents it is often helpful to shock them, to give them the kind of jolt that they are unprepared to meet with a rebuff, a sudden confrontation that helps them realize that the counselor understands exactly the game that is being played. For instance, an adolescent boy who refused to answer the counselor's question was startled when the counselor asked: "Could it be that you came here to make a fool out of me, to show me that you are much smarter and that I, the so called 'expert' can do nothing with you?" This took the boy off guard; he did not know what to say, but his facial expression expressed recognition of the truth in the counselor's statement. The boy said, "Maybe you're right. Still, you have no right to accuse me. Who do you think you are, anyway?'' At least, the shock brought out the boy's anger and it was followed with a conversation. The silence was broken. The effective counselor will then explore the youngster's anger and proceed from there.

The following example is a good illustration of such a case and how the counselor, in the end, won the boy over and effective counseling was then possible.

Counselor: *Did you come voluntarily or were you asked or perhaps forced to come to see me?*

Gilbert: *Nobody forces me.*

Counselor: *Good, then you came because you wanted to come. Now why did you come to see me?*

Gilbert: *I have a problem. I don't like to work.*

Counselor: *You mean you don't want to take a job?*

Gilbert: *I don't like any work.*

Counselor: *Does that include school? Are you still in school?*

Gilbert: *I dropped out two years ago; I never liked school.*

Counselor: *What have you done since then?*

Gilbert: *Oh, lots of things. None which my parents approved of.*

Counselor: *Have you ever been counseled before?*

Gilbert: *I have seen six shrinks in my life.*

Counselor: *That's quite a record. I bet there aren't many youngsters who can beat that. Now, why did you come to see me?*

Gilbert: *I told you, I have a problem; I don't like to work.*

Counselor: *So you told me, but may I tell you my idea of why you came to see me? Could it be that you came to show me that*

I, too, can't help you and you can add another shrink to your collection?

Gilbert: *I didn't say it, you said it.*

Counselor: *Right. You see, Gilbert, I have the impression that it is very important to you to defeat authority and that this makes you feel superior. Is it possible that this is very important to you?*

Gilbert: *What thing?*

Counselor: *Come now, you know very well what I am referring to. But you are right, I doubt if I will be able to help you. Tell me, my dear boy, how many shrinks do you intend to see before you will feel the greatest. After all, you can't see them all.*

Gilbert: (Laughing). *It's up to you to prove to me that you are the superior one. After all you are the expert.*

Counselor: *No, this is not a question of who is the expert in terms of being of help, but who can outwit whom, and I have neither the interest nor the time to get into a power struggle with you. I am not here to prove anything. If you feel that you need help and if you were to accept me as your equal, as another human being who has the experience and may be able to help you understand why you always want to defeat authority, why you refuse to do any work, then we could work together. By the way, how did you get along with your teachers?*

Gilbert: *I don't think that you need for me to answer this. I didn't.*

Counselor: *And your parents?*

Gilbert: *I never got along with my father. I am better with Mom, although we fight a lot.*

Counselor: *Is there any adult with whom you get along, one you trust?*

Gilbert: *Can't say off hand.*

Counselor: *Well, then good luck to you. It was nice to talk to you.*

Gilbert: *Wait a minute. I never said that I don't want you to help me.*

Counselor: *I can't help you, Gilbert as long....*

Gilbert: *Call me, Gib. Everyone calls me Gib.*

Counselor: *All right, Gib. I can only try to help you if the two of us treat each other with respect and trust. I can't help you if it becomes important to you to outsmart me. Not that you couldn't outsmart me, but I can't help you then. Do you follow what I am trying to say?*

Gilbert: *I do.*

Counselor: *So, what will it be?*

Gilbert: *What do you want me to do?*

Counselor: *It's what you want to do, Gib. If you decide to discuss what's really bothering you and give me honest answers to some of the questions I must ask in order to understand how you developed and what influenced you to set such high goals for yourself; when we can talk like two human beings who try to work through a problem, then I might be able to help you. But you must want this and you must, in the first place, want to change.*

Gilbert: *And if I do, what do I do?*

Counselor: *No "if," only really wanting to change will help you. You would then have to agree to come to a minimum of six sessions before you can decide if this is for you or not. But when you come you will have to work with me and not come here to fight me.*

Gilbert: *O.K. I agree.*

COUNSELING JUVENILE DELINQUENTS

The counselor has greater difficulties with children who have already become juvenile delinquents. Often they are referrals from juvenile authorities, a social agency, or the schools. More often than not the crisis will have a long history. However, the counselor is interested primarily in what can be done to alleviate current difficulties.

We suggest that all members of the family be present in the counseling session as other members may have brought about or influenced the present problem. With all members being present, it may show respect by the counselor. Counseling the family together may help to avoid the identified member's suspicion that the family brought him/her for counseling to keep him/her straight and that everyone is going to gang up on him/her. The counselor may consider alternative family sessions with private or individual counseling of the youngster in trouble, but the emphasis should be on family sessions. In other words, in planning a program for prevention or overcoming of alienation between family members, the counselor must concern himself/herself with the total situation. Therapeutic efforts are usually ineffective if they are directed only toward the adjustment of individual offenders. The following case illustrates the effectiveness of involving the entire family in a difficult case of delinquency. The counselor can create high involvement in change by including the whole family in assessing the problems and planning change. Example:

> The family came for counseling because of their concern of their 16 year old son, Kevin. Kevin had been caught drinking on school grounds for the second time. Under the influence of alcohol, he had broken into closed lockers, searching them for drugs. The school authorities summoned the police and Kevin was arrested.

> When talking to Kevin, he felt outraged at the school and at the police. He felt that what he did was just a prank; that he was arrested unjustly. The parents supported this belief. They too were so angry at the school that they sought legal advice from a lawyer. But, then Kevin was again caught in an intoxicated condition on the street, and when the parents had to bail him out of jail, they became frightened and decided (upon the advice of the court) to seek professional help. In talking to the parents, it

became evident that they considered their son's behavior as "typical for youngsters his age," something that the adolescent outgrows." In other words, this kind of behavior was, indirectly, expected of Kevin. One may consider the possibility that Kevin, sensing how the parents felt, lived up to their expectations. He felt that he had no problem; that "all authorities were mean and out to get me."

When we examined the problem further, and when we talked to the other siblings, Helen, 20, Mary 17, they complained that the parents always gave in to Kevin; that "he could always do whatever he wanted, and the parents never punished him for it." It was obvious that both girls resented this kind of treatment and the preference for their brother. Both girls were "good," law-abiding, cooperative, but hostile toward the parents and their brother. They made no secret of it, and often confronted their parents with this accusation. Mother felt that they exaggerated, while father supported the view that "boys will be boys, and let them sow their oats while they are young." Kevin often held his special position up to his sisters. Although the youngest of the children, he treated his sisters with an air of manly superiority; demanding their services; putting them down because of their sex, and sometimes even with physical violence. When the matter was discussed with the parents, they scolded Kevin, reminded him that "a gentleman treats ladies with respect and with concern," which only infuriated the girls the more. They did everything to undermine Kevin's status at home and his prestige. In fact, Kevin was convinced that one of his sisters snitched on him and called the police when he was drunk.

In such a situation, the counselor would have a very difficult time if he/she were to work only with Kevin. This is a family problem; a family issue. It was important to help the parents realize how they reinforced Kevin's attitude of "being entitled to have his way" by their acceptance of his delinquent behavior as "normal" adolescent experimentation. Next the counselor had to focus on the lack of closeness and concern for one another in the family. Parents also needed to be helped to realize how they harm Kevin by turning against the school and against all authorities who imposed any kind of consequences on their son.

The sisters had to be helped to realize how their own emotional reaction to Kevin's behavior only reinforced his feeling of *superiority over them. While they do not have to comply with his demands, they could learn how to ignore them in a manner which did not lead to a fight. They also were helped to understand their own feelings of inferiority because of their sex, and how this feeds into Kevin's attitude toward them and toward a general masculine superiority. Kevin was quite attentive when these matters were discussed. He was helped to understand that much of his bravado and daring behavior was due to his own feelings of inadequacy, and how he, perhaps subconsciously, tried to cover these feelings by his macho and provocative behavior. Last but not least, he was helped to understand that the parents, although meaning well, created an atmosphere in the home in which he could draw the conclusions that as a boy, he has greater value; that because of his sex, he is entitled to certain behavior, and that women are there to serve men.* (It was also obvious that the mother occupied a much inferior position to the husband. He led the discussion, seldom letting her answer questions, and now and then interrupted her in a rude manner.)

The counselor could only help the family by focusing on the entire family structure and how the behavior of one, directly or indirectly, influenced the behavior of the others. In other words, every member of the family had to make changes and to view his/her own behavior before one could help Kevin.

The counselor should explain that he/she is not interested in blame seeking. That he/she will focus on the current situation and not spend much time on what happened in the past. The counselor should find out what the parents are doing to exacerbate the difficulty and influence them to give up the ineffective methods they are using. This should follow with teaching the parents effective methods and encouraging communication with their youngster. Parents who use punishment as a corrective measure should be helped to realize its ineffectiveness in today's society.

Parents will accept this if the counselor helps them understand that their punishment, which they have used for years, has not been effective. If it had, their youngster would not now find himself in a predicament.

Parents of teenagers will often complain, after only two or three sessions, that corrective measures suggested do not work. The counselor should then explore in very specific detail how these were implemented and check with each member of the family on the accuracy of the information. It is also helpful to point out that difficult situations develop over a long period of time, and time and patience are needed to improve relationships in the family.

Counselors will frequently discover that in some families relationships are so hostile and revengeful that there is little hope of achieving other than an uneasy truce between adolescent and parents until such time when the youth can leave home and strike out on his/her own. This is often true of sixteen and seventeen year olds. Several sessions are usually sufficient to reveal the real level and intensity of such hostile attitudes. The counselor is advised to use bold methods in such cases. If a teenager is truly out of control, continually violates school or home structure, and comes and goes as he/she pleases, the counselor should recommend that parents seek help from juvenile authorities. In difficult cases when it is obvious that the family will not change without intensive, long range counseling, the counselor should recommend foster home placement. Although much less common than was once the practice, consideration can be given to placement of the recalcitrant youth with relatives. Placement in foster homes or with relatives has the added advantage of removing the youth from his/her immediate peer environment which often provides the setting for the more serious misbehavior. This is particularly true of youth who are deeply into drugs, alcohol, or sexual promiscuity. It is sometimes necessary to hospitalize youth who are addicted or habitually under the influence of drugs or alcohol in order to "dry them out." Counseling anyone effectively is not possible when they are under the influence of drugs and in an altered state of consciousness. The case study on Candy is a typical example of such a situation.

How one family solved their problem:

Candy, near 16 and in the ninth grade, came for counseling with her parents. Her academic achievement had been consistently low, but her main problem was the use of alcohol and drugs. She had managed to get high on beer, wine, pot, or pills almost every day since she was thirteen. Outwardly, she appeared cheerful and friendly, but her need to be accepted by her peers was so strong that she cooperated with their behavior and their demands. Candy was always neat and orderly. She took care of her household chores and adhered to most of the rules set by her parents except for coming home on time. The counselor soon realized that Candy's father was an extremely rigid man and overbearing. It became obvious that the father was not going to change. The counselor then suggested that Candy be hospitalized for a month in order to "dryout" and to effect a separation from her immediate home and neighborhood environment. The parents agreed to this suggestion. After hospitalization, Candy was placed in a group, residential home where she remained for six months. After that, she went to a foster home for another six months. Today, Candy lives at home, works and pays her own way, and is on friendly terms with her parents.

It is usually quite obvious that disruptive youth are not giving much thought to their future. Often parents have totally unrealistic ambitions for the future of their children. The counselor should focus on this aspect of counseling as an indirect approach to improving family situations. It is often possible to involve the entire family in planning and setting goals for the youth. This process is invaluable to the adolescent, but also has the indirect effect of diffusing the level of hostility among family members.

Another bold approach in working with families, when the level of hostility is extremely high, is that of temporary separation of most family members. An illustration:

A family of eight came for counseling. Mom, Dad, and five children from ten to seventeen and a niece, also seventeen. The father, a 13 year old girl, and 10 year old boy were the only ones who got along at all. The mother previously had been under psychiatric care for three years and had been continuously advised to "express her hostility." She had done this faithfully and inadvertently had taught the other members of the family to do the same. After ten months of counseling by one of the authors the situation was little improved. Bold measures were recommended. Mother and the son, 8, went off to Maine to visit an aunt, the daughter, 17, went to one grandparents' home. The niece, 17, went to the other grandparents. The son, 15, went to camp all summer. Dad stayed home with the daughter, 13, who could cook, and his 10 year old son. This trio lived amicably for four weeks and then the other members of the family returned at intervals and were successfully incorporated into a more cooperative living arrangement. Modified versions of this approach can usually be worked out by counselors in varying family situations.

Bold approaches are often necessary, as they have a dramatic impact on families with respect to their realization of the seriousness of their situation. This often motivates them to make necessary changes. Such dramatic approaches pay off; the counselor should not be afraid to use them. We do not mean to imply that the counselor should use drastic measures with most adolescents. While it may be necessary in some cases, the counselor's major purpose must continue to help the alienated youth to examine his/her values, understand himself/herself and his/her behavior, and to find positive ways to relate to the community.

In addition to the usual family counseling sessions, the counselor should make every effort to incorporate adolescents into group counseling efforts. Teenagers are difficult to influence at best and peers are generally far more successful than counselors or parents on impacting attitudes and behaviors. One counselor reported a unique approach originating in a high school group counseling situation formed to discuss school attendance problems. The group, recognizing that Joseph was acting out his rebellion by cutting school frequently, convinced the principal that Joseph should be told that he could no longer attend that school. Joseph became highly incensed at the idea that an adult should dictate to him what to do when the principal told him that he was suspended. Joseph began to attend regularly to show that he controlled the situation and not the principal. Some readers may believe that many students would like to be told that they could no longer attend school. However, members of this counseling group understood their friend and unerringly chose an effective approach. The counselor should avail himself/herself of such assistance. However, we strongly advise the counselor to be cautious and to know the youngster well before making such a suggestion.

The importance and necessity of establishing and maintaining rapport is never so essential as with counseling adolescents. The counselor must continually be sensitive to the relationship with the adolescent and maintain rapport if he/she is to maintain credibility with difficult youth.

In working with difficult teenagers and their families, the counselor often may be tempted to depart from the basic theory and practice that has been successful in the past, but does not seem to be working now. However, we cannot over emphasize that it is most imperative to remain consistent when cases are difficult. The counselor may experiment with new and innovative techniques, but be certain that these are theoretically sound. Otherwise, the counseling effort will become inconsistent, ineffective, and the adolescent will again have succeeded in manipulating the adult world to his/her own advantage.

BIBLIOGRAPHY

Dreikurs, R., Grunwald, B., & Pepper, F. (1982). *Maintaining sanity in the classroom.* New York: Harper & Row, Publishers.

Ginott, H. (1969). *Between parents and teenagers.* Toronto, Ontario: Macmillan.

Gould, S. (1977). *Teenagers: The continuing challenge.* New York: Hawthorn Books.

Manaster, G. (1977). *Adolescent development and life task.* Allyn & Bacon.

Shulman, B. (1959). Group counseling for adolescents. In Dreikurs et al., Chapter X *Adlerian family counseling.* Eugene, OR: University of Oregon Press.

Walton, F. (1980). *Winning teenagers over.* Columbia, SC: Adlerian Child Care Books.

SPECIAL FAMILIES

Counselors are finding that an increasing proportion of families coming for help can be classified into special categories, i.e., different from the usual father, mother, and children family unit. One in five children are living with a single parent. The divorce rate is well over forty percent and even greater for some ethnic groups. Live-in mates without benefit of marriage are common. All of these situations present some special problems for the family counselor as these special families seek assistance.

Basic principles of human relationships discussed in earlier chapters continue to apply in special families. However, some difficulties often occur in various special families not usually found in traditional family units. The purpose of this chapter is to present these special difficulties and suggest corrective measures that are congruent with the basic approach found throughout this book.

SINGLE PARENT

Under "single parents" is distinguished the widow and widower, the divorced and separated, the never married, and those parents who are separated from their spouses for an extended period of time. Others include women whose husbands may be in the military service, those whose jobs require that they live away from home, or parents whose spouses are in prison or in other types of institutions.

Divorced Parent

The authors do not support the belief that it is always better for children to live with only one parent with whom they have a good and loving relationship than with both parents who bicker and hurt each other; however, in many families the children are happier and develop more secure feelings when the parents separate. How the children accept the separation or divorce usually depends on the relationships the children have had with their parents and on how they view the parent's relationship. Older children especially suffer when parents quarrel and abuse each other and often actually wish that the parents would separate. Another important factor in how children perceive a divorce is the way they were prepared for such a possibility. Children should be reassured that divorce is not their fault, that it does not change the parents' love for them, and that they are not "losing" a parent but that they will not live with this parent in the same household as before. The less parents criticize and abuse each other verbally in front of the children, the easier it will be for the children to adjust to their situation.

The counselor will need to help the children understand that sometimes when married people have such great difficulties with each other, divorce is inevitable. However, this is no indictment of them as people or as parents, and their mother and father need their understanding and support more than ever. At the same time, the counselor must show empathy and understanding of the children's grief and often of their anger.

With all the love for the child, it may still happen that a parent harbors ambivalent feelings about the responsibilities involved in having full custody for it requires great sacrifices. A single parent may feel very much restricted in his/her freedom. The parent is not always free to go whenever he/she wishes or receive friends of the opposite sex without risking the children's suspicion or resentment.   Single parents may resent the children's demands on them. The counselor must put this situation in proper perspective and help the parent not to feel guilty for wanting to go out and enjoy a social life, and the children need to be helped to understand and respect this situation.

When parents and children discuss their emotional needs and when the counselor confronts children with their ability to help Mom or Dad, they usually show compassion and accept that the parent needs a social life and, either leave them home alone, or secure a sitter. Children will feel even more empathetic when the parent recognizes their needs and agrees to come home at a specified time or not to go out on certain days. The problem usually arises when the parent wants to date immediately after the separation or divorce. The children may not yet be ready for this change. We suggest, if possible, that the parent give the children a period of adjustment before discussing with them the need to date or the parent's involvement with another man or woman. Once the single-parent family has made the general adjustments, the single parent may discuss with the children a new social life on which the parent is about to embark.

Single-Parent Children
Often Mature Faster

In many single-parent households, children mature much faster and assume responsibilities at an earlier age than in two-parent homes. This is because of sheer necessity, especially if the parent is employed and away from home all day. Often these children assume the responsibilities of preparing the meals, cleaning the house, and shopping—groceries or other items. This increases the child's development of self-reliance. If the relationship between the single parent and the children is a good one—based on honest communication, consideration, and trust—the children will accept these responsibilities as matter of fact without resentment. Should the relationship be a poor one consisting of criticism, constant nagging, and demands by the parent, the children may resent these responsibilities. They may neglect school or find solace in the company of peers who are themselves rebels, and the parent may have great difficulties communicating with or influencing the children.

The counselor will need to help everyone recognize that the behavior of one ultimately affects other members of the family, that each must think in terms of, "What can I do to improve this situation?" The parent, especially, needs help in refraining from criticism and anger. Children, who are treated with consideration and with willingness to meet them half-way, are apt to be more cooperative and contribute to the welfare of all. All are in the same boat and nobody should have the right to take special privileges for himself/herself. So often, because the parent is working and away from home, the parent feels justified to be excluded from doing certain chores. They sometimes take certain privileges which are not granted to the children. Youngsters do not understand such double standards. They ask, "Why is mother allowed to throw her coat on a chair in the living room when she comes home from work, but I get scolded when I leave my coat or my books in the same place?" "Why must I always take out the garbage because mother hates doing this job? I hate it also." Or, "The dog belongs to all of us, why must I be the one to walk him every day? He/she is not my dog alone." Fathers, especially, if they have the custody of the children, may refuse to help with household chores (many refuse in any family, considering this kind of work not masculine). They claim that they work all day while the children do nothing. This is not true, of course, and is not fair to the children. Children do not play or go idle all day. They go to school which essentially is comparable to going to work. Parents should recognize this fact. If they do, their children are apt to be more cooperative if all members of the family join in doing the household chores.

Widowed Parent

After the death of a parent, especially if the parent died suddenly and there was no time for an emotional preparation, the family experiences several weeks or months of disorientation and severe emotional pain. These emotions may be mingled with fear of the future. There is little the counselor can do to alleviate this difficult adjustment period other than to reassure the family that this is a most natural reaction. However, the family does need to recognize that a readjustment is possible after they go through the initial period of mourning. Wolfelt (1983), a psychologist and experienced thanatologist, has identified several dimensions which are typical of what frequently is exhibited by children experiencing grief. For each dimension, he provided caregiving behaviors that can be utilized by counselors. His book, film strip, and audio cassette serve as excellent tools for working with families.

Children need to be reassured that there is no reason for them to fear that now they will be losing the other parent and be left alone. They also may need help to understand that initially they may feel anger at the deceased parent (and feel guilty about it) who left or abandoned them. These feelings are normal and understandable; but, the family needs to deal with the reality of the situation and concentrate on what can be done to resume a normal life.

If the deceased parent did not provide adequate financial means for the family, it may be necessary for the mother (if it is the father who died) to seek work outside the home. This requires an additional understanding and adjustment. It is of utmost importance that the parent be totally honest with the children, let them know what the situation is, and appeal to them for understanding and support in mother's decision to get a job. This situation may require greater independence on the part of the children, assuming certain responsibilities which mother had assumed before and greater cooperation between the members of the family.

When a mother dies, the widowed father may have a much harder time adjusting to new responsibilities for which he is often unprepared. He may have to hire a housekeeper, or he may have to place the children with relatives until such time when a housekeeper is found or until he remarries. This would be a much more painful and difficult time for the children. They may have to change schools, leave their friends, and be exposed to many new adjustments. If at all possible, we recommend that the father remain with the children in the same physical environment. Older children may now assume responsibilities for themselves and perhaps for the younger siblings which they had not had to assume before. But, it requires, as with the mother who loses her husband, an honest evaluation of the situation and of solicitation of suggestions from the children as to the best solution for the new problems arising. They should be reassured that if their suggestions do not work out well, the family will discuss the matter again and seek new solutions. The children usually will be more cooperative if they are participating in the solution of the problem than if father makes all the decisions.

Mother and Son

When the husband dies or moves away from home, a mother may cling more than ever to an oldest or only son. He may become the man of the house, or perhaps, the man in her life until she forms another attachment. The mother may feel lonely and consciously or subconsciously encourage the attachment of the son. She may even be flirtatious in the process. For instance, a mother who was counseled by us because of difficulties she had with her ten year old daughter constantly referred to her thirteen year old son, Lenny, as "such a doll," who knew how unhappy she felt and never let her down. She then added, "You're my big man now, and I don't know what I would do without you." The daughter openly assaulted her brother. A mother may convey with looks and gestures, if not necessarily with words, the pleasure she derives from having a son. Some mothers ask their sons what to wear, if a particular outfit is becoming to her, and should she use a certain kind of make-up. To the adolescent son this may become a problem in future sexual relationships with women. It may become a burden in having to assume too great a responsibility toward his mother. It may become an attachment to mother so big that the boy refuses social contact with other people, wants to stay home with mother or go out with her, and becomes jealous whenever the mother gives her attention to somebody else.

In such a case, the mother needs to be helped to change the relationship. She must separate from him without making him feel rejected. She should seek other companionship, go out frequently, treat her son with love and consideration in all matters, and keep the communication open. The other children should at no time feel that the son occupies a preferential place and that he receives special treatment. Mothers who attach themselves to one child almost always have difficulties with the other children. The mother must indicate and behave in a manner that conveys to her children that she can handle her problems although she feels lonely at times and that having them is a great solace to her. She should also discuss with her children that she needs the company and social relationships with people near her own age.

SEPARATING PARENTS

A common problem with children whose parents separate is their lack of preparedness for such a possibility. Children often believe that their parents are quite happy in spite of the latter's quarrels. The sudden realization that one parent is moving out often comes as a shock. We suggest that the parents should tell the children in advance that a separation is possible and that the time after the separation will decide whether this may or may not lead to a permanent separation or a divorce. The children should be reassured that this is not their fault and that this separation will not diminish the individual parent's love and concern for them. They also should be helped to realize that there is no stigma attached to a separation or a divorce and that they need not be ashamed to face neighbors or schoolmates in case they should be asked. Of course, this depends to a great degree on how the parents themselves feel about the separation. If they are ashamed and if this feeling is conveyed to the children, then the latter may draw the conclusion that there is something shameful and humiliating about what the parents are doing.

Child Custody Questions

Counselors often are asked if parents should decide with whom a child should live after the divorce. The counselor has no right to make such a decision for the parent. This should come from the parents. In some cases, it may be decided by the child. The counselor may ask the child with whom he/she would like to live but leave the final decision to the family. Frequently, the court decides. If the decision is contrary to what the parent had hoped for, and if the parent is unhappy, the counselor could help this parent accept the inevitable. The counselor should help the parent find ways of maintaining a good relationship with the child. The parent should be cautioned not to criticize or berate the former spouse, and encourage the child to have a good relationship with the parent with whom he/she is living. Criticizing the spouse and pointing out all the negative qualities of this parent to the child may give the parent satisfaction, but it may hurt the child's relationship with both parents. Nothing positive can ever result from one parent "bad mouthing" the other despite conditions that might be considered overwhelmingly compelling to do so.

FOSTER PARENTS

Foster parents often have superior parenting skill because they are not emotionally involved in the same way as natural parents. Foster parents may have the same kind of problems with children that adoptive or natural parents experience. There are some significant differences. Children do not usually consider foster parents as permanent parents. Foster children usually relate to two sets of parents. This relationship in itself may cause problems as the children have to shift from values of one set of parents to those of another.

Sharing the children with natural parents may be a continuing problem for foster parents. Often both of the children's families are a part of his/her ongoing experiences and frequently they are in conflict. There is often tension in such situations. In a sense, the foster parents may compete with the natural parents. They often are critical of them. "Why would they not have kept their children?" The children may resent any kind of discipline, maintaining that "you are not my mother/father and have no right to punish me." Foster parents have boundaries as to the roles they play in the child's life while adoptive parents do not usually have such limits. Foster parents are never sure how long the child will stay with them. This uncertainty has caused many heartbreaks for foster parents who learn to love a child and who must later return a child to the natural parents. The counselor has to prepare foster parents to deal realistically with these possibilities.

The main complaints that foster parents bring to the counselor are usually no different from the complaints from any other family, i.e., the child does not want to wash, is fresh, refuses to clean up after himself/herself, and so forth. For such problems we have no other recommendations for foster parents than those we suggest for natural parents. Foster parents may aggravate situations if they pamper a child, accuse him/her of ungratefulness, or threaten that they will get rid of him/her if he/she doesn't behave.

THE UNWED PARENT

Many unmarried mothers decide to keep their children. In some ways, these mothers have problems that the widowed or the divorced mothers do not have. For one, to some extent, society still often reacts unfavorably to the child that is born out of wedlock. An even greater problem to the mother is her lack of funds; she usually is completely financially responsible for her children; whereas, the divorced or the widowed mother may be receiving child-support or a widow's pension.

Children of never-married parents never experience the child-father relationship. They may come to feel deprived when comparing their home life with that of their peers. They may retaliate because of feeling socially inferior and may be pampered if the mother tries unwisely to make it up to them because she feels sorry that the child does not have a father.

The counselor who encounters such families should be acquainted with agencies that provide financial aid to unmarried mothers. The use of the Big Brother/Big Sister program is often helpful. If the family has the kind of problems that other "normal" families encounter with their children, we suggest that the mother follow the same suggestions given throughout this book. The counselor must help such families accept the reality of their situation and learn to cope with it effectively. These children must be helped to a better self-image and to develop healthy social relationships. They particularly need encouragement. The counselor should take care to teach the never-married parent and children to encourage each other. The same methods outlined for the counselor in working with disrupted families are the counselor's source in working with these families.

ADOPTING PARENT AND ADOPTED CHILD

Many adopted children are well adjusted and feel secure in their relationships with the new family. People who adopt children are usually highly motivated to be loving and devoted parents. But these families rarely come for counseling. The families counselors see are those who have problems and are unhappy. One of the major reasons why parents of adopted children are unhappy is their disappointment in a child because he/she did not live up to their expectations. They do not realize that frequently the parents create problems with the child. Adopting parents often indulge a child because of wanting to be loved and because of a fear that the child may believe the natural parents might have loved him/her more. The adoptive parents try "to make up" or prevent the feeling of not being loved enough; they spoil the child. The more they spoil him/her, the more the child starts making unreasonable demands. Often these children become literal tyrants in the way they treat their parents and the parents may become exasperated and angry. Inwardly, some parents start resenting the child although they seldom admit this feeling. When counseling such parents, the counselor may hear them complain about the ungratefulness of the child. The parents often tell of the frustration they feel because they are afraid to discipline the child or show disapproval lest the child feel rejected and unloved. It becomes a vicious circle. Some parents admit that they feel cheated. It is not uncommon for a parent to say, "To think that I have chosen this child when I might have chosen another. It is different when you have your own child. You have to accept it no matter what you get. You have no choice in the matter. But here I had the choice and what a mistake I have made."

Children are quick to sense parents' feelings regardless of how much parents try to hide them. Once the child senses that parents are disappointed in him/her, the child may provoke the parents to anger rather than cooperate in order to evoke friendly feelings. Often the children literally want to punish parents and are usually successful.

Counselors need to gain the confidence of both parents and the adopted child and help them realize how each is acting out his/her hurt and what each does to the other.

It is not uncommon to hear from these children comments such as, "My parents behave as though they care for me, but they really don't love me. They never make me feel like I am the kind of child they really wanted." These children feel that they are not good enough for any parents, for if they had been good enough, their own parents would not have given them up for adoption.

Some adopted children are convinced that their natural parents were bad people, either criminals or immoral, and that they have inherited bad characteristics from them. Many are ashamed to admit that they are adopted and try to hide this fact from teachers and from their peers. We find that these children may use any of the mentioned rationalizations in their attempt to defeat the parents or to get away from them. This is especially true when these children reach adolescence.

Adopted children often have high moral standards, especially those who are critical of their natural parents. Because of their high moral standards they do not admit, even to themselves, that they don't like their adopted parents. They may try to mislead the counselor by blaming themselves. "I am no good; I should be more grateful." In this way they try to prove to the counselor that their adoptive parents deserve something better. Such children may want to leave home and want the counselor to believe that they do this out of consideration for the adoptive parents.

The counselor must be alert and pick up every nuance of the child's feelings and attitudes toward the adoptive parents and the ways he/she is acting out his/her feelings. After the counselor has established good communication with the adopted child, the counselor must confront the child with the real reasons for his/her attitude. This must be done sensitively, with empathy and understanding. At the same time, the counselor must help the child recognize that he/she may not have given the adoptive parents a chance; that his/her own feelings of not being loved by them prompted him/her to test them and to alienate them. Afterwards, the child can tell himself/herself, "I was right, they do not love me."

Parents need to be helped not to feel guilty or ashamed of what they did or felt, but to concentrate on ways to improve the relationship with the child. It also might be helpful to discuss this with the parents who may feel that a child of their own flesh and blood might have been loved more. This belief is fallacious. Love grows out of a relationship, and loving the child usually does follow when the relationship is good.

Parents need to be helped to treat adopted children the same way they would treat their own children. Parents should not allow themselves to be blackmailed by the child who accuses them with, "You would not do that if I weren't adopted but was your own child." The counselor must caution parents to avoid being manipulated.

The counselor might ask the parents to use paradoxical intentions in such situations. The parent could hug or kiss the child and say, "You are probably right." It is important that this be done with affection. The child is usually shocked by the parents' remark although usually the child knows how it is meant. Such an answer stops all further explanations and reassurances that the child has heard so many times before. This technique should be used with great caution. The counselor may ask the child what life might be like for him/her today if he/she had not been adopted. The child's response often indicates what he/she is trying to avoid or his/her goal for his/her present behavior.

For example:

> One boy said, "If I weren't adopted I wouldn't have to feel grateful for everything my parents do for me." This helps the counselor investigate how much the parents expect of the child and if they remind the child of what they, the parents, do for him/her and how grateful he/she should be to them. For this deduction, the counselor may proceed into discussing with both what each can do to change the situation and move toward a better relationship.

Should the mutual antagonism and distrust be so strong that neither is willing to make any changes, we advise that the rebellious child be placed in a foster home until such time when the adoptive parents and the child would be willing to try anew and develop a satisfactory relationship.

STEPPARENTS AND STEPCHILDREN

One may say that divorce and remarriage has practically become a way of life in this country and it is predicted that this phenomena will continue to increase. It is, therefore, imperative that the family counselor be well prepared to deal effectively with family problems that may arise because of divorce and remarriage.

It cannot be ignored that many people still cling to the myth of the mean stepparent, especially the "stepmother." They often associate these parents with the characters described in fairy tales. The immediate reaction to a child that has a stepmother is often pity. Children's attitudes to a stepmother also are influenced by what they read. One father, who had custody of his child and who was about to get married again was asked by his daughter, "Is she going to be my stepmother? Will she beat me and then send me away from home?" Stepparents will have a difficult time if they have not prepared themselves for this new role and its possible pitfalls and disappointments. They could avoid many problems if they and the children were to receive guidance before marriage.

One of the problems that stepparents encounter stems from an overeagerness to excel in this role. They fantasize about the great times they will have with the stepchildren and how the latter will appreciate and love them. They enter the relationship with excitement and great hope. While many succeed, others end up disappointed and hurt. The children do not always respond to the stepparents no matter how much effort is put forth. Some children even resent the stepparents' efforts to treat them well. As one adolescent boy told the counselor, "I'd prefer it if my stepfather would not try so hard, because I would not feel so guilty. I feel guilty for not being nice to him and I feel guilty toward my own father when I am nice to my stepfather." It often happens that the stepparent, who meets with rejection, gives up trying and withdraws from the child and often even dislikes the child who defeats all the well intentioned efforts.

Children whose parents are divorced and who then remarry are exposed to two great shocks which must be considered. To many children the divorce of the parents is a great tragedy, but when the parent remarries it gives children an additional shock. Some children are relieved when the parents get divorced, especially children who grew up in an atmosphere of continuous fighting and hurt. However, in many cases, both the divorce and the remarriage are catastrophic for children. It is not unusual for children of divorced parents to cherish the hope that some day the parents will be reunited and that they will again be a happy family. Such hopes are now shattered when the parent marries another. Others are convinced that it is their fault that the parents divorced. Children may fantasize how they will make it up to parents once the parents get together again. This hope also is taken away when the parent remarries.

If the child is close to the natural parent, the child may feel threatened by the stepparent who will now take away mother's or father's love. The child may fear that the remarried parent will now devote less time to him/her. The age of the child in such situations is an important factor; another is the length of time that the parents have been separated; still another important factor is the relationship that the child had with the parent who moved away. For instance, if the mother gets custody of the children, and if the children are still very young, they may have not yet formed a close bond with the natural father; therefore, they will adjust to the stepfather more readily than the older children.

Younger children may sometimes even be excited at the prospect of a new father. They may accept the new man as the authority in the home and respect and obey him. If, on the other hand, a child has enjoyed the mother's full attention for a number of years, he/she may react to the parent very much as an only child often reacts to a new sibling. The child may resent the stepparent and do everything to cause friction between the parent and the new spouse. The child may not cooperate, deliberately become destructive, provoke, and punish. The child often hopes that this kind of behavior will ultimately break up the marriage.

An example:

> *Mrs. Winkler, a widow who had a nine-year old daughter, Sarah, married Max who was still a bachelor. The prospect of becoming a father was very challenging and exciting to him. He was a man of high standards with definite ideas about what children should and should not do. Sarah resented him, not so much for his mannerism, as for no other reason than being married to her mother and for living with them in the same house. She did everything to upset the marriage and admitted to the counselor that she spends hours plotting strategy which would cause problems for her mother and stepfather and that she hoped that it would lead to a divorce.*

> *The mother, not understanding Sarah's behavior, disciplined her daughter in a manner which she had never done before. Max, disillusioned in the child and feeling hurt, also punished her. This caused resentment on the part of the mother. She started to feel sorry for her child, and began to think that she had made a mistake in marrying Max. The mother had no idea that she fell right into Sarah's trap.*

The counselor needs to help all three involved understand the role that they have played in this situation and encourage them not to give up but work out this problem cooperatively. Max needs to be helped to understand that it was too early for him to discipline the child. He should make no demands at this time and remove himself from every corrective measure until such time when Sarah will show signs of acceptance and willingness to form a relationship. While mother should be the one to discipline the daughter, she also must be helped to understand how Sarah feels, having been the only child (and no father) for so many years. In addition, the mother needs to understand the purpose of Sarah's behavior and not reinforce it by getting involved in a power-struggle, nor by showing pity when her husband and Sarah have a confrontation. Mother should discuss the situation with Sarah making it clear that she has no intentions of divorcing Max. Sarah and Max will have to learn to get along. Mother may appeal to Sarah for help and come to a mutual agreement. The family should be encouraged to have a Family Council as described in Chapter VI.

Stepparents should proceed cautiously and neither become too demanding or over solicitious. They should refrain from criticism and retaliation. Stepparents should not take the child's hostile behavior personally as the child probably would react in the same way no matter whom the natural parent might have married. If the child senses that mother or father feels sorry for him/her, the child may deliberately provoke the stepparent in order to get the natural parent's sympathy and protection. Parents are usually not aware of how perceptive children are, even very young children, and how ingenious they are to use the parent's soft spot.

Stepparents are advised not to insist that stepchildren call them "mother" or "father," especially if the children have a natural mother or father. While some children may like to do so, many may resent it. This may be regarded as a betrayal of loyalty to their natural parent. It is best to allow children to decide for themselves what they want to call stepparents. They often start by calling them by their first names, but gradually, as they form a relationship, they start on their own by referring to them as "Mom" and "Dad."

The difficulties that parents will encounter in the new marriage will depend greatly on the relationship between the natural parent and the children. It also will depend on the length of time they had been married to the now divorced spouse. The friendlier the natural parents are toward each other after the divorce, the easier it will be for the children, and fewer will be the problems. Serious problems arise when the natural parents use a child to hurt each other, or when a child plays one of the natural parents against the other. A frequent complaint of the stepparent is the child's tattling to the natural parent how the stepparent abuses his/her rights, that mother encourages the stepfather to discipline him/her, and that he is very mean. The father then complains to his former wife, insisting that "this man has no right to dictate to my children and to tell them what to do as long as I am alive." If mother reprimands the child, it starts an all-around war. Ultimately, it may affect the new marriage.

Blended Family

This is a family that consists of parents who bring children from their previous marriages into the new marriage. Thus, mother may bring her children and the stepfather may bring his children and they may, then also have children of their own.

What are the problems that arise in blended families? Many stem from competition between the two sets of children and from the attitudes that the natural parent takes toward the stepchildren. The counselor needs to work with all members concerned, help them understand that such competition—feeling of being less than the other—of not measuring up, and so forth is very natural at first; that it takes time to make the adjustment to such drastic changes in their lives; and that this is a difficult time for everyone. The counselor should reassure the family that problems can be lessened, if not completely solved, if all concerned work towards a solution. As Kirby (1979) stated, "A second marriage resulting in a merged family offers parents a new opportunity to develop the kind of social system they desire" (p. 99).

We encourage blended families, as we do other families, not to get involved in the children's squabbles but let them work out the difficulties. This reduces competition between the children and the individual children's schemes to get the parent to feel sorry for them and come to their aid. The moment a parent is drawn into the children's arguments, there is bound to be a child that feels unfairly treated and hurt, and one who feels triumphant and is encouraged to provoke a sibling. Again, establishing a Family Council is highly recommended.

Extended Family

This family consists of relatives such as grandparents, aunts, uncles, and others who are involved and often are closely associated with the family and sometimes live in the same household.

Grandparents. Some of the influence that grandparents may play in the upbringing of children was previously discussed. The counselor should explore the relationship that relatives have with the parents of the children, with the children themselves, and the extent of involvement. Parents who have not yet freed themselves from needing their own parents' approval, often allow grandparents to intimidate and dictate to them on how they should rear the grandchildren. One mother reacted to the counselor's suggestion to allow a child to wait until the next meal, if the child dawdled or refused to eat what was served, in the following manner. "I would do it if I weren't afraid of my own mother. She would kill me if I were to do what you suggest. I'm afraid, I just can't do it." Or the comment an eight-year old girl made when the counselor suggested that her mother should not get involved in the fights she had with her sister. She said, "Oh, I don't care because I will tell my grandmother and she will stick up for me. She always does because I am the baby in the family." It is very difficult for a parent, especially a mother, who is still seeking her own mother's approval, to go against grandmother's wishes. The counselor should show understanding and not insist that, "It is high time that you cut the umbilical cord," but, slowly help the mother assert herself and do what she believes must be done under the circumstances. Gradually, the grandparent or grandparents will learn to accept that the real parent must have the final say about rearing the children. If the counselor could succeed in getting the grandparents to come to the session, this process of readjustment might go much faster.

MOTHERS WORKING OUTSIDE THE HOME

Much controversy exists regarding the importance that mothers should stay home and always be available to the children. It is assumed that the child's self-esteem, his/her sense of being loved and of being secure depends on the ever-present mother. Research reveals ample evidence that this assumption is a myth, especially once the child enters school. We find many unhappy children in homes where the mother is always present, always ready to serve the child, always fearful of leaving the child with a baby-sitter.

In examining such relationships, it is often found that such mothers are resentful of being housewives. They spend much time yelling and criticizing the children, watching every move they make, and making constant demands that they behave and obey. This kind of relationship is more devastating to the child's development than that of the mother who works outside the home. The children then experience their mother in a more friendly and accepting way. In most research, it is found that the quality of parenting is more important than the quantity. How a parent spends time with the child is more important than the length of time spent.

Women who work outside the home, but who are influenced by the still prevailing belief that a good mother stays with her children until they are old enough to take care of themselves, often feel guilty which affects relationships with the children. Such parents frequently try to make up to the child through overindulgence and spoiling. Such practices usually make tyrants of the children. Counselors can help such mothers shed their guilt feelings and help them see that they are overcompensating for the guilt feelings through methods which only hurt their children. They should help the mother with suggestions of how to talk to the children, how to delegate responsibilities to them, and how to have a good time and enjoy them. How the children interpret mother's absence from home depends more on the relationship and how she trains them than her physical presence. If properly trained, the children usually become more self-reliant, independent, and better adjusted.

The situation of the working mother again provides an excellent opportunity for all members of the family to share in the responsibilities of keeping the household running. Under no circumstance should the working mother, who works full days, come home and attempt to accomplish all the household chores done by full-time housewives. Counselors must help working mothers avoid such mistaken practices. If the mother assumes that it is normal and not harmful to go to work and if she trains the child to assume certain responsibilities (depending on age), the child will react more positively than if mother feels guilty for "neglecting" the child

Anna Freud (1973) researched this topic during the Second World War when so many children had to be separated from their mothers in England. She found that parents who remained calm and reassuring had fewer difficulties with their children than parents who cried and showed their worries about how the child would fare.

The counselor also should educate the working mother to take some time for rest, relaxation, and leisure. Leading a balanced life is a necessary insurance against the working mother resenting her overworked lot in life.

JOINT CUSTODY

Until recently, the inevitable tendency regarding healthy homes for children was to view the mother as the most influential parent, the one whom the children needed more than the father. Therefore, the mother usually was awarded custody of the children. Only under very extreme circumstances was custody awarded to a father. Today, many couples accept the logic of the two-parent principle, allowing the parents to share the time they spend with the children and to assume equal responsibility toward their upbringing and welfare.

Studies indicate that essentially, children need warmth and caring, consistency and continuity of the relationship, rather than the caring of either one of the parents. Furthermore, it is recognized today that the fact of being a mother does not in itself indicate a capacity or willingness to care for the children better than the father. More and more men want to share responsibility for their children. Our present cultural climate requires that both parents share this responsibility because the family is undergoing tremendous change which affects the societal attitude toward custodial care. We find more women who are seeking careers outside the home, and others who are not willing to be tied to household duties. These women demand that these responsibilities be shared equally between them and the male spouse.

Those who share custody of their children are usually willing to work out their difficulties. If problems arise, they are usually cooperative with the counselor; they are willing to divide the time they give to the child, for dropping him/her off at school and picking him/her up afterwards, for looking after the children's belongings, and for providing time for having fun with them. Thus, for many parents, joint custody works well.

Evidence points to the fact that joint-custody couples feel less hostile toward each other and that most children adjust to this new way of life readily with good results. Children often enjoy having friends in two neighborhoods and like to have two homes. This often is supported by the children of joint-custody parents when we counsel them. The problems that individual parents usually have with these children are not any different than those we find in traditional homes. Again, we must stress that a friendly relationship between the parents is a great factor in the child's adjustment to joint custody.

OTHER SUGGESTIONS FOR
SINGLE OR SPECIAL PARENTS

In addition to those previously presented other suggestions pertinent to the situation should be emphasized.

1. Be honest with the children about the situation that caused you to be a single parent.

2. In case of a divorce, assure children that this situation is not their fault.

3. Show understanding for children's feelings of anger and anxiety or possible embarrassment.

4. Do not change the routine of your life as a family, if possible.

5. Try to share responsibilities as much as possible. Do not try to make up to the children for the loss of a parent by taking over the responsibilities for them.

6. Be honest when you discuss your own feelings toward your spouse but not in a way that makes the children hurt or disrespect their other parent. Do not give the children hope that your spouse will come home, unless you see such a possibility, or it may give the children false hopes and they may later feel let down.

7. Do not use your children as a pawn or as a bargaining agent between you and your spouse.

8. Do not encourage tattling by asking your children to report everything the spouse said when they go to visit.

9. Assure the children that they will be loved and cared for as before.

10. Do not talk against your spouse's family.

11. Children, even very young ones, should be informed. White lies, like "Father has to take a trip for a few months" are inadvisable.

12. If possible, keep the children in the same neighborhood and in the same school. This prevents too many drastic changes in the lives of the children at one time.

BIBILIOGRAPHY

Baruth, L. (1979). *A single parent's survival guide.* Dubuque, IA: Kendall Hunt Publishing.

Carro, G. (1980). *Surviving the breakup: How children and parents cope with divorce.* New York: Basic Books.

Cohen, D. (1975). *Going it alone.* New York: Basic Books.

Cohen, D. (November 1977). Adopted Children. *Psychology today.*

Freud, A., & Goldstein, J. (1973). *Beyond the best interest of the child.*

Fry, W. F., & Heersema, P. (1963). Conjoint family therapy. *Problems: psychotherapy, 5,* 147-153.

Kirby, J. (1979). *Second marriage.* Muncie, IN: Accelerated Development.

Roman, M., & Haddard, W. (1978). *Joint custody: The disposable parent.* Holt, Rheinhart, & Winston.

Satir, V. (1967). *Conjoint family therapy.* Palo Alto, CA: Science and Behavior Books.

Visher,E. B., & Visher, J. (1979). *Step families.* New York: Brunner/Mazel, Publishers.

Weiss, R. S. (1975). *Marital separation.* New York: Basic Books.

Wolfelt, A. (1983). *Helping children cope with grief.* Muncie, IN: Accelerated Development.

CASE STUDIES

The authors have repeatedly used examples, illustrations, and abbreviated case studies to illustrate principles and techniques delineated throughout this book. Students and counselors can study complete counseling sessions from beginning to end in order to gain an overall perspective. The cases presented are verbatim reproductions of actual counseling sessions recorded by the authors. Explanatory comments are inserted at appropriate places for the purpose of delineating significance and interpretation of information forthcoming in the dialogue. This indicates the thinking of the counselor as he/she proceeds. The reader should take special note that the cases concentrate on current situations and are devoid of extensive history taking.

CASE OF MISIDENTIFIED PROBLEM
A COMPLETE COUNSELING SESSION

Members of the family include:

Bob and Brenda . . . . , father and mother — *lack of respect*
Jeffrey, 11, in the 6th grade
Pamela, 10, in the 4th grade
Ann, 8, in the 3rd grade
Child who died a few minutes after birth, would be 6 years old now
Jason, 1 years of age

The problem, as identified by the parents, is Pamela. The session proceeded with the parents.

Comment 1: The counselor often will learn that the identified problem is not necessarily the major problem, but that the so-called "good" child creates more difficulties. In this case, we learn that Ann provokes more difficulty than does Pamela. It is unfortunate that Jeffrey did not attend; however, missing family members are not uncommon so the counselor proceeds with whoever attends the session.

Counselor: *I am Mrs. G., and I am your counselor. I am glad to meet you.*

Father: *I am . . . ., and this is my wife . . . .*

Counselor: *Please sit down. I hope that you feel comfortable being here.*

Mother: *I am very nervous. I know that I have no reason feeling nervous, but I do.*

Counselor: *I can understand that. It is a new experience for you. But I hope that you will feel more relaxed in a short time. All we will do is discuss the problems you have with your children, those you care to talk about. We won't discuss anything that is highly personal. How do you feel, Mr. . . . .?*

Father: *Oh, I feel fine. I only wish Brenda wouldn't feel so nervous.*

Mother: *I will be all right. I am already more relaxed.*

Counselor: *I am glad. How should we call each other? Do you prefer to be addressed as Mr. . . and Mrs. . or would you like that I call you by your first names?*

Mother: *I would like to be called Brenda, if this is okay with you.*

Counselor: *Sure. My name is . . . .*

Father: *I, too, prefer the first name.*

Comment 2: It is a matter of courtesy and respect to address people by their preferred names. Often, family counselors may use the terms, Mom/Dad, Mother/Father, when rapport has been established, but the counselor should always ask for permission.

Counselor: *All right, Brenda and Bob. May I ask you a few questions so that we get acquainted and that I learn to understand the nature of your problem. How many people live in your household?*

Bob: *Six of us.*

Counselor: *Who are the six?*

Bob: *My wife and myself and our four children.*

Counselor: *Does anyone else live with you, a housekeeper or a grandparent?*

Comment 3: The reason for this question is to ascertain if anyone else is in daily interaction with the family who may influence the children or counteract what the parents are trying to do.

Bob: *No.*

Counselor: *Would you please tell me the names of your children, starting with the oldest, their ages and their grades.*

Bob: *Our oldest is Jeffrey, he is 11 and in 6th grade. Then comes Pamela, she is 10 and in 4th grade. Then comes Ann, who is 8 and in 3rd grade, and the last one is Jason who is 18 months old.*

Counselor: *Were there any other children or miscarriages?*

Bob: *Yes, we lost a child. It lived only a few hours.*

Counselor: *Between which of the children was this child? How much younger was it from the previous child?*

Bob: *This child, a boy, by the way, was born 2 years after Pamela.*

Brenda: *Two years and two months.*

Bob: *That's right.*

Comment 4: This comment is the first time that mother spoke. We may speculate that father is the domineering part in the marriage. Does mother take a back seat all the time?

Counselor: *Then Ann was the youngest child for 6 ½ years.*

Bob: *That's right. She was our baby.*

Comment 5: Possibly Ann occupies a special position in this family. She may have been more indulged and overprotected than the others. Possibly she now feels dethroned by Jason. We must check this fact later.

Counselor: *What problems do you have with the children?*

Bob: *As I see it, Pamela is very resentful of the others. She is beligerent, disrespectful, but isn't this typical of a middle child?*

Comment 6: Fathers appears protective of Pamela, or he tries to justify her behavior through rationalization.

Counselor: *Brenda, how do you feel about what Bob said?*

Brenda: *You mean about Pam? Well, I find her impossible to live with. She does everything to upset me, but just everything.*

Counselor: *It would help me if you could give me an example of what Pam does that upsets you so.*

Brenda: *I feel kind of funny to describe all the things she does. I get upset.*

Bob: *Brenda gets upset, and of course, this upsets me. I really don't think that some of the things that Pamela does are so terrible, but my wife thinks so.*

Comment 7: Possibly Pam plays one parent against the other. Possibly mother resents that father sticks up for the daughter, and this creates further friction between her and Pam.

Counselor: *I sense that it is very difficult for you, Brenda, to talk about this and I am sorry that I have to ask you to give me specific examples of what Pam does or says that upsets you so. This would help me understand the problem.*

Brenda: *Well, for instance, she likes to wear the most outlandish, most inappropriate clothes and no matter what I say or do does not help. Finally I give up.*

Counselor: *What do you say or do before you give up?*

Brenda: *I yell; I tell her that she can't go out like that. Sometimes I hit her.*

Counselor: *What happens then?*

Brenda: *Nothing, except that she just won't change, and she wins out. It's always the same story. She either has no idea of what she looks like, or she doesn't care, or she loves to upset me. I sometimes feel that I can't understand my own child. Nothing I say or do pleases her.*

Comment 8: Mother is not only very angry but seems to be discouraged and feels defeated. But also, possibly she feels sorry for herself.

Counselor: *How do you see this, Bob?*

Bob: *I am not home when many of these things happen. My wife tells me about them when I come home. What can I do? I don't see this behavior from Pam when I come home. We get along fine. I don't know why this is, and naturally, I am concerned about Brenda's feelings, but I don't know what to do.*

Comment 9: Our first guess seems confirmed. Father indirectly conveys to his wife that there is something wrong with her, and that he, in a sense, is superior to her in his relationship with Pamela. Mother may consider this unfair and resent Pam even more for it. Perhaps, she unwittingly creates problems with Pam in order to prove to her husband how unfair he is.

Counselor: *May I ask you, Brenda, how you feel when Bob explained his reaction to what you said a while ago.*

Brenda: *Well, I am used to this. He isn't home, as he said, and he does not get this obnoxious behavior from Pamela that I do.*

Counselor: *But, how do you feel about his reaction?*

Brenda: *It's all right.*

Comment 10: Brenda seems reluctant to express her feelings. Counselor must respect this desire and not pursue this for the moment.

Counselor: *Could it be, Brenda that you feel helpless and defeated by the way Pamela reacts and that you also feel discouraged, perhaps wondering what you do wrong and angry because you cannot control the situation?*

Brenda: *Yes, I feel all of these things. Don't misunderstand me. I love my daughter, and I keep telling her this, and because I love her, I want her to look nice, I mean, maybe not exactly "nice" but decent and presentable. I don't want her to run around like nobody cares. Would you let your daughter go in shorts to school? Well, she goes to school in shorts, and I want you to know that this is against school regulations, and she knows this too. Oh well, I don't know. I just wish I knew what to do and this is why I am here. What shall I do?*

Comment 11: Mother seems to be more concerned with her image as a mother, with how others may judge her than with what Pam wears. She also is displaying this need in her justification for why she feels as she does. "I do this out of love."

Counselor: *I hope that, by the end of the session, we can all come to some decisions as to what you might do. But, it would help you if you tried to sort out your own feelings why it disturbs you so what Pamela wears. This seems to be so very important to you.*

Brenda: *It is against school regulations.*

Counselor: *Would you mind letting the school handle this?*

Bob: *That's exactly what I have told her.*

Brenda: *Why should the school have to handle this? She has parents.*

Comment 12: The school personnel set the rule about girls wearing shorts to school. The rule is the school personnel's and not the parent's; therefore, after the parent helps the child understand the consequences that may result from defiance, let the school personnel deal with the problem. It will relieve mother of one more chore, and she has enough problems already. More important, it is an excellent example of advising the parent to withdraw from a power struggle.

Counselor: *I am questioning the price you pay for handling this. Is it worth it, or is this such a serious problem that you would allow this to impair your relationship with your daughter? I wonder what would happen if you said nothing and let her decide what she should wear. In fact, if you would even compliment her on her choices?*

Brenda: *What would happen? What would . . . . she would wear just what she wants to wear, I suppose. Why not? Nobody would stop her.*

Counselor: *I meant what would happen if you decided not to get upset no matter what she wears, and if this goes against school regulations then let the school talk to Pamela. You could stay out of it.*

Brenda: *She already wins anyway, so now she would always feel that she can win. So, she wins anyway. It would really make no difference.*

Comment 13: Mother has a hang up about winning. She may see most human interaction as a "win" or "lose" situation. The counselor will need to re-educate her toward the ideas of cooperation if this attitude is the case.

Counselor: *I think it would make a difference, namely, that winning without upsetting you may take out all the fun in "winning." She wins only if you try to stop her and when she can defeat you. But if you remove yourself from the power-struggle—are you aware that you both are in a power-struggle?—the moment you remove yourself, there is no more winning. But, may I ask you, could it be that "winning" is very important to you?*

Brenda: *I don't know if insisting that a child obey her mother is "winning."*

Bob: *Come on, Brenda. You know that you have to win. I think that "winning" is very important to you.*

Brenda: *All right, so winning is important to me.*

Comment 14: The counselor's previous surmisal is verified.

Counselor: *I have a feeling that your daughter admires you very much. Can you see what gives me this feeling?*

Brenda: *No.*

Counselor: *I wonder if she wants very much to be like you. If you must win whenever you and she disagree, then she may feel that "winning" is very important in life. And as most children, she is much stronger and can hold out much longer than an adult. "Winning" then is a triumph to her. I wonder if "winning" would still be so important to her, if it were less or not important to you. You could find out. Would you want to?*

Comment 15: Children usually pattern themselves after the parent whom they most admire.

Brenda: *You mean, I should just let her do whatever she wants to do?*

Counselor: *No, not exactly. I mean, in this case, let her make the decisions about what she wants to wear. What do you think?*

Brenda: *Well, I could try. Let's see what will happen.*

Counselor: *I have the feeling that you don't expect good results from this and that, perhaps, you don't really like my suggestion.*

Brenda: *No, I said I will try.*

Counselor: *We have had the experience that when a parent says "try," they usually are skeptical, and then it doesn't work. You must really believe in what you are doing, and do it. Not just "try."*

Brenda: (Laughs). *I'll do it. I'll do it.*

Counselor: *Do it, and then you will see how things work out. Before I go into other disagreeable areas in regard to Pamela, could you tell me a little about your other children?*

Brenda: *You want me to tell you or my husband?*

Counselor: *Whoever wants to start. It would help if both of you tell how each of you sees them and how you individually relate to them.*

Bob: *Jeffrey is completely the opposite from Pam. Just everything. He is an extrovert, while she is an introvert. He is very gregarious, a leader, very outgoing, and liked by people.*

Comment 16: This is a typical example of two older children developing opposite characteristics and personalities. If the counselor had had a thumbnail description of Jeffrey at the beginning, she could have known what Pamela was like. Such guesses will be accurate 75-80% of the time.

Counselor: *How would you describe him, Brenda?*

Brenda: *I would agree with Bob. He is an easy child, and we have not problems with him.*

Counselor: *Have you any idea why he is so different from Pamela?*

Brenda: *I . . . I . . . I guess he is just different. Some children are . . . some have one kind of character, and others have a different character.*

Counselor: *This is true. However, all our studies indicate that this is not due to an inherited trait, that there are external influences that shape character. For instance, we found that in most cases, the first two children are most different from each other. If one is good and cooperative, the other may choose to be just the opposite—this is not a conscious process. A child has no idea why he or she is behaving as he or she does. But each child wants more than anything to feel belongingness and be important. Each tries to find this belongingness through his/her own unique way. Possibly if Pamela would be more cooperative and easy to raise, Jeffrey may have tried to find his place by being different from her. This must not be so, but this may have happened. I wonder to what extent, Jeffrey's popularity, easy-goingness, and delight to you may have*

discouraged his sister. She has certainly succeeded to get a lot of atten-
tion from you through her opposition and defiance. How do these two
children get along?

Bob: *Jeffrey is not much involved with Pamela. He has his own life.*

Counselor: *Do they fight?*

Bob: *No more than most children.*

   Comment 17: Father avoids direct answers. He justifies children's
behavior through generalizations.

Brenda: *They do fight, not very often, but they fight. You have seen*
them fight, Bob.

Counselor: *When they fight, what do you do?*

Brenda: *We used to interfere, but now we try to let them fight and we*
stay out of it.

Counselor: *It seems that someone came ahead of me. How did you*
decide to stay out of their fights? What made you change?

Brenda: *Somebody told us that this works, so we tried it, and it does*
work.

Counselor: *I am glad to hear it. We found that it works in most cases.*

Brenda: *But she fights with Ann, and these fights are to the bitter end. I*
can't remove myself when they fight.

   Comment 18: Mother's comment, "I can't remove myself when
they fight," is a goldmine to be probed further. Why can't she? For what
is she looking out? What basic attitudes on her part motivate her to
react? What do these attitudes lead her to do and what effect do they
have on the children's behavior?

Counselor: *Why not?*

Brenda: *I just can't let the big girl hit a much smaller child. You have no*
idea how vicious Pamela can be. She really hurts.

Counselor: *So what do you do?*

Brenda: *Just what do you think I do? I do all the things that I probably shouldn't. I separate them; I scream at them; I sent them to their rooms, and sometimes, I deprive them of privileges. I don't know what to do (none of these things work).*

Bob: *Except that Pamela doesn't go to her room.*

Brenda: *She goes, and she comes out after a few minutes.*

Counselor: *What do you do, Bob, when Ann and Pam fight?*

Bob: *For one, they don't fight as much when I am home. But when they fight, I, too, separate them; only I don't punish them as Brenda does.*

Comment 19: We can see here that children know exactly which parent will react and where provocation pays off, and which parent would not react to their provocation, and therefore, there is no fun in provoking.

Counselor: *You have just told me that staying out of the fight between Jeffrey and Pamela works; why, then, don't you apply the same principle to the fight she has with Ann? Could it be that you feel sorry for Ann?*

Brenda: *Well, she is younger, and she can't defend herself. Pamela can defend herself when she fights with Jeffrey. Ann is very sensitive, and she cries; she doesn't hit back. It would be unfair to her to leave her to the mercy of Pamela.*

Comment 20: Mother feels sorry for Ann. She doesn't have faith that Ann can handle her own problems.

Counselor: *I wonder if Ann is not playing on your sympathy; knowing that you feel sorry for her, she may not even try to defend herself. She may love it when you come to her defense, and, of course, this may only add fuel to the fire. Pamela may punish her for being Mama's little girl. Is she your little girl? She was the youngest for over six years. Did you ever call her "my baby?"*

Brenda: *I did. She was my baby.*

Bob: *We both did. In fact, although Jason is now the baby, we sometimes call her our "little baby girl."*

Comment 21: Parents do not realize how they reinforce Ann's sensitivity and her use of tears. She was the baby for a long time, and she loved it. She is now doing everything to keep this place.

Counselor: *Can you, perhaps, figure out why Ann would not defend herself? I am not so sure that she couldn't defend herself if she were to decide.*

Bob: *Yes, I think that I can see that as long as we call her "our little girl," she has to keep this place. The moment she shows independence and stands up for herself, she gives up the position of being our little girl and helpless.*

Counselor: *What do you think, mother?*

Brenda: *I have to think about this. I never looked at it that way, but I suppose that maybe you have a point there. She likes it when we call her "our little baby girl;" she loves it.*

Counselor: *You have to decide what it is you want to do. Keep her your little baby girl, or give her a chance to grow up.*

Brenda: *Right. I realize that I have to let her grow up. It's so hard. Gosh, it's so hard to be a mother. You have to always think of what is right and what is good for the kid. Can't you ever think of your own feelings?*

Comment 22: The Counselor must seek the client's private logic in such situations. Mother probably is saying to herself, "Life is so difficult, especially for a mother. I never can think of myself—it's always the kids first." Next the counselor looks for Mom's behavior that stems from this mistaken attitude.

Counselor: *It's hard to be a parent, and I can understand your feelings, but feelings can be changed. I know that this is a hard concept for most people to accept, but when you see your child unafraid of life, assuming responsibilities and enjoying her relationships with others, wouldn't you have happy feelings?*

Brenda: *I suppose so. I know that this is so.*

Counselor: *You love your children, and you want to do what prepares them for a happy life. This requires that parents often do what is best for the child, and this acceptance changes your feelings—you are not as resentful or angry, nor do you feel that you must win or else you are a bad mother or that you don't count. What do you think?*

Brenda: *Yes, I realize this. This is why we came. It is not always helpful to realize what must be done. You want to hear it from an expert. This helps a lot. Really. I think I can do some things now which I would not do before. But if I can stand by and watch Pamela beat up Ann, that, in all honesty, I don't know if I will be able to do.*

Counselor: *I did not suggest that you watch.*

Brenda: (Laughs). *No, you didn't. But I know that I will watch. I know that.*

Comment 23: Brenda's statement supports the previous point that Ann cannot take care of herself. It also is possible that Brenda needs the involvement with the children to insure her own importance.

Counselor: *You must decide what you will do. But, then you must also accept that things won't change in this respect. It is damaging for both girls. Tell me a little about Ann.*

Brenda: *As I told you, she is very sensitive. I have to be very careful how I say something to her. She gets hurt so easily, and she cries so bitterly, that it breaks your heart to see her. But she is a very good child. She helps me in the household, which Pam just never does. And I mean never. She doesn't even help with the baby. But Ann helps. Thank God we don't have any problems with her or Jeffrey. I don't know what I would do if we had.*

Comment 24: Undue sensitivity by a child, or adults also, always has a purpose. It usually results in others being very careful not to hurt the very sensitive individual. Usually, so called over sensitive people are exercising goal two—power. They attempt to mask their true intentions by being good, tender, and loving.

Counselor: *Could you put yourself into Pamela's skin for a moment. How would you feel if you sensed that your parents appreciate the other children but not you? She has only one route open to her in order to be* noticed and important, and that is to be a rebel, to provoke you and keep you busy with her. This may make no sense to you, but this makes sense to a child. And you have to see it from her point of view.

Brenda: *But when you have to live with it and put up with it every day—-day after day—believe me, you can't take it, no matter how much you may understand that it is hard for her being a middle child.*

Counselor: *Of course, it's difficult. You see, it's not just being "a middle child." Not all middle children have Pamela's problems. It all depends on the personalities of the two other children and on how the parents react to all of them. In your case, Pamela has found her place by keeping you worried, angry, busy with her, making you feel guilty, and so on.*

Brenda: *I am sure of that.*

Counselor: *You might want to consider all that has been discussed here when you go home. Perhaps, some changes will take place. Is there any area which is easier—appears easier for you to follow?*

Brenda: *Well, as we discussed, I think that I will be able to let her decide what to wear and not tell her what I think.*

Counselor: *Anything else?*

Brenda: *I'll try to, no, you said "don't try," so I will do it; I won't mix into the fights between Pammy and Ann, and I will—I forget what else you suggested.*

Counselor: *Nothing else. That is already plenty if you could do these two things. Next time, and I hope that you will want to come back, we might add another area where you could change. What area would that be?*

Brenda: *I hate when she asks me, I mean she tells me, "I am ugly and dumb."*

Counselor: *Perhaps you can find an answer to that too, what you should do in such a situation. You have been listening very intensively, Bob. Would you like to comment?*

Bob: *All I want to say is that I hope that Brenda will really stick to it. I know that if she should do what we discussed here, it would help a lot. Will you really do it, Brenda?*

Comment 25: Bob is not convinced of Brenda's ability to implement the recommendation. He discourages her by this show of lack of confidence.

Counselor: *Brenda, how do you feel this very moment?*

Brenda: *I feel that Bob has no confidence in me. Of course, I will do it. I said so, didn't I?*

Counselor: (To Bob). *I hope that you understand that your remark was discouraging to Brenda. It implies no confidence in her. You may not realize this, in fact, I am sure you don't, but this is no different than telling a child who said that he/she will do something, "Are you sure?" It implies, "You may promise, but you won't keep to your promise," and that discourages a person. Does this make any sense to you?*

Bob: *Yes, it does. I will have to be more careful.*

Counselor: *It would be even better if you didn't think that way. Then you need to be careful. I wanted to go over a typical day with you, but it is getting late, and I haven't yet seen the children. However, since it would be too much for you to cover more grounds in one session, it doesn't matter if we don't discuss the typical day now. I would like to see the children and then talk to all of you. Is this all right with you?*

Comment 26: The counselor often will need to alter a structured plan for the interview. The typical day description can be used in subsequent sessions if needed. The counselor can't cover every problem in one session.

Bob: *Sure.*

Brenda: *I am really curious what they will have to say.*

Parents leave. Children enter. Ann came first, smiling, taking a seat, and changing to another. Pamela walked slowly, looked at the floor until she came close to the counselor. She stopped and stood there.

Counselor: *Hello, you must be Pamela and you are Ann* (shakes hands with both). *Won't you sit down Pamela? I am Mrs. . . . I am a family counselor. People come to me to help them with whatever problems they have in the family. Did you know why you came to see me?*

Ann: *Because we have problems, and we will talk about them.*

Counselor: *What did you know, Pam?*

Pam: *Nothing.*

Counselor: *What did you think would happen here?*

Pam: *I don't know.*

Counselor: *What would you like to happen here?*

Pam: *I don't know.*

Counselor: *What about you, Ann?*

Ann: *Talk.*

Counselor: *Did you want to come?*

Ann: *I did.*

Counselor: *What about you, Pamela?*

Pam: *Yes.*

Ann: (Whispers). *No, she didn't. Mother had to make her come.*

Counselor: *May I ask you, Ann, why you told me this?*

Ann: (Shrugs shoulders).

Counselor: *Would it be all right if Pamela would speak for herself and tell me what she wants to tell me about herself, and you tell me what you want to tell me about yourself?*

Ann: *Okay.*

Counselor: *Pamela, how do you feel about what I just said?*

Pam: *She always tells on me.* (Stuck tongue out at Ann.)

Ann: *I do not.*

Pam: *You do so, and you know you do.*

Counselor: *Perhaps you would want to discuss this after we get acquainted. The parents told me that they do have some problems. Are you aware that they have problems?*

Ann: *Yes.*

Counselor: *And you, Pam?*

Pam: *I guess so.*

Counselor: *What, in your opinion, Pam, is a problem to them?*

Pam: *I don't know.*

Counselor: *Do you know why you always tell me that you don't know?*

Pam: *I don't know.*

Counselor: *May I tell you what I think? Could it be that you decided that you won't tell me a thing, that you will show me that I can't make you talk?*

Pam: *Maybe.*

Counselor: *You are right. I can't. You have a right not to talk, if you don't want to talk. I have another thought. Could it be that you often feel that "Nobody will make me do anything? I will do only what I want?"*

Pam: *Yes.*

Comment 27: Usually the counselor will confront the child with all four goals. However, when one goal seems obvious, the counselor may skip the others. In this case, the counselor was confronting Pam with Goal Two—power.

Counselor: *How about you, Ann?*

Ann: *I will talk; I want to talk.*

Counselor: *Your parents told me that sometimes you cry for no good reason and that you are sensitive. Is that right?*

Ann: *Right.*

Counselor: *Do you know why you do this?*

Ann: *Yes, because I feel sad.*

Counselor: *I have another idea. Could it be that you cry so that your parents would feel sorry for you and give in to you?*

Ann: *Maybe, but they don't always give in.*

Counselor: *But you try with your crying, hoping they would give in.*

Ann: *Yes, I can't help it.*

Counselor: *Nobody is accusing you, Ann. I just tried to explain why you cry. You can cry if you wish. On the other hand, perhaps, you could find a different way to handle such situations.*

Pam: *She always gets what she wants. She can shed more tears than there is in the ocean.*

Ann: *I do not.*

Pam: (Mimics). *"I do not." You know that you cry and then they (parents) give in.*

Counselor: *How do you feel when they give in?*

Pam: *I hate it, and I hate her, and I hate my parents, and I don't care.*

Comment 28: Pam's response indicated that she also may operate on Goal Three—revenge, in respect to her sister. Later, the counselor became aware that he/she did not check this out.

Counselor: *What do you do when you feel so angry at Ann? Do you just hate her? Do you walk away?*

Comment 29: The counselor is moving from the general to the specific.

Ann: *She hits me, that's what she does.*

Counselor: *And then what happens?*

Ann: *Then there is a fight.*

Counselor: *What happens when you fight?*

Ann: *Nothing, we just fight.*

Counselor: *You mean nobody says anything? Your parents say nothing?*

Pam: *My mother tries to break up the fight and then she gets mad, and then she gets mad at me, especially at me, and then she either sends us to our room, or she just yells at us.*

Counselor: *How do you feel when she does this?*

Pam: *I don't care.*

Counselor: *How about you, Ann?*

Ann: *I hate these fights, and I don't think it's right.*

Counselor: *How does your mother know that you are fighting? Is she always in the room where the fight is?*

Pam: *She tells her.*

Counselor: *Do you?*

Ann: *I have to, and it isn't fair that she should always hurt me and fight me, and I should let her.*

Counselor: *Could it be, Ann, that you like to get mother involved in the fight?*

Comment 30: This confirms the previous thought that mother unwittingly communicates to Ann that life is unfair and that she was still unable to handle her own problems.

Comment 31: (Shrugs shoulders. Ann is on guard—afraid to admit.) (Recognition reflex possibly meaning unwillingness to acknowledge.)

Counselor: *Could it be that you like when mother comes and scolds Pam, and tells her that you are much younger—well, maybe not so much, but that you are younger and that she should not hurt a younger child. Could it be that you feel good about it because mother pays attention to you and, in a way, indicates to Pam that she is a bad girl. What do you think?*

Comment 32: Counselor realized that this was to much explanation. It would have sufficed to use the straight forward confronting question—"Could it be . . . . ?"

Ann: *No, I don't.*

Counselor: *Would you rather not have the fight?*

Ann: *I don't want to fight.*

Counselor: *Good. Do you think that there can be a fight if one person doesn't want to fight?*

Ann: *Yes.*

Counselor: *I don't quite see how there can be a fight if only one person wants to fight. How about you, Pam, do you like to fight?*

Pam: *No, but I am not going to let her get away with things.*

Counselor: *But do you, in general, like to fight?*

Pam: *No.*

Counselor: *If neither one of you agrees to fight, how can there be a fight? How about scheduling a time for fighting?*

Pam: *What do you mean?*

Counselor: *Simply, once a week you may discuss if and when you want to fight, like Thursday at two in the afternoon. How about that?*

Ann: *That's funny.*

Counselor: *I guess so. You can then fight when you want to fight, but since both of you say that you don't like to fight, then this should be no problem. You just fight when you want to—Wednesday, or Thursday. But, then the fight must be only between the two of you. This is not your mother's business. I suggested to her to let you fight if you wish and not to mix in. Do you think she will do it?*

Comment 33: This shows respect for the children and their right to decide. It gives them an opportunity to take charge of themselves. Bringing in humor enables the counselor to break the tension.

Ann: *She already does it when Pam fights with my brother. She doesn't mix in.*

Counselor: *She is smart. And I think she will not mix in now when the two of you fight. Fighting will be up to you. Ann, do you think of yourself as a little girl who is completely helpless?*

Comment 34: This question is used as an introduction to the next point.

Ann: *No.*

Counselor: *Well, then, since you are a big girl, mother should respect this. What about father? Does he mix into your fights?*

Ann: *Sometimes, but he doesn't get so angry, and we don't fight when he is around.*

Counselor: *That's interesting. Why not?*

Ann: *We just don't.*

Counselor: *What is your opinion, Pam, about not fighting when father is around?*

Pam: *We fight sometimes but when mother gets angry, she is so angry, and she gets so mean, and she punishes me.*

Counselor: *Could it be, Pamela, that it is not as much fun fighting when father is around than when mother is around? After all, father doesn't get involved but mother does. Perhaps, you like to get mother upset?*

Maybe you never thought of it, but when you think of it now, could it be that you enjoy seeing mother upset?

Pam: (Grins). *That's funny.*

Comment 35: Pam responded to the Counselor's confrontation with a typical affirmative reflex.

Counselor: *You know what I enjoy now, Pam? You don't answer me with "I don't know," but you talk to me and that helps me a lot to understand the problem. I appreciate it.*

Comment 36: Counselor gives encouragement to Pam by showing appreciation for her help.

Pam: *You're welcome.*

Counselor: *How do you feel about mother not getting involved in your fights?*

Ann: (Looking sad). *I don't know.*

Counselor: *What about you, Pam?*

Pam: *It's okay with me.*

Counselor: *I have all the confidence in the two of you that you will settle your problems without mother's interference. But, mother has another problem. She tells me that you, Pam, often tell her that you are dumb and that you are ugly. Why do you do this?*

Pam: *If I feel that way, I want to tell her. She is my mother, and I want her to know how I feel, and I don't always say this to her, only sometimes.*

Counselor: *Do you think that you are ugly?*

Pam: *Sometimes.*

Counselor: *When do you think that you are ugly and when don't you?*

Pam: *I don't know.*

Counselor: *Maybe I have an idea. Could it be that you want mother to reassure you, tell you how pretty you are, and pay attention to you?*

Pam: *Yes.*

Comment 37: Several of Pam's answers indicate that one of her goals also is "attention." Although the counselor did not use the standard format for confronting Pam with Goal One, the information reveals clearly that Pam is pursuing attention in this situation.

Counselor: *You are very honest, dear. You want mother's attention, and why not? Tell me, could you get mother's attention in a different way?*

Comment 38: The counselor is using every opportunity to be supportive to Pam and to win her over.

Pam: *I don't know what you mean?*

Counselor: *Well, instead of saying you are ugly, which you know that you are not, and mother knows that you really don't believe it, is there any other way that you could get her attention?*

Ann: *I know.*

Counselor: *So does your sister; I want to hear it from her.*

Pam: *I could do better in school.*

Counselor: *Oh, don't you do well in school?*

Pam: *Yes, but I goof off.*

Counselor: *Why do you do that?*

Pam: *I like it; it's fun.*

Counselor: *Pamela, you are a very smart girl. I wonder if you can tell me what you get out of goofing off in class? See if you can see a similar pattern to the one you use at home with mother?*

Ann: *I know.*

Counselor: (To audience). *I wonder if Ann feels that I am neglecting her? Maybe I did for a while. You and I will talk in a minute, Ann. Can you wait?*

Ann: (Nods affirmatively).

Counselor: *Well, Pamela, what do you think about what I said?*

Pam: *I don't know.*

Counselor: *Could it be that you like to keep many people busy with you and have them pay attention to you; mother at home, the teacher at school. What do you think?*

Pam: *I guess so.*

Counselor: *Pam, do you believe that this is the only way you can get attention by goofing off, by annoying, by asking the same questions knowing all the time what mother will say when you tell her that you are ugly? Can you think of other ways to get attention?*

Pam: *Yes.*

Counselor: *Like how?*

Pam: *Like not goofing off in class.*

Counselor: *But, will you get attention then?*

Pam: *I don't know.*

Counselor: *Do you ever help other children who can't do the work as well as you do?*

Comment 39: The Counselor is presenting an alternative way for Pam to get attention. This is encouraging to Pam because the counselor shows her faith that Pam can be a helper and shows no disapproval of her need for attention.

Pam: *No. The teacher wouldn't let me.*

Counselor: *How do you know? Have you tried?*

Pam: *I just know.*

Counselor: *Maybe you are right, but perhaps you are wrong. Would you want to find out? Tell your teacher that you would like to help children who can't do the work as well as you can. Would you be willing to try?*

Pam: *Yes.*

Counselor: *When? How soon will you ask the teacher?*

Pam: *Tomorrow.*

Counselor: *Good. Let's see what happens! What could you do to get different kinds of attention from mother? We call it "positive" attention.*

Pam: *I could help with the baby. I do help sometimes.*

Ann: *No, you don't. It's either me or Jeff.*

Counselor: *Ann, you have been trying to say something for some time. I'm sorry I let you wait. Before we discuss the remarks you made, would you tell me again, would you rather be a big girl or a little girl?*

Ann: *Mmmmm. That's a hard one. I don't know. Sometimes, I want to be little and then sometimes I want to be big.*

Counselor: *That is difficult. Could it be that you want both, to be the baby, and to have everyone pamper you. And at the same time you want to be bigger and smarter than Pamela?*

Ann: (No answer).

Counselor: *Do you know that all the time while I was talking to Pamela, you tried to show me how much smarter you are than she is and that you know all the answers? I know that you never realized what you were doing, but could it be that you like to push her down so that you can go up? Do you know what I mean?*

Comment 40: Some non-Adlerian trained people may consider such a direct confrontation objectionable. However, if the confrontation appears true to the children, the relationship with the counselor may actually improve because the child feels understood. Furthermore, Adlerians have great confidence that even very young children can face realities and mistaken ways of their behavior, even when they don't like what they hear. Adler referred to this as "Spitting into the soup." The child may still continue eating the soup, but it will never taste the same.

Ann: (No answer).

Counselor: *What do you think?*

Ann: *I didn't know that this is what I was doing. I wouldn't have done it (if I had understood). I can't help it if I didn't know it.*

Comment 41: Ann is actually operating on the active-constructive power level. She wants others to consider her as a good child who always wants to do the right thing.

Counselor: *Right. And nobody is accusing you. I am only making you aware of something you do without realizing it. But now that you know, what do you want to do?*

Ann: *I won't do it anymore.*

Counselor: *You may find that you will want to do it, but you can always catch yourself, and say to yourself, "Must I push her down in order to be noticed and to show how smart and good I am? I can be smart and good without pushing Pamela or anybody down." Does this make any sense to you?*

Ann: *Yeah.*

Counselor: *I am about to call your parents and together we will decide what each one of you could do to get along better with the other members in the family. Would you like to stay and be in on the discussion?*

Ann: *I would.*

Counselor: *You, Pam?*

Pam: *Yes.*

Comment 42: We always ask children if they want to stay for this part of the interview. Most of them do, but occasionally there are children who do not. We always respect their wishes. It is important to discuss the counselor's findings and evaluation with the parents.

Parents returned.

Brenda: *I am sure anxious to know how things went.*

Comment 43: The "good" mother has to know everything because it gives her some feeling of being in control.

Counselor: *What did you expect?*

Brenda: *Okay, I guess.*

Counselor: *You have two very pretty and very smart girls. I enjoyed very much talking with them. We ought to be able to summarize this session at this point. Each one of you has a clear picture of the situation and what other choices you have instead of doing what you did until now. For instance, Brenda, what might you do when Pamela tells you that she is ugly and dumb?*

Brenda: *Walk away and do nothing.*

Counselor: *No, Brenda, walking away is not doing nothing, it is doing something. You might shrug your shoulders and tell her that you are sorry that she feels that way and then walk away. You see, Pam knows exactly what you are going to tell her when she tells you that she is ugly and dumb. It is not a matter of what you say to her as it is to keep you busy with her. You could say anything, as long as you pay attention to her, she will be pleased. But, you should pay attention to her. Is there anything she does that pleases you?*

Brenda: *Sure. I am always pleased when she listens to me and when she helps me in the household.*

Comment 44: This is "conditional" acceptance. Mother needs to be helped to accept the children as they are, without setting conditions.

Counselor: *Brenda, I don't know if you are aware of what you are really saying. If you say that you are pleased with her if she listens, then you are not recognizing qualities Pam must have which have nothing to do with listening. Let's see if there is something you like that has nothing to do with her listening to you?*

Brenda: *I always like that she is so independent in the morning and gets ready for school by herself.*

Counselor: *Did you know, Pam, that this pleased mother?*

Pam: *No.*

Brenda: *Come on, Pamela, you know that this makes me very happy.*

Pam: *You never told me.*

Counselor: *Perhaps, this little incident will help you, Brenda, to be more conscious of telling your children the things you like about them. Don't take it for granted that they know. What I am suggesting here is encouragement built on positive attention and building on strength of the child and not on weakness. If you consider carefully, I am sure you can find many such situations where you can give them positive attention. Do you spend any time with each child in a way that is fun?*

Brenda: *Not enough. I am always rushing and tired. I should spend more time with them.*

Counselor: *What could mother do to encourage you, Pamela, and to make you feel good about yourself?*

Pam: *Nothing.*

Counselor: *You like her just the way she is and you don't want any changes.*

Pam: *I guess so.*

Counselor: *It's very wonderful that you accept mother as she is. But there will be some changes, Pamela. Like mother will not yell as she did before; she won't get involved with your fights with Ann, not explain over and over things you know any how, like that you are a pretty girl. There will be some changes.*

Pam: *That's all right.*

Counselor: *What can your mother do to encourage you, Ann, and to make you feel better.*

Ann: *She could listen to me more when I talk to her, and she could play with me, like she could play Monopoly or such with me.*

Counselor: *What do you think, Brenda?*

Brenda: *I will take more time to play with you, Ann, and I will listen when you talk to me.*

Counselor: *All right, Ann?*

Ann: *Okay, that's all I wanted to hear.*

Counselor: *What can father do to each one of you to make you feel happier?*

Ann: *He could do the same as Mom. He never has time for us. He could come home earlier and just be with us.*

Counselor: *What do you say, Bob?*

Bob: *I am really sorry, Ann, that I don't spend enough time with you—with all of you. I promise that I will do everything in my power to change this.*

Counselor: *What can each one of the three do to encourage you, Bob?*

Bob: *Well, I don't feel too discouraged. I have much confidence in my wife and in my children. If they stop aggravating Brenda, I will feel much better.*

Counselor: *What about you, Brenda, what can each one do so that you would feel happier.*

Brenda: *I really would feel much better if Pamela would talk nicer to me and not be so fresh, if she would not provoke me so.*

Counselor: *What do you say, Pamela?*

Pam: *I will try.*

Counselor: *You know, Pam, I explained to your mother about "trying."*
Trying usually doesn't work out well. You must decide if you want to
stop sassing mother or if you don't want to stop. You have every right to
make this decision.

Pam: *I will stop.*

Counselor: *Good. What can Ann and your husband do to encourage*
you, Brenda?

Brenda: *My husband could encourage me if he would stick up for me.*
Well, I don't mean "stick up for me" but sort of be on my side when I
see that he lets them do what they want and lets me do all the disciplin-
ing.

Comment 45: Mother has indicated throughout the conference how
life and how people are unfair to her. It becomes more evident how Ann
has learned some of these attitudes from mother.

Counselor: *What exactly would you want him to do?*

Brenda: *I would want him to tell Pam or any of the children, "your*
mother is right, and I won't have it when you talk back to her or don't
listen to her." That would make me feel much better.

Counselor: *You want his support.*

Brenda: *Right.*

Counselor: *When you tell your children "no," do they then go to father*
and he says "yes?"

Brenda: *Yeah, that happens also.*

Counselor: *Bob, this often encourages children to play one parent*
against the other. Would it be hard for you to tell a child, "this is be-
tween you and mother, and the two of you must work this out?"

Bob: *Not at all. I will be glad to do this.*

Counselor: *Would that help you Brenda?*

Brenda: *Some. It would be better.*

Comment 46: Our suggestion to parents is to not interfere with the spouse's way of handling or disciplining a child. If a parent has any criticism or suggestion, he/she should discuss this later when they are alone.

Counselor: *Do you think that we have accomplished anything here today?*

Pam: *I guess. Yes.*

Ann: *Yes, I think so.*

Counselor: *Brenda?*

Brenda: *Oh, yes. Thank you very much.*

Counselor: *You are a very lovely family, and I enjoyed very much talking to you. We will schedule you for a follow-up. Would you want to come back and tell me how things went and then we can discuss whatever other problems the family has?*

Bob: *Okay.*

Brenda: *Do I arrange this now or do you call me and tell us when you want us?*

Counselor: *Miss . . . . will discuss this with you after the session and make the arrangements.* (Shakes hands with all.) *Good-bye, thank you for coming.*

THE CASE OF THE SINGLE PARENT
AND ONLY CHILD

Joe is not only an only child, but is also a 16 year old adolescent. His father died when he was four. Mother has never remarried. Joe is a senior in high school, wears a suit, tie, and vest to the session. He is neatly groomed. Joe came alone for counseling.

Counselor: (After preliminary warm-up). *Tell me about yourself. Why did you come to see me?*

Joe: *I have a problem wherever I go.*

Counselor: *What kind of problem?*

Joe: *I want to know my identity as an individual. Not that I want to be something special.*

Counselor: *Would you please give me specific examples when you have a problem.*

Joe: *For instance, I want to wear what I want to wear and not what I am told I should wear. I want to please myself and not others.*

Counselor: *What does it mean to you "to strive for identity?"*

Joe: *I want to be myself.*

Counselor: *May I tell you what I think? Could it be that you want to be special, different from others, and that you want to have the right to do whatever you want, and that you resent anyone who tries to stop you?*

Comment 1: The client began the dialogue with generalized language. The counselor responded with a confrontation in order to move the discussion to specific issues. He/she may or may not have been accurate, but moving the discussion to specifics is necessary if the counselor is to help Joe with his problem—whatever it is.

Joe: *Doesn't everyone have this right? I mean shouldn't everybody have this right?*

Counselor: *May I tell you what you do, Joe? It seems to me that when you don't want to answer a question, you answer it with asking a question of your own. This is a technique people use to avoid answering questions they don't like. What do you think?*

Joe: *But I do think that everyone should have this right.*

Counselor: *Are you putting yourself in the category of "everybody?" Would you like to be included in the concept of "everybody?" This would put you in the category of "no better and no worse than anyone else."*

Joe: *I don't think that this is a fair question.*

Counselor: *May I tell you what other techniques you use to avoid answering? If you don't like the question, you attack the person who asks the question. But tell me, why is this unfair?*

Comment 2: The counselor again confronts Joe. She points out how Joe is trying to avoid the real issue.

Joe: *Because you are trying to pin me down. I don't like that.*

Counselor: *Why not?*

Joe: *I just don't. I am not a snob, but I don't think that anybody likes to be just like anybody else.*

Counselor: *May I tell you what other techniques you use to avoid answering? You intellectualize and use generalizations, and righteousness.*

Comment 3: The counselor continues to confront Joe with the techniques that Joe uses to avoid the real issues. Although some counselors would feel that such repeated confrontations would alienate the client, the counselor is showing Joe that she understands him and feeling understood, Joe will respond positively. This point is verified in the next exchanges.

Joe: *So what's wrong with that?*

Counselor: *This is not a question of what is right or what is wrong. I am not sitting here in judgment of you, Joe. I am concerned in helping you see why some things are so important to you, how you think, and why you have problems in life. That is, if you want to find out. I can't force you to listen or to buy what I am saying. Tell me do you want to find out?*

Joe: *Sure.*

Counselor: *May I tell you what I think?*

Joe: *If you wish.*

Counselor: *Could it be that you want to be special, but that you are careful not to admit this even to yourself? Could it be that you want to be so good and so fair and you're afraid that if you openly admit that you want to be better than others you may lose their respect for you?*

Joe: *No.*

Counselor: *Could it be that you think "yes" and say "no?"*

Joe: *Why would I want to be special? I told you that I am no snob.*

Counselor: *Yes, you did. Maybe I was wrong. Tell me are many people unfair to you?*

Comment 4: The counselor moves to a more specific question designed to get at Joe's real problem.

Joe: *I don't know what you call "unfair," but I run into them often.*

Counselor: *Give me an example of when someone was unfair to you.*

Joe: *Well, like this matter of what I wear. I like to look nice. My family brought me up to look my best—presentable. I never understand radicals. I don't want to break rules, and I think that I am right at this. This is how I was brought up.*

Counselor: *How does this show that people are unfair to you?*

Joe: *Oh, yes. The other students in my class think that this makes me odd; they often joke about it; they even laugh at me. Just because I like to dress differently, and I like to look my best.*

Counselor: (Just sat and said nothing. There was a minute's silence.)

Comment 5: The counselor is allowing time for Joe to think through his previous remark and to make his own deduction as to why he really prefers to dress the way he does. He got the point.

Joe: *I guess you will think that this way I try to be special.*

Counselor: (Silence.)

Joe: *I guess that you think that I try to be better than the others.*

Counselor: *Any other problems, Joe?*

Joe: *Only in that area, I do everything to be different than others, but not because I want to show off or something. I don't tell people what they should do, and they should not tell me what I should do. This is only fair. They should just leave me alone.*

Counselor: *In what other areas are you different, Joe?*

Joe: *I am colorful, not dull. I like to play hooky. I goof off.*

Counselor: *Do you know why you do this?*

Joe: *Yeah. I don't want to be dull.*

Counselor: *Do you want my opinion?*

Joe: *What is your opinion?*

Comment 6: Joe obviously has been impressed with the counselor's interpretations. He is now really interested in what she has to say. The counselor has established her credibility with the client. Rapport is present.

Counselor: *Could it be that you depend too much on being the star of the show? That you think very little of yourself unless you are the star?*

Joe: *Why do you always ask questions that one can't answer with "yes" or "no?" Yes, I want to be different, I said that.*

Counselor: *What do you want to be? You'll make an excellent lawyer. Was anyone ever strict with you?*

Joe: *What makes you think that I would make an excellent lawyer?*

Counselor: *You seem to be overambitious, Joe. Interesting that you did not respond to my questions, but you seem impressed with my diagnosis. Do you feel flattered?*

Joe: *I would really like to know why you think that I'd make an excellent lawyer.*

Counselor: *You seem to be good in talking around a subject and getting people confused. Are you aware of this? Did anyone ever tell you that you talk like a lawyer?*

Joe: *Only my teachers.*

Counselor: *But teachers don't count, right?*

Joe: (Laughs). *Maybe.*

Counselor: *They are not smart enough for you, right?*

Joe: (Laughs very hard). *Maybe.*

Counselor: *What kind of student are you now?*

Joe: *A poor student. I argue with teachers.*

Counselor: *Why?*

Joe: *They try to prove that they are right, and I try to prove that I am right.*

Counselor: *You are not concerned with what is right, only with who is right. Only with being right. Could it be that you would rather flunk than give in?*

Joe: *Perhaps.*

Counselor: *Do you do anything to get attention?*

Joe: *Yes, I goof off.*

Counselor: *Do you know why?*

Joe: *Yes, because I want to.*

Counselor: *That's right. Nobody can tell you what to do. What do you do especially well?*

Joe: *Play hockey.*

Counselor: *Is it possible that you do well only in areas where you can have a special position?*

Joe: *Perhaps.*

Comment 7: Joe is beginning to see the accuracy of the counselor's interpretations.

Counselor: *Are you pleased with yourself? Do you want to continue life as it is now?*

Comment 8: The counselor is assessing Joe's desire to change.

Joe: *I wouldn't have come if I did.*

Counselor: *Not necessarily. You may have come for other reasons.*

Joe: *I wouldn't know what other reasons. Would you mind telling me what you mean?*

Counselor: *For instance, you may have come to please your mother, to show her that you, coming from a family where good manners and obedience is valued, are doing what is expected of you. And then, you may have come to outsmart me and to show that you're superior to me, that you can draw circles around me. You are very good at this. Are you aware of it? That's quite a talent you have.*

Comment 9: The counselor admits to Joe's talent and superiority over her if he chooses to use it. She withdraws from any play for Joe to use his power.

Joe: (Big grin). *You're much older and wiser. I would not do this to you even if I could.*

Counselor: *"Even if you could." Could it be that you think, "I could?" You see, good manners are very important to you, and therefore, you could never admit that. But I don't see why you should change if you are happy. You could even throw away your outward good manners and make it real tough on teachers and everybody. It's your life, and you have the right to do as you wish. Good-bye Joe. I enjoyed talking to you.*

Comment 10: The counselor concedes Joe's rights to decide how he will live his life, thus placing the responsibility squarely on Joe's shoulders.

Joe: *What do you suggest that I do?*

Counselor: *Do you really want to know? You may not like to do what I will suggest.*

Joe: *I would like to hear it first.*

Counselor: *You could start by accepting yourself as being human, having faults, having problems, and not to think less of yourself because of it.*

Joe: *But I do.*

Counselor: *No, my dear. You don't. You have to show the world that you're better, superior. You don't touch anything where you don't shine as you do in hockey. Being special is too important to you.*

Joe: *I didn't know.*

Counselor: *That's right. Would you want to see me again?*

Joe: *Yes, I would like to.*

Comment 11: It is obvious that Joe accepts the counselor's interpretations. He wants to return.

Counselor: *Think about what I said, and come, and see me again.*

A CASE STUDY OF ROLE PLAY
IN COUNSELING

Counselors are discovering an increasing variety of techniques that prove effective in re-educating family members. One of these, which has proven very effective, is role playing. This technique is illustrated in the following case. A mother has come for help with a daughter. She is extremely worried about late hours, and strange friends that the daughter alludes to; drugs, and the cessation of communication with the daughter. Mother is in a real dilemma as to her daughter's situation. This case also illustrates how even very brief counseling sessions can be effective in promoting changes in family relationships.

Mother: *I don't know where my daughter is when she goes out at night. When she was little, she did not go out in the evening except when she went with us. I always feel tense and worried when she is out at night. When I try to talk to her about it, she gets mad and rushes off to her room. There is no way I can talk to her about it.*

Counselor: *Would you mind if we role played this kind of situation, with me playing your daughter. Now, how late does she usually come home.*

Mother: *Anywhere between eleven and twelve midnight. Sometimes even later.*

Counselor: *Now, let's imagine that I am Iris, and I just came home at midnight. Where would you be at this time?*

Mother: *I usually stay up and wait for her in the living room.*

Counselor: *Okay. You are waiting in the living room. How do you feel?*

Mother: *I feel worried, but I also feel angry, very angry. She knows that I won't go to sleep until she comes home and why would she do this to me?*

Counselor: *Okay. I am Iris. I just came home. You are waiting in the living room. Now show me what you do or what you say when she enters.*

Mother: *This is a hard one, but I will try. I say to her that she had no right to . . . . .*

Counselor: *No, Mrs. Wanda. Talk to me exactly the way you would to your daughter, using the same words and the same tone of voice.*

Mother: *Do you know what time it is? You said you would be home at 11:00 at the latest, and it is almost midnight. Where in hell have you been? You run around with those bums, those good-for-nothing bums.*

Yes, that's what they are and that's what you are getting to be. I just won't have it . .

Counselor: *Now let's change roles and you will be Iris, and I will be you. Show me what she says or does when you talk to her the way you just did. I will repeat the last few words you said, and then you show me. "You run around with bums, and that's what you're becoming now. I won't have it."*

Now you show me what she says and does.

Mother: (Making a disgusting face). *Well, it's just too bad. And then she goes into her room, and she locks it.*

Counselor: *How do you know that she locks it?*

Mother: *I know because I go after her, and I can't get into her room.*

Counselor: *How do you suppose your daughter feels when you talk to her the way you have just shown me?*

Mother: *How I think she feels? What do I care how she feels? It's how I feel that is the question here. I did not do anything wrong.*

Counselor: *I understand how you feel, and I am not saying that you're wrong. I just want you for a moment to put yourself into Iris's skin and imagine how she feels. Would you try, please?*

Mother: *It's not easy when you are so mad, but I will try. I would feel guilty and apologize. But I don't suppose that this is what you want.*

Counselor: *It's not a question of what I want. I think it would help if you, knowing how your daughter reacts to criticism and scolding, might react in this case.*

Mother: *I guess she thinks that I am a hysterical woman and that I wouldn't understand or give in to her.*

Counselor: *If you were she, feeling the way you describe her, what would you do?*

Mother: *I don't know. I really can't know.*

Counselor: *Let's see if we can find another approach to the same situation. You are angry because Iris broke her promise and came home late. How could you have handled this situation differently, so that Iris might have listened to you?*

Mother: *I don't know. You tell me.*

Counselor: *I am not sure if I know exactly, but I might have told her that I was glad to see her, told her "Good-night," and discussed the matter with her the next day when both of you might be calmer. I might have told her of my concern, not that I did not trust her but that one hears and reads of so many incidents where young girls are being attacked at night. I would have asked her to help me with my fears. I would probably not say anything of a derogatory nature about her friends, because I might only antagonize her, and I want to win her over and trust me. Once you change the relationship, you might ask her about her friends and if she feels that they are the right kind of people for her. You see, Mrs. Wanda, you would first have to establish a relationship built on trust and respect before you can have good communication with your daughter. Right now, both of you are too angry. You might then discuss possible consequences when she breaks her agreement. This can not happen overnight; it is a slow process and calls for a great deal of self-control, but it can be done. What do you say?*

Mother: *I certainly want a better relationship with my daughter, and I am willing to do anything, but I don't know if I can carry through what you suggest.*

Counselor: *Start, and then we shall see what difficulties you have and discuss what you might do next. But do begin right away. Find a good moment for the two of you to talk about your concern and appeal to Iris to help you. Perhaps, she can start with one thing first, like coming home at 11:00 on week days or three days a week. Then once she keeps her agreement, you can show how pleased you are, and perhaps you can negotiate with her further. Remember that she needs much encouragement from you, not criticism or punishment. But make sure that she is aware of your concern.*

Try it this week and come and see me next week. Perhaps Iris would be willing to come also.

Comment: The reader might be interested to know that mother and daughter improved their relationship within a few weeks. Iris did not trust the change in her mother at first, but gradually, she began to talk to her mother and listen to her with understanding. When the counselor last saw the mother, Iris was coming home before eleven when she went out evenings, and on days when she stayed out later, she told her mother where she would be and that she would be home no later than one in the morning. She asked mother not to wait up for her. Iris seldom stayed out late. While it was not exactly what mother had originally wished for, namely that her daughter always should be home at ten in the evening. She accepted this arrangement as it proved to be more satisfactory in their relationship and it led to better communication.

SUMMARY

Today's children often challenge the parent's ideas of appropriate behavior. Parents who have rebellious children are bound to get into a terrible power-struggle with their adolescent children, one which leads to the loss of the youngster's confidence, and to the final power-struggle which the parent is bound to lose.

APPENDICES

APPENDIX A

THE FAMILY COUNSELING CENTER

Adler demonstrated his theory and approach to understanding problems between parents and children by counseling the entire family in an open counseling center. Parents, children, and often the children's teachers were interviewed in front of an audience. Parents with children older than ten years generally were interviewed together while parents with younger children were interviewed separately. This was explained in more detail in Chapter V. In this way, observers as well as the identified family benefited from the counseling sessions and discussions which followed.

Establishing and Operating a Family Counseling Center

A center may be an independent, nonprofit organization, or it may be one of an integrated chain of centers sponsored by the community, church, school, settlement house, or any other interested group.

Each center needs a coordinator, counselor, recorder, playroom director, and a social worker if possible. The social worker is more essential when a community has several centers and he/she serves all of them. All staff members may serve more than one center.

Most centers hold sessions once a week for an hour and a half to two hours depending on the involvement of the audience. At the stated opening time, the audience takes seats in the counseling room. The parents to be counseled sit next to the counselor while the children go to the playroom where they are observed by the playroom director. The recorder sits near the counselor. The counseling session may be preceded by a presentation on selected parenting principles and techniques.

Parents who intend to be counseled attend two to four counseling sessions as observers prior to being counseled. This procedure is suggested in order that the parents may acquaint themselves with the procedure and observe the educational process that takes place during a counseling session. Most parents identify their problems with some of the problems of the parents who are being counseled. This helps parents who are being counseled to relax and not feel threatened by the forthcoming experience.

When parents wish to be counseled, they see the social worker or intake person who is in charge of recording a brief history of the family. Most centers have an intake form which the social worker completes and gives to the counselor before the counseling session takes place. The purpose for this is two-fold, it helps the counselor focus on those areas which are more urgent, and the center has a record of the family that schedules counseling.

Most centers operate on the basis of voluntary support. Usually, a group of interested citizens sponsor a center. This means that they provide a place to meet and facilities for the children to wait while the parents are being counseled. In some situations, they may have to underwrite the expenses for conducting the sessions. The money is usually raised through drives, donations, rummage sales, dances, or dues that members pay. Volunteers usually are parents.

The personnel for such an organization usually is composed of four general groups. These are as follows:

—A Board of Directors which sends delegates to meetings which the staff hold. The Board of Directors integrate the activities of each center.

—Volunteer workers who act as receptionists, raise funds, prepare refreshments, and so forth.

—Other nonprofessional assistants such as assistant playroom worker, recorder, or registrar.

—Professional workers such as counselor, social worker, and playroom director. However, the latter does not necessarily have to be professionally trained.

Counselors should be trained in the Adlerian philosophy and in the techniques of Adlerian family counseling. We have found that professional counselors, with other than the Adlerian approach, prove unable to carry on the process described.

The Role of the Social Worker

While the staff of the centers must operate as a team, each of them performs a specialized task independently of the others. The social worker's responsibilities are to contact individual families who have indicated a desire to be counseled and to schedule appointments. The social worker also may contact school personnel including teachers of the child with school problems. The social worker does the initial intake and keeps a record of the case.

The Role of the Recorder

The function of the recorder is to take notes during the interviews, edit them, and rewrite them in an organized fashion. These notes help the counselor to review the previous interviews with respect to the problem, the family interaction, the goals of the children as diagnosed by the counselor, and the recommendations made.

The recorder's report should be brief and to the point. Example:

Merle refuses to do her homework unless a parent sits with her.

Mother is convinced that Merle would never do her work unless a parent "makes" her do it.

Mother was reluctant to accept counselor's suggestion to leave homework to Merle and let the school handle it.

Counselor decided not to work on this problem at this session but wait until mother experienced some success in other areas.

Father was disturbed about the hassle that goes on each morning when the girls had to decide what to wear to school.

Merle complains that mother yells a lot.

Stella agreed to take a bath each evening without having to be reminded and forced.

Merle seems to operate on goals one and two.

Counselor's recommendations:

1. Parents should not get involved in what the children decided to wear in the morning.

2. Express appreciation when Stella takes a bath without having been reminded.

3. Mother should catch herself each time she wants to yell and lower her voice.

4. Children should realize that the parents are discouraged and unhappy, and they should think of ways to encourage the parents—with words or deeds.

5. Establish a Family Council.

While it is important to record the exact recommendations made by the counselor, it is not necessary to write down every word a family member says. The recorder has to eliminate irrelevant details.

Role of the Playroom Director

The playroom director needs to have an understanding of the basic principles of child behavior. He/she must treat the child with respect and acceptance. The playroom director must be observant and alert to the children's interaction, who takes leading roles, who follows, who bullies, who withdraws, and who uses charm to feel accepted.

The playroom director may engage the children in organized games, singing, acting, or leaving them to their own devices to play with materials provided by the center, or with each other in any manner they wish.

The playroom director's role is primarily to observe children and to report observations to the counselor. The playroom director gives the report after the counselor has interviewed parents and before the children enter. The purpose of the playroom director's report is to assess the children's attitudes and behavior in the playroom as compared to what the counselor was told by the parents. After the playroom director gives the report, the children enter the counseling room and are interviewed by the counselor.

The parents return after the counselor has finished talking with the children. The children may remain or may leave, depending on their wishes.

The counselor summarizes the interview with the parents and the one with the children. He/she gives recommendations to the parents. At this time, if the children decide to remain, the counselor may encourage both parents and children to come to constructive agreements.

For extensive information on Adlerian open center counseling see the chapter by Christensen and Marchant (1983).

BIBLIOGRAPHY

Christensen, O. C., & Marchant, W. C. (1983). The family counseling process, Chapter III in Christensen, O. C., & Schramski, T. G., *Adlerian family counseling*. Minneapolis, Minnesota: Educational Media Corporation.

Lowe, R. N., & Morse, C. (1977). Parent-child education centers in Hatcher, C. and Brooks, B., Editors. *Innovations in Counseling Psychology: Developing New Roles, Settings, and Techniques.* San Francisco, California: Jossey-Bass.

APPENDIX B

SHARING RESPONSIBILITIES

(Sharing Responsibilities was prepared by the Community Parent-Teacher Counselor Education Center of Tucson, Arizona.)

In today's changing society, children are challenged to become "working partners" with parents and teachers. Such a challenge can be met in many ways: mutual respect, sharing of opinions, acceptance of decisions, cooperative setting of goals, standards, or limitations, and permitting certain rights and privileges.

Assuming responsibilities can enhance the individual interpersonally and intrapersonally. As the child learns the benefits of order resulting from cooperation, he/she begins to view himself/herself as a person who is capable of making a contribution to others. Growth in this area is best acquired developmentally, whereby the child becomes useful and needed at an early age, with the expectation of becoming more self-reliant and independent as time passes.

Adult's personal experiences and situations may lead him/her to find many ways in which a child can contribute. Sometimes parents and teachers aware of the need to giving children responsibility, are stymied at knowing what to do and what to expect. The following is intended to meet this need.

In training for these responsibilities, it may be wise to proceed gradually. First establish a relationship, and then through friendly discussions, the adult and the child together may determine the manner in which the child can become a contributing member.

Before assigning duties, it would be helpful to keep some of the following principles in mind:

Children have rights as well as responsibilities. If these rights are arbitrarily or impulsively withdrawn by the adult, the child may feel dominated or revengeful and will resist any efforts to elicit his/her cooperation.

Children should be consulted about jobs that need to be done. After they have helped identify the work, then they must set standards of work, and be involved in the evaluation of the completed jobs.

Allow the children choices in which jobs they would like to do. (Not doing anything is not one of the choices.) They must then follow with their choice or experience the consequences.

Allow the consequences to follow logically from the uncompleted job. Do discuss beforehand what will happen if someone does not fulfill the commitment.

Place appropriate time limits on when a task should be completed. If the child participates in setting these time limits, he/she will be more willing to meet them.

Vary the tasks to do. Children become easily bored with the same thing. They like the challenge of a new or unusual job.

Use common sense in the number of tasks expected of each child. He/she may stage a "sitdown" strike if he/she feels used.

Remember you are a model of "order" to your child. Do not expect an orderliness or cleanliness from him/her that you would not expect of yourself.

Examine your own standards. Perhaps you are a perfectionist about your house or classroom, feel uncomfortable if things are slightly out of order, or are concerned about what others will think. Learn to accept the house or classroom as a place of work and communication for the members, and not as a reflection of your own personal worth.

Never do anything for a child that he/she can do for himself/herself, except in an emergency.

HOME RESPONSIBILITIES
FOR A 3-YEAR OLD

1. Pick up unused toys and put in the proper place.

2. Put books and magazines in a rack.

3. Empty ashtrays.

4. Carry napkins, plates, and silverware to the table.

5. Clean up what they drop after eating.

6. Clear own place at the table. Put dishes on the counter after cleaning the leftovers off the plate.

7. Simple hygiene—brush teeth, wash and dry hands and face, and brush hair.

8. Undress self—dress with some help.

9. Wipe up own accidents.

10. Carry boxed or canned goods from the grocery sacks to proper shelf. Put some things away on a lower shelf.

HOME RESPONSIBILITIES
FOR 4-YEAR OLD

1. Set the table—with good dishes, too, with some help.

2. Help mother put the groceries away.

3. Help with grocery shopping under close supervision.

4. Follow a schedule for feeding pets.

5. Help do easy yard and garden work.

6. Help make the beds.

7. Help do dishes or fill dishwasher, with some help.

8. Dust furniture.

9. Spread butter on sandwiches.

10. Prepare cold cereal.

11. Help mother prepare plates of food for family dinner.

12. Help make a simple dessert (add topping to cupcakes, jello, pour toppings on ice cream).

13. Hold hand mixer to whip potatoes or mix a cake.

14. Share toys with friends (practice courtesy).

15. Get the mail.

16. Tell parent his/her whereabouts before going out to play.

17. Play without constant adult supervision and attention.

18. Bring in milk from the milkbox.

19. Hang socks, handkerchiefs, and washcloths on a lower line.

HOME RESPONSIBILITIES
FOR A 5-YEAR OLD

1. Help with meal planning and grocery shopping.

2. Make own sandwich or simple breakfast and clean afterwards.

3. Pour own drink.

4. Set dinner table.

5. Tear lettuce for salad.

6. Put in certain ingredients to a recipe.

7. Make bed and clean room.

8. Dress himself/herself and choose outfit for the day.

9. Scrub the sink, toilet, and bathtub.

10. Clean mirrors and windows if they are low.

11. Separate clothing for washing. Put white clothes in one pile and colored in another.

12. Fold clean clothes and put them away.

13. Answer the telephone.

14. Help with yard work.

15. Pay for small purchases.

16. Help clean out car.

17. Help take out garbage.

18. Decide how he/she wants to spend his/her of the family entertainment fund.

19. Feed his/her pets and clean the pet's living area.

20. Tie own shoes.

HOME RESPONSIBILITIES
FOR 6-YEAR OLD
FIRST GRADE

1. Choose own clothing for the day according to the weather or a special event.

2. Shake rugs.

3. Water plants and flowers.

4. Peel vegetables.

5. Cook simple food (hot dogs, boiled egg, and toast).

6. Prepare own school lunch.

7. Help hang clothes on the clothes line.

8. Hang up own clothes in the closet.

9. Gather wood for fireplace.

10. Rake leaves and weeds.

11. Take pet for walk.

12. Tie own shoes.

13. Responsible for own minor injuries.

14. Keep the garbage container clean.

15. Help clean out inside of car.

16. Straighten or clean out silverware drawer.

17. Set the table.

HOME RESPONSIBILITIES
FOR 7-YEAR OLD
SECOND GRADE

1. Oil and care for bike and lock it when unused.

2. Take phone messages and write them down.

3. Sweep and wash patio area.

4. Run errands for parents.

5. Water the lawn.

6. Take care for bike and other outside toy or equipment.

7. Wash dog or cat.

8. Train pets.

9. Carry in the grocery sacks.

10. Get self up in the morning and to bed at night without being told.

11. Be polite, courteous, and respect others.

12. Carry own lunch money and notes to school.

13. Leave the bathroom in order; hang up clean towels.

14. Do simple ironing, flat pieces.

15. Scrub floors.

HOME RESPONSIBILITIES
FOR 8-9 YEAR OLDS
THIRD GRADE

1. Fold napkins properly and set silverware properly.

2. Mop or buff the floor.

3. Clean venetian blinds.

4. Help rearrange furniture. Help plan the layout.

5. Run own bath water.

6. Help others with their work when asked.

7. Straighten own closet and drawers.

8. Shop and select own clothing and shoes with parent's assistance.

9. Change school clothes without being told.

10. Fold blankets.

11. Sew buttons.

12. Sew rips in seams.

13. Clean storage room.

14. Clean up animal "messes" in the yard and house.

15. Begin to read recipes and cook for the family.

16. Babysit for short periods of time.

17. Cut flowers and make a centerpiece.

18. Pick fruit off trees.

19. Build a campfire, get items ready to cook out (charcoal, meat).

20. Paint fence or shelves.

21. Write simple letters.

22. Write thank-you notes.

23. Help with defrosting and cleaning of the refrigerator.

24. Feed the baby.

25. Bathe younger sister or brother.

26. Polish silverware, copper, or brass items.

27. Clean patio furniture.

28. Wax living room furniture.

HOME RESPONSIBILITIES
FOR 9-10 YEAR OLDS
FOURTH GRADE

1. Change sheets on the bed and put dirty sheets in hamper.

2. Operate the washer and/or dryer.

3. Measure detergent and bleach.

4. Buy groceries using a list and comparative shopping.

5. Cross streets unassisted.

6. Keep own appointments (dentist, school, and so forth, if within bike distance).

7. Prepare pastries from box mixes.

8. Prepare a family meal.

9. Receive and answer own mail.

10. Pour and make tea, coffee, and kool-aid.

11. Wait on guests.

12. Plan own birthday or other parties.

13. Be able to apply simple first aid.

14. Do neighborhood chores.

15. Be able to sew, knit, or weave (even use a sewing machine).

16. Wash the family car.

17. Learn to bank and to be thrifty.

HOME RESPONSIBILITIES
FOR 10-11 YEAR OLDS
FIFTH GRADE

1. Earn own money (babysit).

2. Do not fear to be alone at home.

3. Handle sums of money responsibly.

4. Be able to take the city bus.

5. Be responsible for personal hobby.

HOME RESPONSIBILITIES
FOR 11-12 YEAR OLDS
SIXTH GRADE

1. Be able to take responsibility as a leader in outside organizations.

2. Put very young siblings to bed.

3. Clean pool and pool area.

4. Run own errands.

5. Mow lawn.

6. Help father build things and do family errands.

7. Clean oven and stove.

8. Be able to schedule himself/herself the time for studies.

9. Be responsible for a paper route.

10. Check and add oil to car.

HOME RESPONSIBILITIES FOR
JUNIOR HIGH STUDENTS

1. Be able to determine how late he/she should stay up during the week. Also be able to determine how late he/she should be out for evening gatherings (Through mutual child-parent discussion and agreement).

2. Accept responsibility of preparing family meals.

3. Have social awareness: good health, necessary rest, nutritious food, exercise, correct weight, physical examination.

4. Anticipate the needs of others and initiate the appropriate action.

5. Have a realistic acceptance of capabilities and limitations.

6. Have self-respect or individual worth.

7. Take responsibility for one's decisions.

8. Show mutual respect, loyalty, and honesty in the family.

APPENDIX C

INSTRUCTIONS FOR ADMINISTERING
FAMILY RELATIONSHIP INDEX

Materials Required:

1. Instruction sheet
2. Double-sided rating form
3. Pencils

Procedures:

1. *Before passing out forms* tell parents: "I shall give you instructions for filling out this form. Please wait for instructions."

2. *Now pass out the forms.* Ask if anyone wants a pencil.

3. When all have a form say: "This form will help show problem areas in your family. Please fill in your name and the date and check 'mother' or 'father'."

4. "Fill in the name, sex, and age of the children living at home, beginning with the oldest child, going down by age."

5. "The word *rating* refers to the degree of difficulty you are having with that child overall. An '0' means *no problem,* '1' means *minor problem,* '2' means *moderate problem,* '3' means *serious problem,* and 'X' means you *cannot rate* the child. An example of inability to rate is: a one-year-old would not be in school and therefore would have an 'X' rating for the item 'home-school'."

6. "Only you can judge the degree of difficulty. Please fill out the forms independently."

7. "I will now read each item with a brief explanation and you are to put in the boxes the degree of problem you are having with each child by

writing in the box a '0', a '1', a '2', a '3', or an 'X'." If parents show an understanding, turn to reverse side of this sheet and *read verbatim each item,* allowing some time for decision-making on the part of the parents.

8. After the 24 items have been read, suggest: "You may have a problem not listed here. Please put them in spaces labeled *other problems,* and rate them accordingly."

General Information for Administrator.

An individual administration will last about ten minutes. A group administration will last about fifteen minutes. The reverse side of the rating form is for post-counseling or study group evaluation and for research purposes.

PROBLEM AREAS AND SPECIFIC QUESTIONS

1. *Getting up* (Any difficulty in getting children out of bed in the morning?)

2. *Dressing* (Any problems about getting dressed: selection of clothing, color combinations?)

3. *Eating* (Does child decline to eat properly, refuse certain foods, show bad manners?)

4. *Cleanliness* (Does child resist washing, bathing, tooth-brushing?)

5. *Home/school* (Are there problems about school that spill over at home, notes from teachers?)

6. *Bedtime* (Do you have difficulty persuading child it's bedtime; does child keep getting up?)

7. *Conformance* (Does child comply with family rules without resistance—and parent pressure?)

8. *Chores* (Does child do assigned work without hassles, remember what to do and do it properly?)

9. *Own room* (Does child keep own room clean and neat, make bed, put things away?)

10. *Clutter* (Does child leave toys, papers, books cluttering up house and/or yard?)

11. *Possessions* (Does child take adequate care of own toys, books, games?)

12. *Fighting* (Does child quarrel and fight with brothers, sisters or other children?)

13. *Car behavior* (Any problems with fighting, fidgeting, making noises, teasing other children?)

14. *Public misbehavior* (Are there problems in stores, restaurants, visiting in friends' homes?)

15. *Aggression* (Does child show aggressive or brutal behavior with persons outside family?)

16. *Social* (Is child shy, fearful, critical of or uncooperative with others?)

17. *Attention seeking* (Does child demand undue and/or constant attention—show off, whine, talk back?)

18. *Dawdling* (Is child slow to do what is requested or required—draggy about getting started?)

19. *Temper displays* (Does child get upset too easily, cry without real cause, throw tantrums?)

20. *Fears and terrors* (Is child afraid of dark, strangers, animals, being alone?)

21. *Harmful habits* (Does child bite nails, suck thumb, pull hair, eat dirt, put objects in nose?)

22. *Bedwetting* (Not much explanation needed here...)

23. *Incontinence* (Is child unable to retain urine or feces during day?)

24. *Character* (Does child lie, cheat, steal?)

1 FAMILY RELATIONSHIP INDEX FRONT

( ) Mother
Family Name _____ ( ) Father Date _____

Please fill in below, using the following ratings:

RATINGS: 0 — No problem   2 — Moderate problem   X — Cannot rate
          1 — Minor problem   3 — Serious problem

Names of children at home - oldest first.

Child	Age	Sex	Rating	Child	Age	Sex	Rating
I _____	( )	( )	( )	IV _____	( )	( )	( )
II _____	( )	( )	( )	V _____	( )	( )	( )
III _____	( )	( )	( )	VI _____	( )	( )	( )

	CHILD								CHILD						
	I	II	III	IV	V	VI			I	II	III	IV	V	VI
1. Getting up							13. Car							
2. Dressing							14. Public							
3. Eating							15. Aggression							
4. Keeping clean							16. Social							
5. Home-School							17. Attention							
6. Bedtime							18. Dawdling							
7. Conformance							19. Temper							
8. Chores							20. Fears							
9. Own room							21. Habits							
10. Clutter							22. Bedwetting							
11. Possessions							23. Incontinence							
12. Fighting							24. Character							

Other problems:

(1) _____ Rating ( )

(2) _____ Rating ( )

Comments: _____

_____

FAMILY RELATIONSHIP INDEX developed by Ray Corsini, Ph.D.

2 FAMILY RELATIONSHIP INDEX   BACK

( ) Mother

Family Name _____ ( ) Father   Date _____

Please fill in below, using the following ratings:

RATINGS: 0 — No problem   2 — Moderate problem   X — Cannot rate
           1 — Minor problem   3 — Serious problem

Names of children at home - oldest first.

Child	Age	Sex	Rating	Child	Age	Sex	Rating
I _____ ( )	( )	( )	IV _____ ( )	( )	( )
II _____ ( )	( )	( )	V _____ ( )	( )	( )
III _____ ( )	( )	( )	VI _____ ( )	( )	( )

CHILD
I II III IV V VI

1. Getting up
2. Dressing
3. Eating
4. Keeping clean
5. Home-School
6. Bedtime
7. Conformance
8. Chores
9. Own room
10. Clutter
11. Possessions
12. Fighting

CHILD
I II III IV V VI

13. Car
14. Public
15. Aggression
16. Social
17. Attention
18. Dawdling
19. Temper
20. Fears
21. Habits
22. Bedwetting
23. Incontinence
24. Character

Other problems:

(1) _____ Rating ( )

(2) _____ Rating ( )

Comments: _____

_____

PRACTICAL PARENTING PUBLICATIONS Box 1635   Columbia, Missouri 65205

APPENDIX D

PARENT SELF-HELP CHECKLIST

The counselor can often get the parents more involved in counseling process by asking them to complete the following Self-Help Checklist. Such activities will usually result in parents becoming sensitive to the various ploys the child uses to control and manipulate the parents.

Does your child:

1. demand service like, "Mom, get me a glass of water, a fork, a pencil, my shoes, etc.?

2. wait for you to wake him?

3. have to be reminded to practice his music lesson; do his/her homework, write a "thank-you" note, not to be late for a doctor's appointment, be home in time for dinner, and so forth?

4. expect you to remind him/her to take along his/her lunch, library book, homework, mittens, note to the teacher, and so forth?

5. refuse to do homework unless you sit with him/her?

6. watch television every spare moment?

7. tell you that he/she is bored and that you "do something about it" or that you tell him/her what he should do?

8. refuse to go even very short distances by himself/herself?

9. refuse to play unless others play the game that he/she wants?

10. cry when he/she loses a game?

11. throw up or indicate other digestive symptoms when he/she is forced to eat something that he/she doesn't want to eat?

12. "forget" to take care of his/her pet?

13. let you carry things that he/she could very well carry himself like books, clothes, when you walk with him/her?

14. demand that you go to school to tell the teacher that the children tease and mistreat him/her?

15. demand that you go to school to straighten out unpleasant situations that he/she created?

16. ask you, "what shall I say?" when he/she has to talk to someone about a situation or a problem?

17. demand frequently that you tell him/her that you love him/her?

18. get upset because you did not tell him/her that he/she is a good boy/girl?

19. want to be praised for everything he/she does?

20. demand that you tell him/her what to wear and pick out his/her clothes?

21. refuse to go to school with other children and demands that a parent take him/her there?

22. refuse to work in class unless the teacher sits with him/her?

23. say, "I can't" when asked to do something for the first time?

24. refuse to go into the doctor's office unless a parent goes in with him/her?

25. come to you at night because he/she has nightmares?

Dependency takes on many forms. Not all of them can be found in textbooks. Some can be found under "Attention" or "Power" or *"Assumed Inadequacy."* Much of children's dependency may be in having his own way and a constant reassurance of being loved.

When you check out the above possibilities, always find out how the parent handles the situation because then you will be in a better position to understand why the child behaves as he/she does.

INDEX

INDEX

A

words 132-3
Encouragement of children, definition
  132
Encouraging, right to participate 129-30
Equal worth 124
Equality 124-5
Establishing rapport 34-5
Exploring alternatives 38-9
Extended family 260-1

F

Factophelia 77
Facts, gathering 36
Families, special 245-65
Family
  blended 260
  encouragement 83
  encouraging 40
  extended 260-1
Family constellation 68, 69-77, 81
Family Council 82, 144-8
  basis 147
Family counseling 5-24
  basic steps 33-41
Family Counseling Center 83, 311-5
  establishing and operating 311-3
Family Education Center 82
Family members, counseling together and
    separately 100-10
Family Relationship Index
  form 332-3
  instructions for administering
    329-33
  problem areas 330-1
  specific questions 330-1
Family routine, elements 155-6
Fears, children's 207
Feelings
  confrontation 63-4
  inferiority 7-8
Fighting, children
  solutions 174
Fighting, sibling 170-5
Follow-up session 110-2
Foster parents 251-2
Frankl, V 142, 167
Freud, A 262, 265
Fry, W F 265

G

Ginott, H 24, 243
Giving attitude 192
Goal
  four, assumed disability 54
  one, attention 53
  three, revenge 54
  two, power 53-4
Goals
  alignment 114
  disturbing behavior 12, 44-55
Goals of misbehavior 3
  assumed disability 12
  attention getting 12
  power 12
  revenge 12
Goals, setting
  encouragement 129
Goldmines 79-81
  definition 79
Goldstein, J 265
Gould, S 243
Grandparents 260-1
Grey, L 136, 141, 167, 181, 217
Group approach in therapy 3
Grunwald, B ix, 12, 24, 65, 81, 118,
    172, 217, 243
Guidelines, television problem 193

H

Haddard, W 265
Having faith, encouragement 126
Heersema, P 265
Help, asking for
  encouragement 126-7
Hidden goals 37
Historical antecedents 135-6
Historical overview 1
Holistic
  nature of man 9
  view of persons 10
Home responsibilities
  3-year old 319
  4-year old 319-20
  5-year old 320-1
  6-year old 322

P

Painter, G 131, 166
Painter, J 174, 217
Pampered children 13-23
Pampering, types 17-23
Paradoxical intentions 141-4
Parent
  adopting 253-6
  divorced 246-7
  overprotective 22
  self-help checklist 335-7
  single 246-50
  unwed 252-3
  widowed 248-9
Parent driving, child disturbing 190-1
Parents
  do's and don'ts 158-66
  foster 251-2
  separating 250-1
Parents and children, counseling
  together 101-10
Participation, principle 139
Passive receptor 192
Patterns of behavior 78
Pepper, F 12, 24, 65, 172, 217, 243
Personality traits 69
Playroom director, role 314
Power, goal two 53-4
Power acting child 50
Power struggle
  avoid 31
  withdrawing 154-5
Power struggles, clients
  avoid 81
Powers, R 64, 65
Praise 133
Premises, psychological 43-65
Principle
  choice 137-8
  consistency 139-41
  immediacy 138
  meaning 137
  natural and logical consequences
    136-41
  participation 139
  prior knowledge 137
  relatedness 137
Prior knowledge, principle 137
Private logic 37

defined 43
Problems, specific
  working with 169-217
Promoting agreement 39-40
Provocations, dealing with 211-3
Psychological disclosure, confrontation
  techniques 43-4
Psychological goal, individual's
  clues 47
Psychological premises 43-65
Psychological processes, private logic
  44

Q

Questions, openended 78-9

R

Rapport 242
  establishing 34-5
Rationale 5-7
Reason, hidden
  guessing 55-60
Recognition reflex 93
  definition 51
Recommendations 39-40
  make specific 82
  share with children 89
Recorder, role 313-4
Redoubling, child
  efforts 121
Reflex, recognition 51
Reframing 142
Reimer, C 132, 167
Relatedness, principle 137
Relationships to others 10
Respect, mutual 123-4
Responsibilities, sharing 194-5, 317-28
Revenge, goal three 54
Revengeful child 50
Rewards and punishment, system 130
Right to participate, encouraging 129-30
Riley, D P 265
Robert's Rules of Order 145
Role-play 111
Roman, J 265

ABOUT
THE
AUTHORS

Bernice Bronia Grunwald

Bernice Bronia Grunwald is on the faculty of the Alfred Adler Institute, Chicago, and the annual Rudolf Dreikurs Summer Institute
sponsored by the International Committee for Adlerian Summer Schools
and Institutes (ICASSI). Ms. Grunwald was trained in Adlerian Dreikursian methods by Rudolph Dreikurs and worked with him for over 25
years.

Speaking several languages fluently, Ms. Grunwald is in constant
demand as a consultant and workshop leader both in the U.S. and
abroad. In addition to workshops presented in the United States and
Canada, she has most recently conducted workshops in West Germany,
Austria, and Greece.

Ms. Grunwald is a co-author of the widely accepted book *Maintaining Sanity in the Classroom*. This book also has been published in Ger-
man.

Harold V. McAbee 464-2359

Long active in the fields of family and Adlerian Counseling, Dr. Harold V. McAbee currently serves as Professor of Counseling Psychology and Founder and Director, The Adler-Dreikurs Institute of Human Relations, Bowie State College, Bowie, Maryland, and is President, The Alfred Adler Institute of Washington, D.C. In addition, Dr. McAbee conducts a private practice specializing in marriage and family counseling and conducts demonstrations of marriage and family counseling for a variety of groups.

Dr. McAbee has extensive education in counseling and therapy. He has attended eight international institutes where he studied with leading Adlerians from many countries. Adlerian related topics have been the focus of several articles by Dr. McAbee published in *The Individual Psychologist*.

Dr. McAbee maintains membership in a variety of professional organizations. He also has served on numerous committees and commissions including: President, North American Society of Adlerian Psychologists, 1978-79; member of the Delegate Assembly, NASAP, 1976-80; Administrator, International Committee for Adlerian Summer Schools and Institutes, 1975 to present; and Secretary General, International Association of Individual Psychology, 1979-85.